Executive Coaching with
Backbone and Heart

JB JOSSEY-BASS

Executive Coaching with Backbone and Heart

A Systems Approach to Engaging Leaders with Their Challenges

Second Edition

Mary Beth O'Neill

John Wiley & Sons, Inc.

Published by Jossey-Bass
A Wiley Imprint
989 Market Street, San Francisco, CA 94103-1741 www.josseybass.com

Jossey-Bass books and products are available through most bookstores. To contact Jossey-Bass directly call our Customer Care Department within the U.S. at 800-956-7739, outside the U.S. at 317-572-3986, or fax 317-572-4002.

Jossey-Bass also publishes its books in a variety of electronic formats. Some content that appears in print may not be available in electronic books.

Library of Congress Cataloging-in-Publication Data
O'Neill, Mary Beth, date.
  Executive coaching with backbone and heart : a systems approach to engaging leaders with their challenges/Mary Beth O'Neill. – 2nd ed.
    p. cm. – (The Jossey-Bass business & management series)
  Includes bibliographical references and index.
  ISBN 978-0-7879-8639-1 (cloth)
1. Executive coaching. I. Title.
  HD30.4.O53 2007
  658.4'07124 – dc22   2007017893

Printed in the United States of America
SECOND EDITION
HB Printing   10 9 8 7 6 5

The Jossey-Bass Business &

Management Series

Contents

In memoriam:
To my late husband, Don Werner,
who taught me the difference
between nagging and coaching,
and never to coach without a contract!

To my parents, Madeline and Walter O'Neill,
who have shown me the value of bringing
both backbone and heart into the world.

Preface

I did not intentionally set out to become an executive coach. I evolved into coaching. As an internal consultant in a corporation, I encountered leaders who were often inattentive to parts of their management style that rendered them less effective than they wanted to be. In my early experiences with organizational development work, I was also fortunate to have upper management bosses and clients who were willing to show me the ropes for achieving business results while remaining open to my expertise in project management and facilitation. Thus, I was privileged to work with these key decision makers on issues and undertakings about which they cared deeply.

My career development was also aided by the fact that I often found myself in the executive office sitting across from a leader and discussing crucial business issues. A leader was sometimes disappointed with a project's progress. I had two choices: door number one—take his negative feedback personally and conclude that I, along with the rest of the executive team, had let him down; or door number two—search for a pattern in his leadership behavior that inevitably led us all to this point. (Throughout this book, I alternate *he* and *she*, using them interchangeably as pronouns for the coach, the executive, and the employee.) For my first year as an internal consultant, I chose door number one. Chalk it up to inexperience and a false sense of omnipotence ("it must always be my fault"). Given more time and a broader perspective, I noticed door number two opening frequently.

Discovering a Passion for Coaching

So there I was, across from a disgruntled leader. I began to invite him into conversations about his frustrations and to ask him what he thought the external causes were and what he might be contributing, albeit unintentionally, to the slowdown. These discussions were brief at first. As I became more skillful, I incorporated them into regular conversations I had with leaders regarding their business goals (Chapter Ten explores this transition to executive coaching in depth).

Another developmental thread in my coaching practice evolved from my work as a trainer in management development. Now let me say right off that the classes I offered in leadership training were *good*. They were engaging, experiential, and practical. However, the managers basically tolerated the training. They felt pretty smug and satisfied with their level of management skill back on the floor, or at least until they got stuck. However, when faced with pressing and immediate dilemmas about high turnover, troublesome employees, low productivity, or a failed change effort, they would come to my office for help. Their motivation to explore options for action was dramatically keener than their interest in the same issues in my classes. When the managers came to me one-to-one with their issues, I was happy to help them navigate through dilemmas regarding tasks or team challenges that they found personally daunting.

I was midstream in my own coaching practice before I thought of myself as an executive coach. It developed naturally out of these organizational projects when leaders came to me for help. I was ten years into coaching when I began to articulate the coaching method outlined in this book. Now, many years later, executive coaching, both one-to-one and with teams, is the primary focus of my work.

I find coaching executives highly rewarding because the work is challenging, inspiring, fun, and stimulating. I have been blessed with clients willing to look within themselves for the key ingredients of significant change in their organizations. This kind of journey requires full engagement and risk taking on the part of both client and coach.

My passion is to work with executives at the crossroads of two highways: road #1, developing leadership capacity, and road #2, achieving business results. When executive coaching focuses on this intersection, organizations enjoy a two-for-one deal: executives are developing while they are driving for results. They are not taking time out to develop but taking "time in" to develop while they get their work done. What could be a better contribution to organizations than to work with executives at this crossroads? For too long, companies have segregated these functions of leadership development and bottom-line results. Often the people involved with these functions do not develop ways to work together for greater synergies. The kind of executive coaching I define and describe in this book is a perspective that comes from working at this crossroads and finding those synergies. The essence of executive coaching is helping leaders work through their dilemmas so they can transform their learning directly into results for the organization.

> *The essence of executive coaching is helping leaders work through their dilemmas so they can transform their learning directly into results for the organization.*

Who This Book Is For

People in many disciplines have become interested in the coaching field. Some practitioners have a traditional business background and enter coaching from one of the following organizational roles:

- Internal organizational development specialist
- External consultant
- Human resource staff
- Staff positions that require coaching skills such as project leaders, engineers, and information systems managers

Others enter the field of executive coaching through different routes, such as counseling. Regardless of your background, if you identify with one or more of the following statements, you will find this book useful:

- I have reached a plateau in my effectiveness as a coach, and I need to find my way to the next level.
- I am not sure when one-to-one executive coaching should be expanded to working with the leader's team.
- My clients don't use my services as well as they could.
- I have a gut sense of what works when I coach, but I don't know why it works. And sometimes it doesn't.
- The leader I am coaching resists my advice.
- I want to avoid becoming as anxious as my clients so that I can continue to be useful to them.
- I want to increase my range of coaching within different venues: one-to-one, team, behind-the-scenes, and live action.
- I want to improve the way I give tough feedback.

How This Book Is Different

There are many books on coaching that describe the skills used in coaching individuals to achieve both higher competence and greater motivation in their work. One of the main audiences for these books is managers who are learning how to better coach their employees. Two excellent examples are Hargrove (1995) and Bell (1996). Although the writers focus on managers, business coaches in general can benefit from learning the building-block skills to coaching detailed in the literature. *Executive Coaching with Backbone and Heart* explores a different territory.

First, this book is written for professionals who coach leaders of organizations. These executive coaches have the privilege of working with the men and women who lead and influence the direction of today's organizations. With this privilege comes a responsibility to partner with leaders in significant ways in order to contribute to successful change efforts. The work of executive coaches now has its own literature.

Second, unlike coaching methods that use techniques to leverage changes within the client, *Executive Coaching with Backbone and Heart* focuses on the need for coaches to use their own presence with the client. Executive coaching is not about imposing skills training on leaders. Fundamentally, it is about learning to be with leaders as they navigate through their world and finding key moments when they are most open to learning.

Let me be clear about being, learning, and doing. Being, learning, and doing do not trump the need of our clients to produce business outcomes. Executive coaching has to be relevant to achieving business results, and coaches should be business partners with their clients (Chapter Five). This involves helping leaders face their own challenges in attaining business results, to see how they can hinder their own progress. In these pivotal moments, the manner in which a coach manages the relationship with the executive facing those challenges can make the critical difference in the coaching outcome and thus the business outcome.

Third, this book focuses on the larger systems forces at play that require the attention of the executive coach. By "larger systems forces," I mean an organization's force field that shapes and influences the individuals working within it (I define the interactional force field and its effects in Chapter Three). Individuals subconsciously react to this field with their own emotional responses, either helping or hindering their effectiveness. Executives act and react within this field, along with everyone else they lead. Coaches who fail to see how the system affects their clients will not understand why their interventions sometimes fail. When coaches use skills presented in the general coaching literature and do not incorporate a systems approach, their efforts will yield limited results.

A systems viewpoint allows coaches to see the executive's world in a new way. *Executive Coaching with Backbone and Heart* explores a systems perspective and shows the implications and choices for the coach who maintains that perspective.

Although coaches need a systems viewpoint to understand their client's environment, they also need to realize what effect their client's system has on them. This is the central premise and challenge of the book. Coaches must tune in to how the client's force field affects them, so they can maintain their equilibrium within it and help the client to do the same. When coaches hold this bifocal view, seeing their client and themselves within the system, they can use the skill-building technologies in the coaching literature effectively. In fact, they can finally realize the full power of these skills.

How This Book Is Organized

This book navigates between two cliffs: a way of thinking about coaching and a methodology of coaching. I imagine this book as a river that runs through the canyon created by these two cliffs, needing both for its shape and power.

Just when it seems that a philosophy about presence and systems will lose its practical application, a method emerges to clarify that way. When the method becomes too rational for the topsy-turvy challenges of organizational life, a way of remaining in the moment saves the method from being trivialized. Perhaps the image is more like Alice of *Through the Looking Glass* when she finds herself in the wood of the vanishing path. When one is following a well-worn trail (the method) and that path disappears, one needs a way to attend to the forest (using one's presence in the moment) and orient oneself within it.

Following is an overview and sequence of the content in the book.

Part One: Core Concepts: The Coach's Stance

Chapter One defines executive coaching and explores three core principles that underlie the book: coach self-management, a systems perspective, and a methodology compatible with the first two principles. The chapter explains the use of backbone and heart as it relates to the principle of coach self-management.

Chapter Two addresses the need to develop a signature presence, a way of bringing forward your backbone and your heart as a coach. I describe four conditions that promote a strong presence, benefiting both coach and executive.

Chapters Three and Four cover specific ways of using systemic dynamics to read a client's system and recognize the system created between the client and coach. There are many system variables to study. Chapters Three and Four focus on some of the central ones. As a coach, you will find that when you attend to these systemic concepts, you are more likely to free a client and an organization from the detrimental qualities of their own system.

Part Two: Methodology: The Four Phases of Coaching

Chapters Five through Eight outline four essential phases to the coaching process: contracting, planning, live-action intervening, and debriefing. These can help both beginning and experienced coaches provide a more in-depth service to their clients. The method, however, depends greatly on bringing one's presence to coaching and maintaining a systems perspective. As an important part of the debriefing phase, Chapter Nine explains a way to calculate your clients' return on investment for your executive coaching contracts.

The combination of using systems thinking while bringing forward a signature presence creates a highly engaging and effective process.

Part Three: Special Applications

Chapter Ten is for consultants, trainers, and human resource professionals, internal or external, who facilitate processes and projects in organizations. This chapter explores the instances in which leaders do not seek coaching directly. It also describes the conversations practitioners must have with these leaders before they start to see you as a coach.

Chapter Eleven covers how a coach can help an executive who needs to coach employees. Executive coaches often work with clients who struggle with being effective coaches themselves. This chapter explains how to assist executives in becoming more effective coaches.

How to Use This Book

Executive Coaching with Backbone and Heart can be viewed as a workbook for coaches. Key ideas are in bold type throughout the text so that you can quickly access the areas most important to you. Highlights of the main ideas appear at the end of each chapter. You may wish to look at the highlights first as an overview before delving into the chapter or scan them quickly for a review.

Appendix A contains the four essential activities, with matching outcomes, for each of the coaching phases. You can use it to prepare for a coaching session and then check back afterward to see if you covered all the essential bases of that coaching phase. Appendix B has an extensive self-assessment survey organized by the activities and skills needed for each coaching phase. You can identify your strengths and weaknesses regarding the coaching method in this book. Appendix C covers key questions to ask clients during the contracting, planning, and debriefing phases of the coaching method. Finally, Appendix D explores the territory of combining coaching with consulting. It lists the competencies you need to have if you want to broaden your practice to include larger organizational consulting efforts.

There are stories from my coaching practice and typical vignettes throughout the book that illustrate the coaching concepts and the methods you can apply to the challenging situations you encounter when you coach clients. I invite you to use the material in this book to visit your past, present, and future coaching experiences with new eyes.

Seattle, Washington   Mary Beth O'Neill
May 2007

Acknowledgments

I have increasing gratitude to those who contribute to my professional and personal journey. Their generous companionship creates a richly textured path for us to travel. It is with this appreciation that I thank the following people:

Roger Taylor, Dr. Judy Heinrich, and Rob Schachter: highly experienced consultants who practiced and used this approach to executive coaching with me. I acknowledge the significant contribution that Rob has made to my perspective and practice while we worked as a consulting team to many diverse clients. Roger's partnership while working in client systems, training the Executive Coach Training Seminar Series with me, giving feedback on both editions, and his coaching during our case consultations has been invaluable in keeping me on track and creative in this work.

Dr. Donald Williamson, Dr. Pamela Johnson, Dr. Timothy Weber, and Cheryl Cebula: faculty colleagues at the Leadership Institute of Seattle/Bastyr University who critiqued the book and offered perspectives from their disciplines and experience in organizational development and family systems.

Jack Fontaine, Dr. Ron Short, John Runyan, Christine Frishholz, Dale Scriven, Dr. Philip Heller, Diane Robbins, and Ellen Tichenor: colleagues who gave feedback that significantly influenced the direction of the book.

Peter LaFemina: a colleague and chief financial officer who gave me invaluable consultation regarding return-on-investment calculation in Chapter Nine of this second edition.

Byron Schneider, Julianna Gustafson, Margi Fox, Erwin Karl, and Janna Silverstein: Byron and Julianna, my editors for the first edition at Jossey-Bass, were delightful. Their clarity of purpose gave this book added consistency while their gentleness urged me forward. Margi and Erwin gave me the editing guidance I needed to nudge the book to a final manuscript. Janna taught me to write a book proposal that publishers would read.

Don Werner, my late husband: he supported my work on the first edition, helped with initial graphics, and put up with having "the book" invade our home for longer than he ever imagined.

My clients and students: for their thirst for learning and willingness to risk new ways of seeing, being, and doing.

Michael Waters: for comparing notes regarding our experiences of the creative process in different media and supporting me during the writing of the second edition with much dance and laughter.

Barbara Guzzo, Libbie Stellas, Pat Lewis, Maureen Reid, Mary Hartrich, Judy Ryan, and Susie Leonard: Godsisters giving many decades of support and friendship—they buoyed me during the writing process, as they have in all of my other life transitions.

The Author

Mary Beth O'Neill is an executive coach, leadership consultant, author, and leader of the Executive Coach Training Seminar Series.

O'Neill has coached a range of leaders, from CEOs to senior vice presidents, vice presidents, and directors. She works with executives and their teams as well as one-to-one with leaders. Her specialty is live team coaching, encouraging individual initiative and leadership from a systemic perspective. The outcome of team coaching is the creation of clearly defined stretch goals and business results that are achieved through the executive's and leadership team's development. Some of her clients have included Premera Blue Cross, Nike, Microsoft, Waggener Edstrom, REI, Simon Fraser Health Region, Catalyst Paper, Marguerite Casey Foundation, Harborstone Credit Union, and TransAlta Utilities Corporation.

The Executive Coach Training Seminar Series in Seattle, Washington, is sponsored by the Leadership Institute of Seattle/ Bastyr University. As lead trainer for two of the three seminars, O'Neill uses the approach and methodology from this book, particularly in how to create a synergy between the client's leadership development and the production of bottom-line business results. The three seminars specifically cover the skills required to use the book's four phases of executive coaching (registration is online at www.mboExecutiveCoaching.com).

For eleven years O'Neill was a graduate faculty member in the master's program at the Leadership Institute of Seattle/Bastyr

University, which offers degrees with an emphasis in organization consultation and coaching, or systems counseling. She taught courses in executive coaching, managing organizational change, change agent and consulting skills, action research, creating business goals and measures, and systemic intervening in organizations. She continues to teach the executive coaching class in the master's program.

Previously she was the director of training and development at the Sheraton Seattle Hotel and Towers. She received the 1988 President's Award for her contributions to productivity and quality at the Sheraton.

O'Neill has a master's degree from Whitworth College in applied behavioral science, with an emphasis in organizational development. She also holds a master's degree in theology from Vanderbilt University.

She has been the cochair of Human Systems Development Professionals, an association of organizational development practitioners in the northwestern United States and Canada. She is a member of the International Consortium for Coaching in Organizations as well as the Organization Development Network.

Part One

CORE CONCEPTS

The Coach's Stance

1

AN INTRODUCTION TO EXECUTIVE COACHING

Coach: What are the most pressing business challenges you face?

Leader: We've got to get our division out of the cellar. Consistently we perform behind the other four divisions, and the CEO's patience with us is wearing thin. I don't think he's going to put up with it much longer.

Coach: How much time have you got?

Leader: At the outside, maybe twelve months.

Coach: What obstacles prevent you from getting the results that you want?

Leader: My executive team isn't operating as a unit. They're pursuing their own business goals, not coordinating overlapping interests with other departments. In our meetings, when I ask for their opinions, they address issues only in their functional area. We're not doing any creative problem solving.

Coach: What impacts do these disappointing results have on you personally?

Leader: I have to work two jobs: my own and the vacancy on my team. In my first year as senior vice president, I had three positions in a row vacated, and it's taken too long to fill each one. It's like trying to drive a car with one wheel constantly missing: it prevents me from looking at the big picture.

Coach: This sounds like a great setup for self-perpetuating burnout, for both you and your team. You'll never get the results you need to succeed if you don't carve out the space to lead your team.

Leader: So tell me how to do it when I'm fighting fires!

Coach: You may, by default, be managing only what you know how to do rather than doing what is needed. You may need to go beyond your own leadership strengths to achieve significantly different, breakthrough results. What is challenging for you about this situation in the face of these disappointing results?

Leader: Leading this effort is a big challenge for me. It's the first time I've ever managed multiple functions. I've never spent energy on managing as a discipline in itself. I achieve success through technical know-how. I could use some help figuring out where to start.

Coach: Let's start by defining more specifically which actions on the part of your team would directly lead to the results you need. Then we can look at how you will achieve those results with your team.

Leaders hold a special position in the landscape of change. A leader's clarity of purpose and her ability to connect the people in her organization to that purpose go a long way toward mobilizing the necessary forces for change. Sometimes executives need help to fulfill the responsibilities of their special position. Executive coaches, who understand the demands and requirements of the change process, can help these leaders.

Leaders hold a special position in the landscape of change.

What would you do if the leader from the preceding dialogue were referred to you for coaching? What would be your goal with him? What would you want to accomplish? How would you determine if you were being effective?

These are the questions that effective coaches ask themselves every time they enter a new coaching relationship. They are also the questions that keep coaches, even experienced ones, up at night when the client or the situation reaches a particularly dicey phase.

A well-managed coaching relationship, along with an adequate period of time and a motivated executive, can lead to impressive results. That was the case for this leader, whose division became the top performer in the company within eight months.

This book explores how to think and act in ways that empower the executives you coach. It will help you become a valued resource to the leaders who need you most.

What Is Executive Coaching?

The coaching partnership begins when the leader faces a dilemma and feels stymied. The essence of executive coaching is helping leaders work through challenges so they can transform their learning into results for the organization.

Coaches possess the trained yet natural curiosity of a journalist or an anthropologist to the client's work situation. In addition, coaches typically:

- Share conceptual frameworks, images, and metaphors with executives.
- Encourage rigor in the ways that clients organize their thinking, visioning, planning, and expectations.
- Challenge executives to expand their learning edge and go beyond their current level of competence.
- Build clients' capacities to manage their own anxiety in tough situations.

By "executive," I mean leaders who are in the top and upper levels of their organizations: the CEOs, senior vice presidents, plant managers, and executive directors of organizations. I define the executive's job in three broad areas:

1. **Communicating the territory,** that is, the purpose, the vision, and goals of the organization to key constituencies, as well as outlining opportunities and challenges.
2. **Building commitment, building relationships, and facilitating interactions** that result in outstanding team performance.
3. **Producing results and outcomes** through the direct efforts of others as well as the executive's own efforts.

Executive coaching is the process of increasing the client's effectiveness in meeting these three responsibilities. For example, in the opening story, the executive was clear about the third responsibility: the results. He even had a sense about what was missing in the second area: the interactions he needed from his team. But he had yet to act on that knowledge: he was not defining the expectations he had for his team. Neither was he communicating to his team, with any conviction, the territory ahead and his vision for where they needed to go.

Some of you coach one-to-one with leaders exclusively. Others, myself included, use coaching as one tool in the toolbox used for larger organizational change projects with leaders (see Appendix D). Although my practice encompasses larger change efforts, this book focuses largely on the one-to-one executive coach work relationship because it is so critical.

It is easy to assume that this coaching relationship happens in isolation from the dynamics of the executive's team. Of course, it does not, even when you coach only the leader. Whether coaching the executive happens with the team or independently, that relationship must take into account the team and the organization. One of the purposes of executive coaching is to turn the leader toward his team so he can lead them more effectively. This approach can enhance the contributions of both the leader and the team.

I do wish to acknowledge the special concerns of executives at the very top of their organizations. Top executives deal with issues of stockholders, owners or partners, succession, loyalty, strategic alliances, and positioning in the marketplace. Many believe that they should not ask for help, which exacerbates their "lonely at the top" experience.

The biggest difference I find in coaching top executives as opposed to middle executives is one of tone and pace. Top executives require more toughness from those who partner with them. By toughness, I mean knowing when to sacrifice tact for directness to reach the punch line sooner. Although the pace is quicker and the tone may be blunter with top executives, the coaching approach of this book works well for middle executives too.

How to Be the Most Hard-Nosed Businessperson in the Room

For as much as American and Western culture corporations have the reputation for being tough-minded and bottom-line oriented, too many organizational customers of executive coaching services invest in coaching with less rigor and outcome focus than they should. Organizations deserve to see a return on the investment they make in their executives through coaching. I make sure that I am seen as a business partner with my clients by sticking to these parameters regarding my work:

- **Refuse to be satisfied with executive coaching as "finishing school."**
- **Refuse to undertake an initiative that has no business measures associated with it.**
- **Refuse to be a substitute for your client's boss.**

By "finishing school," I mean those vague requests for coaching that come because someone's boss said she needed to "develop more executive presence," or "prepare herself for the next level of management," or "I'm not sure what my boss meant, he just said that coaching might benefit me." There needs to be an established need for coaching expressed in ways that mobilize the client toward a specific goal.

Attaching business measures to a coaching effort makes clear the connection between investment in the executive and the return that the organization will receive. It goes well beyond finishing school and starts delivering two-for-one results for organizations: they get both a developed leader and greater bottom-line results with the same investment dollars.

Everyone is overworked in the business environment, clients' bosses included. I do not blame bosses for wanting to offload some of their supervisory work onto their subordinates' coaches. It is just that I do not let them succeed at their attempts to do it. Executive coaching is not a substitute for performance management. The executive coach is an adjunct resource, not a replacement for the boss–direct report relationship.

> *Executive coaching is not a substitute for performance management.*

What is your most pressing challenge right now?

Four Essential Ingredients of Executive Coaching

Let's revisit the coach-executive conversation at the beginning of this chapter. The coach's sequencing of questions reveals four essential ingredients of executive coaching. **The first ingredient is maintaining a results orientation** to a leader's problem ("What are the most pressing business challenges you face? . . . How much time have you got?") To lose sight of outcomes is to waste the leader's time, money, and energy. The organization needs him to stay focused on what will produce the key goods, services, or information that define that organization's success. A coach's job is to support the leader's drive for results.

The second ingredient is partnership. The coach becomes a partner in the executive's journey toward greater competence and effectiveness. During the conversation (and in the question, "What obstacles prevent you from getting the results that you want?"), the coach begins to stand shoulder to shoulder with the executive in untangling and assessing the many factors, forces, and dilemmas facing the leader. Within this collegiality, the coach inquires, stimulates, and challenges the leader to perform at his optimal level.

The third ingredient is the ability to engage the specific leadership challenges that the executive faces ("What is challenging for you about this situation in the face of these disappointing results?"). This helps him explore what drives him off course and what he typically avoids—for example, seeing the waves he creates for others as he works through his agenda. Leaders naturally resist concentrating on their own actions while looking to others for results. Within the coaching partnership, the coach confronts the executive to look at the ways in which he may be his own worst enemy and thus prevent himself from achieving the results he wants.

In the fourth ingredient, the coach links team behaviors to the bottom-line goals and points out the need for executives to set specific expectations for their teams. ("Let's start by defining more specifically which actions on the part of your team would directly lead to the results you need.") This is an essential connection. Coaches help clients define specifically the people processes that are most relevant to the business goals. **They keep leaders focused on their results orientation but also widen their view of what their teams need to do to get there**. It is important in the conversation linking results to team behaviors that the leader's responsibility remains central (note the coach's last comment in the dialogue: "Then we can look at how you will achieve those results with your team").

Core Principles That Guide Executive Coaching

When I coach executives, I adhere to three core values or principles. When diligently observed, these principles result in an exponential improvement in coaching effectiveness. The first two principles—bringing your signature presence to the coaching process and using a systems perspective in your practice—are discussed extensively in the Core Concepts section in Part One of this book. The third principle—applying a coaching method—is fleshed out in the Methodology chapters in Part Two.

PRINCIPLE 1: *Bring your own signature presence to coaching. It is the major intervention tool that you have.*

Coaches challenge executives to lead authentically and bring a more integrated self to their work. When we coach our clients, we must bring ourselves forward as well.

Bringing your unique signature presence means that you inhabit the role of coach in ways that no one else does. You do not perform *techniques* on executives. You know how irritating it is when someone is doing a technique *on* you? Leaders can instantly detect a cookie-cutter technique. Instead, leaders need true partners in their developmental process. I have already used the word *partner* several times because it is a deep value that I hold in working with executives. They require peers who will join them in their most daunting work challenges. People do not want leaders to hide behind a role. We have to be equally brave ourselves. Our executive clients deserve coaches who are also willing to be who they are rather than hide behind the coach role.

The coaching relationship is built on trust, the ability to give and receive feedback, and genuine presence on the part of both coach and leader. It is a highly interactive process. Your signature presence as a coach can evoke the signature presence of the client.

You can help clients learn that bringing themselves to their goals, challenges, and relationships is crucial to their success.

PRINCIPLE 2: *Use a systems perspective. It keeps you focused on fundamental forces. These forces either promote or impede the interactions and results of the executives you coach.*

A systems perspective is essential to executive coaches. We must pay attention to the system, the nested set of spheres, where our clients work (Figure 1.1). Those forces may have an enormous impact on your client's success. They influence the very challenges, goals, and obstacles she faces, the ones you are working

Figure 1.1 The Leader's System

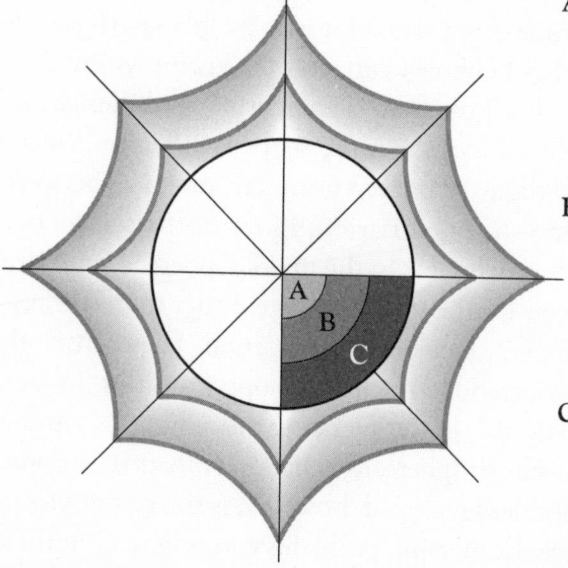

A = Smallest sphere: leader's motivations, traits, goals, challenges

B = Midsize sphere: leader and her team, other departments, vendors, customers

C = Largest sphere: strategic alliances, global economy, the natural environment, geopolitical shifts

Note: Even the image of a nested set of spheres is too confining to convey, among other things, the fluidity of interconnecting systems. To indicate the sensitivity of any system's sphere to the influence of changes in neighboring systems, I chose the image of the web because it connotes strength and responsiveness to changes. Imagine the web intersecting through all the spheres.

on together. This is a nonlinear perspective that allows you as a coach to recognize patterns of interaction within and across spheres.

When you focus too narrowly on your client alone (the smallest sphere), including her personal challenges, her goals, and the inner obstacles that keep her from being successful, you miss the whole grand ecosystem in which she functions. She is both influencing and being influenced by an entire web of interrelationships in and around the organization, including the team, other departments, vendors, and customers (the middle sphere). Also important are external contexts, which include the global economy and the natural environment (the largest sphere).

Viewing an organization systemically constitutes the foundation of Peter Senge's influential work (1990). He emphasizes the effects of feedback loops on a system. Feedback loops are the consequences or repercussions of a system's behavior in interaction with other contexts, and they provide input back to the system by acting as either a brake or an accelerator to people's activity. He focuses on the way slight changes can alter the entire system.

The perspective that I use here is compatible with Senge and the mind-set of feedback loops, but the scope is different. Rather than looking at how the external environment interacts between the largest sphere and the organization, I look at the system of a leader and the other constituents in the middle sphere around her.

Why keep my view on the middle sphere rather than the largest one? Leaders reflexively look out to the horizon. They constantly scan for large themes, trends, threats, and opportunities. In fact, leaders can learn to do this better by being introduced to systems thinking through the largest sphere, as Senge and others have done.

What has been underdeveloped, however, is the systems focus on the middle sphere. Leadership problems can originate in their own backyards, specifically the system of interactions in place between them and the people with whom they work most closely. As coaches, we can help them change their way of interacting by examining the middle system and their role within it. Executives can then unlock an enormous array of the resources they and their teams possess to learn from and work with the larger environment (the largest sphere).

PRINCIPLE 3: *A coaching method is powerfully effective when you incorporate the first two principles together with it: bringing your signature presence and using a systems approach. Otherwise the method will achieve at best short-term results.*

The coaching method I outline in this book follows four straightforward stages: contracting, planning, live-action intervening, and debriefing. Professionals in the organizational development field will recognize the methodology as classic action research applied to coaching. Like action research, this coaching method aims to achieve business results while fostering the sustainable capacity of clients to apply what they learn to other organizational situations.

There is great value embedded in recognizing that leaders already possess most of the resources they need to address the very issues that seem most daunting. This resilience mobilizes clients to use the resources at hand, both in them and in the people around them, to address pressing organizational challenges.

The four phases of the methodology progress in a linear, step-by-step manner. However, nonlinear human responses can undo the most carefully constructed methodologies. Coaching methods unravel in our hands at the very times we depend on them the most: with executives on the verge of implementing a vision, leaders in the midst of large change efforts, or executives in the heat of interdepartmental conflicts. As an antidote to these afflictions of chaos and stress, I advocate mining the resources of one's presence and focusing on what happens within and between the system of the human beings caught in the dilemma. Making the most of the moment can be the leverage point for change when it is explored fully and then linked back to concrete results.

Integrating these three principles into your coaching practice ensures greater success in your efforts to evoke, promote, and challenge the executive to operate from the same principles as well. They need to find **their signature presence** in the unique way that they lead. **A systems perspective** can keep them from getting lost in the patterns and processes of the organization. **Their method** of leading needs to be informed by the ability to mine the moment.

Coaching with Backbone and Heart

In bringing your signature presence, you bring your ideas, biases, and ability to constructively challenge your clients. You also need to maintain strong relationships and connections with those leaders. *Backbone* **means knowing and clearly stating your position, whether it is popular or not.** *Heart* **is staying engaged in the relationship and reaching out even when that relationship is mired in conflict.**

> Backbone *means knowing and clearly stating your position, whether it is popular or not.* Heart *is staying engaged in the relationship and reaching out even when that relationship is mired in conflict.*

These two seemingly opposing functions work quite well together. Each withers in isolation from the other. For example, speaking strongly while shutting others down or being highly empathic without stating your views can diminish effective communication. Executive coaching is a continual dance of balancing backbone and heart while you work with your client.

A healthy backbone is strong and flexible. Having backbone does not mean that you are fixed in your positions. You can still be open to being influenced. You know where you stand, however, even as you are shifting your position with new information.

One way to test for your own ability to have both backbone and heart is to take an inventory of your coaching interactions:

Bringing Backbone

- Does my client know what I think? How often do I say, "I agree with you," or "I disagree with you" and clearly state why?
- Do I identify what I need from my client in our working relationship in order to be most effective with her?
- Can I give my position without blame or defensiveness?
- Can I state my opinion without jargon or arcane concepts?
- Can I give hard feedback when I need to?

Bringing Heart

- Do I empathize with my client's situation?
- Can I clearly articulate his position and reflect it back to him?
- Do I identify and communicate the hunches I have about possible deeper reactions, feelings, and thoughts he is leaving unsaid?
- In the face of disagreement or conflict with my client, do I keep engaging with him, or do I retreat and disengage?
- Do I continue to stay in touch?
- Do I express appreciation for the degree of difficulty in the client's situation and also the degree of accomplishment he has achieved?

Everyone seems to come equipped with the ability to show either backbone or heart more naturally, but executive coaching requires you to do both, whether they come naturally or not. Executives deserve nothing less from you. As an executive coach, you must develop your competence to access and use both functions in your work with leaders.

The main reason we have to be strong in both functions is that a coach helps executives develop both backbone and heart. In my experience with executives, I have rarely found a leader who is a natural in both areas. **Executives have to bring backbone by standing up for and articulating their positions in the face of others challenging them. They bring heart when they have compassion for those they lead and seek to understand their challenges, concerns, and ideas.** The more you learn how to balance backbone and heart in your coaching work, the more you will know how to help clients do the same. The upcoming chapters in this book address some ways to do just that.

Chapter One Highlights

What Is Executive Coaching?

1. Coaching activities

   • Use your curiosity to learn about the client's situation.

   • Share conceptual frameworks.

   • Invite the client to be more rigorous in his thinking.

   • Build the leader's capacity to manage his anxiety.

2. Assess the executive's ability to:

   • Communicate the territory.

   • Build commitment and relationships and facilitate interactions.

   • Produce results and outcomes.

How to Be the Most Hard-Nosed Businessperson in the Room

1. Refuse to be satisfied with executive coaching as a "finishing school."

2. Refuse to undertake an initiative that has no business measure to it.

3. Refuse to be a substitute for your client's boss.

Four Essential Ingredients of Executive Coaching

1. Bring a results orientation to the client's problem.

2. Be a partner.

3. Engage the client in her specific leadership challenges.

4. Link team behaviors to bottom-line goals.

Core Principles That Guide Executive Coaching

1. Bring your own signature presence.

2. Use a systems perspective.

3. Effectively integrate your signature presence and systems perspective into the coaching method.

Coaching with Backbone and Heart

1. Backbone: State your positions clearly.

2. Heart: Tune in to the relationship with understanding and compassion.

2

DEVELOPING A STRONG SIGNATURE PRESENCE

The business arena has risks, opportunities, dangers, and dead-ends that can make any leader flinch. Not surprisingly, dealing with organizational change and dilemmas is not for the faint-hearted. Coaches are colleagues to executives at exactly those times when leaders may flinch, fight back, dig in, or react in an unpredictable manner. A coach is likely to show up in the executive's office when the client is reacting on a visceral level, which is often not the most effective response to a dilemma.

Having signature presence is critical for coaches. A coach must bring her own presence to bear in order to be a contributing partner with her client. Otherwise the client's interactional force field of dilemmas can pull in the coach and neutralize her work with the executive (interactional fields are covered in Chapter Three). When the coach succumbs to the same dilemmas as the client instead of helping, the coach may well contribute to the problem.

Your Central Tool

Presence means bringing your self when you coach: your values, passion, creativity, emotion, and discerning judgment to any given moment with a client. Your resourcefulness and authenticity are crucial dimensions of your work. Coaches must build skills in two arenas when developing their clients: the courage to speak and command attention and the ability to take a back seat.[1]

Presence means **developing and sustaining your tolerance** for a host of situations many people actively avoid: ambiguity, daunting challenges, the anxiety or disapproval of others, and your own personal sources of stress. Coaches with presence stand fast in the midst of all these challenges and face them head-on rather than retreating. In the face of internal or external resistance, you refuse to back away from the challenge at hand. Signature presence is moving through these moments in your own unique way, thus making the most of your own strengths, interests, and eccentricities.

If you do not develop yourself enough to withstand a client's stress, you default to actions that handle your own discomfort but are not useful to your client. The worst-case scenario occurs when you are unaware that you are in this state and you run your client through a methodology that rings hollow to the dilemma your client faces.

> *If you do not develop yourself enough to withstand a client's stress, you default to actions that handle your own discomfort but are not useful to your client.*

When you realize that you have absorbed the anxiety and feelings of responsibility from your client, there is a glimmer of hope. When you can say to yourself, "I'm stuck. I'm as anxious and ineffective as my client is," you begin to find your way back to equilibrium. Questions to ask at these times are:

- Why am I doing what I'm doing?
- Is this truly in the best interest of the client?
- Am I doing this only to lower my own stress, even as I imagine that I act in the client's best interest?

The more you maintain your presence, the more you assist the client. You can clearly get at the core of your client's issues when you both successfully challenge the client and offer genuine support. Presence is easy when you are not anxious and elusive when you are. The problem is how to regain your presence when you have lost it.

Self-Differentiation

One of the keys to maintaining presence in anxious moments is the process of **self-differentiation**.[2] It strikes a balance between two major tasks in working relationships. First, you must clearly articulate where you stand regarding your position, your judgment, your decision, or a limit you set (**backbone work**). Second, you must stay connected and tuned in to those with whom you take a stand or decision (**the work of the heart**).

An image I find useful for representing self-differentiation is that of a gyroscope. It constantly tilts, moves, and rolls with outside forces, yet the inner mechanism stays level, no matter how topsy-turvy the whole system becomes. **Interactional equilibrium** is the ability to maintain yourself and your relationships while being pulled by the forces of fear, conflict, and anxiety.

To coach without a fair degree of self-differentiation can lead to a state of **reactivity** in which we lose our balance internally and respond in an automatic, ineffectual way. We become reactive when we cannot tolerate feeling our own anxiety about something at the moment. Reactivity manifests in many different ways. It throws backbone and heart out of balance. We may alienate others or have a posture that is excessively timid. We may cave in on a position, or become overly rigid and closed to influence. We might cut off the relationship and distance ourselves from others, or pay too much attention to other people's moods by smoothing over rough spots.

No one achieves self-differentiation 100 percent of the time. In fact, even 70 or 80 percent of the time is rare. To achieve this balance a simple majority of the time is a feat. Most of us constantly fall into reactivity, then pull out of it and face the next challenge. **Our goal should be to minimize how often we are**

reactive and recover equilibrium more quickly. With practice, coaches learn to take stands while staying connected, which increases the chances of being effective with clients.

If you learn to recover from your reactivity with less damage to yourself and your relationships, you will become more valuable to those with whom you work. Examples of actions you could take as a coach to maintain the balance of backbone and heart include the following:

- Disagree with a specific process the client is using (backbone) AND continue to understand and support the client's larger goals (heart).
- Show how clearly you see a boss's need to develop his direct report (heart) AND refuse to sell a coaching service to an executive, if the potential client is not mobilized to learn (backbone). Offer to help the boss learn how to address his direct report's lack of commitment to higher performance (heart).
- Offer the client help to become more consistent (heart) AND challenge the client's commitment to a planned course if her actions continue to contradict that commitment. Be clear that you will end the contract if the inconsistency continues and is destructive to the planned outcome (backbone).

Any coach who brings this kind of balance to her work will be in high demand. An effective coach is not intimidated by the client and does not embrace the client's viewpoint too quickly. However, the coach can grasp the client's position and convey understanding and compassion for the client's dilemmas. In other words, the coach has the ability to be an independent thinker while working interdependently with the client.

So, you may ask, *how can I coach with both backbone and heart? Is there a way to strengthen my presence? Are there ways to regain this balance?*

Strengthen Your Presence

Learning to regain your presence in the moment and with creativity can propel you along the path to coaching excellence. The following four approaches promote a healthy resilience in your work with your clients:

- Identify and sustain a goal for yourself in each coaching session.
- Manage yourself in the midst of ambiguity.
- Increase your tolerance for the reactivity within you and in others around you.
- Bring immediacy to the moment.

These approaches are not techniques, and it would be foolish to assume anyone could attain them merely through insight and understanding. They demand a willingness to enter into a maturing process that builds resiliency. They require you to take action, learn from the experience, and set new goals for action that maintains a balance between backbone and heart. A lifelong commitment to honing these actions can lead to a stronger sense of presence. The stronger your presence is, the easier it is to access these approaches. Mastering them is a lifelong process.[3] All four approaches recur continually in the coaching method outlined in Chapters Five through Eight.

Identify and Sustain Your Goal

In some ways, having a goal for yourself in coaching sessions sets the stage for the other three approaches for strengthening your signature presence. Coaches cannot proceed without a goal. When a coach becomes reactive, it is harder to hold on to that goal or even to remember it. It is important that coaches remain mindful of specific goals for themselves in coaching sessions with clients.

What? you may be thinking. *Have a goal for myself! Shouldn't I be helping the client with HIS goal?* Of course, you help the client with his goal. Nevertheless, the clearer you are about what you want to accomplish in the session while you work on the client's agenda, the more valuable you will be to your client. When you are with a client, you have only yourself to rely on to stay on course. If you don't pay attention to what you are doing, who will? You can take the following steps to identify and sustain your goal:

1. **Choose content and process goals for each meeting.**
2. **Know your vulnerability in a reactive system.**
3. **Remain focused on your goal.**
4. **Remain more committed to attaining your goal than to easing your discomfort in the moment.**

The **content goals** define *what* is to be accomplished in the coaching session—the business task. The **process goals** describe *how* you want to conduct yourself in the session. **Content** goals could include any of the following:

- Gain the commitment of the client to a coaching contract.
- Help the client establish outcome measures for her change initiative.
- The client ends up with a prioritized list of the issues that she needs to address.

The following goals demonstrate a focus on a relationship **process** or on parameters for conducting yourself as a coach:

- Show understanding for the executive's world and challenges.
- Stay on track in the session, even if the client grows impatient.
- Give the tough feedback that until now you have been withholding.

It is one thing to establish goals and another thing entirely to sustain those goals. **You must become familiar with your own areas of vulnerability within a reactive system.** By vulnerability, I mean the **triggers** that can jump-start your knee-jerk, subconscious response and cause you to abandon your goals in the session. Triggers differ for each person, but here are some common ones:

> *You must become familiar with your own areas of vulnerability within a reactive system.*

- Being challenged by a dominating person
- Facing high rates of change
- Receiving requests for help from a highly dependent person
- Having a client who rushes from one activity to the next, including the coaching sessions

Reconnecting with your goal when you become reactive goes a long way toward lessening the effects of your anxiety. First, **realize that you will go on automatic when your stress is high.** Adrenaline responses easily take over. Once you acknowledge this without berating yourself, you can get back on track. Here are some clues that you have let go of your goal: either your spine dissolves into jelly or you become as rigid as a stone wall; either you completely lose empathy for your client or you begin to see the world only through your client's eyes. These and other extreme responses indicate reactivity.

After you realize you have gone on automatic, remember your goal in the heat of the moment. (*What was it I said I wanted to accomplish in this session? Oh yeah!*) Once you recall it, **be more committed to your goal than to fighting or fleeing from the intense discomfort you feel in the moment. Then act on that commitment.** This is the big one! Everything in you will want to give up your goal to regain feeling more comfortable. We have been trained to avoid discomfort, but in the people development world, discomfort is a sign of something new happening. Hang in there through the discomfort! To the extent that you thoughtfully identified an appropriate goal before the session, you can still trust that goal when you temporarily lose sight of it. Regaining a hold on it and proceeding provides the anchor that steadies your boat in stormy seas.

Here is an example of what identifying and sustaining a goal can look like.*

Luke

Luke was in a tough position, and I was in a tough position with Luke. His boss, the president, "suggested" that he develop his staff into a stronger team in order to operate more efficiently. Luke would not have chosen to initiate this work. He responded to the president's recommendation because he felt pressured to do it.

After I spent some time with Luke and his staff, three things became clear: (1) the staff was not sure about the purpose of the team development and whether the president truly backed it, (2) Luke needed to have a frank conversation with his boss about issues that festered between the two of them, for example, whether the boss truly supported the department's work, and (3) Luke needed extensive development for himself as a leader in order for this team to take any significant step forward.

My anxiety increased because I sensed Luke's passivity in this project; he was mainly just going through the paces. I believed that to move ahead without a higher investment on his part would accomplish nothing and only waste time and money. Worse, it would damage the morale of the department if they experienced one more false start in a long line of half-baked change efforts. My track record of coaching for successful change efforts was on the line as well.

I established three goals for myself as I went into a critical meeting with Luke: (1) proceed only if he commits to working on his

---

Note: Names and identifying details have been changed to protect the privacy of individuals and organizations.

relationship with his boss as it relates to the department (content goal), (2) proceed only if he commits to developing himself as a leader (content goal), and (3) while working on the first two goals, offer support as well as challenge to Luke during this meeting (process goal).

Luke started the meeting with his usual passive affability. As I talked about what I viewed as necessary changes, his demeanor changed dramatically. He grew silent, then became argumentative: "I don't understand what this project has to do with my relationship to my boss! Why are you making it so difficult to proceed?" We came to an impasse: he was unwilling to commit to the two bottom lines I had established, and I was unwilling to move ahead without them. I was within five minutes of ending the contract.

My bottom lines were extremely challenging to Luke. For a long time, he had avoided dealing with the expectations and judgments that his boss had of him, but I continued to highlight the need for it in this project.

I said, "Luke, I don't think a boss has to be involved in every team development project. But on this one, it is critical, a make-or-break issue. Part of the team development work is to clarify the goals for the department. You are telegraphing to your team deeply mixed messages about what you expect of them. That's not just because you are unclear but because your boss is giving you mixed messages. It's time to clear them up with him. Otherwise you waste this team's time, and we might as well call it off."

Throughout the meeting, I also continuously offered Luke support for his efforts to work on his relationship to his boss should he choose to move in that direction. I let him know that because this step would be so challenging for him, most of our coaching work would focus on that relationship. I was there to help him if he wanted it.

Although he resisted the issue for a long time, Luke understood the stakes were too high for him to do nothing. He found a way to articulate the clarification work he would do with his boss to get the project under way. I decided that was an adequate commitment, and we could proceed with the team project.

These issues continued to be part of the fabric of my work with Luke. This was no magic bullet conversation. However, we had more effective sessions because I kept sight of my goals for the duration of my work with Luke. By sustaining your own goals as a coach in your sessions with the client, you will have more focus, particularly in ambiguous situations.

Manage Yourself in the Midst of Ambiguity

By *ambiguity*, I mean the business situations that are by nature unclear and murky. It's not like people have suddenly lost their intelligence or problem-solving ability. Rather, the issues never seem to sort themselves out. Many leaders try to suppress ambiguity rather than acknowledge it, even to themselves. Others give up in the face of it, believing that choosing a next step may be too treacherous. During times of ambiguity, people fill in gaps of information with rumor, fears, assumptions, and paranoia.

During times of ambiguity, coaches can also lose their bearings. This can be a humbling experience. The root word of humble is *humus*—ground, compost, soil. When you are in a reactive mode, you are not grounded. To reground yourself, you need to assess the lay of the land and see your circumstances for what they are rather than what you either wish or fear them to be.

How you **manage yourself in ambiguity** is the key. Here are five actions you can take, and suggest that your client take, in these kinds of situations:

1. **Acknowledge the ambiguity.**
2. **Distinguish for yourself where you are clear and where you are unclear about the situation. (an internal process)**
3. **Articulate to others the boundary between your clarity and your lack of clarity. (an external process)**
4. **Say what it is you want to do, given the situation.**
5. **Tell others what you need from them, and ask what they need from you.**

With this approach, you can cultivate decisiveness even in the midst of confusion. How refreshing it is to acknowledge both your clarity and your ambiguity rather than hide it or become victimized by it. You can be clear about what you know and what you do not know. This allows others to come forward, seeing their part of the conversation as a contribution rather than an indictment of their inadequacy. Then you can fill in the perceived gaps with real information and discover the remaining actual gaps. Building on this dialogue, you can articulate what you want to do and what you need from others, ask what they need from you, and transform the discussion from free-floating anxiety to collecting information and taking action.

Obviously clients need to learn how to manage themselves in the face of ambiguity. But how is it useful for coaches? *Isn't any lack of clarity in the coach detrimental for the client?* In fact, it can be good modeling for clients to experience a coach's acknowledging areas where she encounters the deep ambiguity of the client's situation. In the following story, after feeling rather humbled myself, I followed the steps for managing myself in ambiguity. You may notice they do not necessarily follow a sequential order because managing ambiguity is not a linear process.

Bill

Bill was the leader of two departments that had recently merged. In addition, the organization had a new CEO who indicated that the company would be reorganizing sometime next year. Bill had formidable tasks at hand, including coordinating new job expectations within the consolidated department, maintaining the same level of productivity that the company needed from them, and responding quickly to any imminent reorganization even though there was no established structure or start date for it. The situation was deeply ambiguous by nature.

Bill wanted help to organize his own people so they could function in the midst of all this uncertainty. The first step he identified was the easier one. Since he wanted to integrate the two departments as one, he decided he would not figure this out on his own, or leave it up to the half of the department that historically took on problem solving. Instead, he engaged the best thinking of his people throughout the whole department.

Bill invited me to join him and his team on a retreat where they addressed these issues. My role was to coach him during the meeting while they designed a process they could use to achieve greater clarity.

The retreat started off well enough but hit an inevitable snag when no one saw a way through all the unknown factors facing them. I did not know how to proceed either and silently berated myself for not conceiving of a clear way out. I was the coach, after all! Bill and the team were all looking at me expectantly. (Action 2: Distinguish for yourself where you are clear and where you are unclear about the situation.) I was clear that this ambiguity was inevitable; Bill and his staff had not missed anything. There truly were many unknowable factors in play. It was also clear that they did not need to be stymied by the innate ambiguity. The design of the retreat was not to blame for the ambiguity of the situation: the right people were in the room; they had all the information that was available from the CEO; they were looking at current realities, future opportunities, and obstacles; they held discussions in matrixed groups; and they were a highly creative group of people.

The ambiguity debilitating their progress occurred because there were true unknowables. I have come to appreciate what they experienced much more now than I did then: the chaos preceding the emergence of a new way of thinking. They were in the position to discover a new way to organize, but they could not see it because this new way did not exist apart from moving through the ambiguity itself.[4]

Bill, continued

All of us were trapped in a patch of deep fog. (Action 1: Acknowledge the ambiguity.) I told Bill and his team that it was time to name what was clear and unclear, and what they needed from themselves or others. I also said that it felt uncomfortable not because they were doing anything wrong, but because the situation was by nature unclear. It could also mean that they were on the verge of a burst of creativity because original thinking could start when they were willing to stop hanging on to the familiar territory and start moving out into the unknown. I told Bill to hang out in the confusion and hold less tightly to their need to have clarity quickly. (Action 4: Say what it is you want to do, given the situation.)

If this had been a pep talk, I would have failed miserably because I was unable to offer a clear path toward resolution. The team continued to struggle with the issues. After a while, however, one of the team leaders thought of a way to arrange the department into groups so that they reenergized their creative thinking around the issues. They discovered how to lightly organize themselves into a fluid matrix so that they could work on current demands from the rest of the organization and also identify internal issues related to reorganization.

I shared with Bill and his team what I knew: no matter how they organized themselves now or identified the issues for restructuring, they needed to find a way to specifically clarify decision-making authority and task responsibility. (Action 3: Articulate to others the boundary of your clarity and your lack of clarity.) Otherwise their quick-response mechanisms would fail at the time they needed them the most and their planning efforts would prove futile. Bill then recognized that it was his responsibility to ensure decision-making clarity. The team members also realized that they needed to insist that Bill be clear with them about what authority they had for which specific issues. (Action 5: Tell others what you need from them.)

I admired their development of a fluid structure that anticipated and serviced changes. I was also glad that we all had managed the ambiguity by staying in conversation, distinguishing what was known and not known, clarifying plans to move ahead, and sharing all team members' expectations of others.

Increase Your Tolerance for Reactivity

In some ways, having tolerance for others' anxiety and reactivity is the essence of presence. In addition, you must deal with your own anxiety about external or internal resistance and rise to the challenges of the moment. We all have our own tolerance levels in uncomfortable situations and our own individual reactive responses: fight, flight, save the day, placate. The list is endless. These responses can prevent us from helping a client or a system regain maximum functioning. Our automatic responses to an overload of input can short-circuit our own resilience like a blown fuse shuts down a fuse box.

When I am in an anxiety-producing situation, I sometimes feel helpless and inadequate. I ask myself, "What good am I doing at this point?" My feeling of helplessness can draw out responses in me that in retrospect seem inappropriate and ineffective in the situation. I turn to the first thing I can think of just to find an expedient resolution. It is not the client I am fleeing; I am fleeing the discomfort I feel. The best way I can help my client is to become more tolerant of my anxiety so that I can truly be with her instead of being distracted by my own reactivity.

To contrast the tendency to be reactive to one's own anxiety with a completely different kind of response, remember back to the kind of learning that we were all capable of in our first years of life. I call it toddler learning or Toddler Mind. We and our clients can work to regain some of the attitude and drive of toddlers in our own learning to become better coaches while helping our clients become better leaders.

When infants are on the verge of becoming toddlers and learning to walk, they have a ferocious drive for competence. Very little distracts them from the goal to walk. How many times have you seen babies endlessly work to get themselves up to stand, then take a step, then tumble and fall, and then start the whole process over again? It is downright inspiring if you think of toddlers as models for how to learn. Here is their approach, which, of course, is subconscious:

1. I must stand and walk.
2. I will get myself upright no matter what it takes.
3. I take a step. The risk of falling does not deter me.
4. I fall. Falling happens a lot.
5. I get up and do it again.
6. Falling is sometimes frustrating. I cry in frustration. Crying is like a rainstorm that passes through quickly and is gone. I'm not embarrassed by my frustration or my tears.
7. I have no negative judgments about falling. Falling is part of this magical thing called walking. I only know to do a continuous set of experiments, to try again. And again. And again. And again.
8. I walked! I took three full steps this time before falling. Yay!
9. Repeat steps 1 through 8.

We all did it this way. It is time to access that early virtuoso learning methodology when it comes to increasing human interaction skills, whether as a coach or a leader.

Learning new skills or learning to contain one's own reactivity is awkward, and no one is great the first time out. I tell my clients to expect to do "100 reps" before even beginning to presume that it will feel like second nature. You can remember Toddler Mind when you feel embarrassed by frustration or anxiety or failure. There was a time when we all learned without negative self-talk as we took risks, failed, added more repetitions, and gradually became competent walkers.

Executive coaching skills and leader interaction skills are no less complicated than the art of walking. It is the repeated experiments of a highly mobilized and motivated person that lead to mastery, whether in walking, leading, or executive coaching. If you can help yourself and your clients recreate the high competency of toddler learning—that feelings of frustration, anxiety, and awkwardness are survivable, expected, and not enough to deter one from one's goals—you will have made a great contribution to this world.

It is the repeated experiments of a highly mobilized and motivated person that lead to mastery.

Increasing your tolerance for your own anxiety is by nature a nearly unbearable experience because the pull of the old reactivity is so strong. However, you can take steps to help yourself arrive on the other side. In some ways, these steps are the adult version of the single-mindedness of toddler learning:

1. **Identify the trigger to your reactivity.**
2. **Learn your typical reaction to that trigger.**
3. **Choose an alternative response to pursue a different path.**
4. **Stay on track with the goal you have set for yourself in the meeting.**

These are necessary conditions, but taking them without the essential mind-set is not sufficient to improve your tolerance for reactivity. You must also be willing to enter the emotional void inherent in reaching beyond your current abilities. Increasing your tolerance means strengthening an emotional muscle that can hold on in that void.

Tolerance can grow with exposure to the situations themselves, just as an emergency room physician's comfort with trauma is higher than that of a medical student's. Of course, education and practice with the methodology help foster greater tolerance and the ability to cope with your anxiety and the anxiety of your client. You can also examine and alter your reactions to stress by revisiting the first "organization" you participated in, your family.[5] Whatever it takes, and it may take all of the above, your job is to strengthen that muscle so you can remain present with your clients.

Although they do not offer a comprehensive solution, these steps act as a potent set of tools. Once you are ready to increase your tolerance, you need to **identify the triggers** for your reactivity in specific situations. Your particular trigger can be anything: your client's tone of voice, a particular subject matter, or a challenge to your competence, for example. The content and the context of the triggers are unique to you.

Reactivity is a response that happens automatically and subconsciously. Your reaction may be taking control before you notice it. What are typical reactive responses on your part? Do you feel guilty and skulk away? Do you get angry and lash out? Do you feel defensive and explain your position? Get to know your habitual responses. **Once you understand what causes your response, you can learn to link your reaction to a specific trigger.**

Plan and choose an alternative response. It gives you time to think before acting. You will rarely be able to plan in the heat of an automatic response, so knowing your own habits is critical. You can see them in the moment ("there I go again") and have something in mind to break the trance. As an example of a planned response, you could deliberately pause, break the chain of reactivity, and give yourself time to think. Or plan to ask about the position and concerns of the other person. Or remember to keep working toward your goal.

Staying on track with your goal is the central point of transforming yourself into a less reactive person because reactivity leads you away from your goal.

Thankfully, the mere fact that you have established and remained focused on a goal can calm you in the midst of your reactivity. Choosing a worthy goal is a necessary condition of signature presence.

I personally experienced the far-reaching impact of reactivity and developing tolerance to it with a long-time client in the following situation:

Annette

Annette, a client with whom I had a collaborative, long-term working relationship, would periodically ask me to take on a role that was not appropriate to my coaching role as stipulated in our contract. This time, she wanted me to manage a committee on human resource standards with her staff. However, there were people in the organization who were much more appropriate than I was for the role. This was a role for an employee to staff, not a role for an external person to take on, which would create undue dependence on an external consultant. My management of the committee would undermine the skill development of others who reported to her. Annette did not see it that way. She knew I was a good facilitator, and she just wanted the job done.

Because everything else in our contract worked well, it was personally difficult for me to refuse her request. Yet I was very sure that saying no was the best response for the organization—and ultimately for Annette. On other occasions in which I had agreed to activities that fell outside the bounds of my role, I always regretted it. I saw that I contributed to a continued weakness in her staff and resented my own compromise. Whenever I found myself in Annette's office in the middle of this conversation, I could feel the internal pull to acquiesce to her request. My anxiety grew as I imagined the degree of disappointment she would have in me if I refused.

Finally, I understood my discomfort: I found it hard to sit in the midst of her disappointment in me and her irritation. Period. Sometimes I flinched in the face of it and would agree to do something just to avoid her disappointment. When I realized this, I resolved to hold my ground no matter what the consequences. One way I thought I could endure her reaction was by being prepared to say, over and over again, "I know you find it disappointing, but I am not able to do it."

In our next meeting, Annette spent twenty minutes cajoling, flattering, threatening, and bargaining with me. For twenty minutes I repeated my mantra: "I know you find it disappointing . . ." It seemed as though it persisted for an eternity. Time can really slow down, almost unbearably, when one is in the void, totally out of one's comfort zone, and continuing to hang on anyway. She finally stopped. I left the meeting convinced that I had broken my relationship with her.

She never asked me to take on the task again. One of her managers did this work instead, and it helped him develop further in his job. After some initial awkwardness on both our parts, Annette and I resumed our productive working relationship.

The amount of time you spend confronting and tolerating your reactivity can vary: twenty seconds, or two hours, or two months. Think of it as increasing the strength and stamina of your tolerance muscle. Investing in gaining greater tolerance for moments of reactivity can lead you to discover a more rewarding coaching experience instead of the same old action-reaction-counterreaction. You experience yourself as an adventurer in a land few travel by enduring reactivity long enough for the new moment to occur. You cannot have this breakthrough by repeating the same old responses.

Like standing on a windy hill in a hailstorm, the process is sometimes bracing and also daunting and a bit nerve-wracking. However, even an incremental increase in tolerance can provide a geometric gain in bringing novelty to a situation, either as a dramatically different form of resistance from the client or a breakthrough with the client, or both.

Executive coaches need this kind of tolerance because in many ways, we are like horse whisperers to our clients. Horse whisperers work with horses that have lost their trust in themselves and their ability to work in concert with humans. One kind of horse whispering literally puts the horse in an extremely confined space (like swaddling an infant) until the horse settles down enough to rebuild its self-trust, resourcefulness, and cooperation with humans. I often think of my work with clients as similar: by being unintimidated by and able to tolerate my clients' anxiety, I show my clients it is possible to hold and tolerate their own anxiety. Over time they learn to trust that they can in fact tolerate their anxiety on their own.

> *I show my clients it is possible to hold and tolerate their own anxiety. Over time they learn to trust that they can in fact tolerate their anxiety on their own.*

Bring Immediacy to the Moment

Immediacy means that you notice a relationship between what the client talks about "out there" and what actually happens in the moment between the two of you. When you notice this parallel occurrence, you can report your experience of her directly in the here and now. Rather than see yourself as outside what the client describes, you put yourself within it. This gives the client a clearer picture of what happens with her in her organization. How you interact with the client and your internal reactions to her can provide her with useful information. She can assess the effectiveness of that particular interaction and identify a potential area for change.

During your coaching conversations with a client, you can increase immediacy by doing the following:

1. **Look for parallels** between the client's actions at work and in coaching sessions.
2. **Identify your internal and external reactions** to the client's actions.
3. **Speak directly to the client about your experience of her.**
4. **Make the connection** between your experience of the client in the moment and the ways she may be acting similarly elsewhere.

Over time, you will begin to notice **parallel occurrences.** People often act consistently across contexts, including in their coaching sessions. The key is to hone in on the occurrences that have the most relevance to the business issue at hand.

There are plenty of ways that we as coaches miss opportunities to be immediate with our clients. You can tell that you are not scanning for parallel occurrences when your mind wanders while you listen to a client's story and you think it is a waste of time. You miss it if you are thinking, "Okay, so what has this story got to do with anything? She's mentioning her victories again." You *do* start to scan and hone in on parallel occurrences when you think, "Am I the only one whose mind wanders off when she talks? How often does she list victories with her team, and how does it affect them?"

Identifying your personal reactions is crucial for immediacy. A here-and-now conversation with your client requires that you mention your reactions because your reactions reveal useful information. *Here* means focusing on what is going on between you and the person you are with, not you and someone else. And *now* means this very moment, not the past or the future. Here-and-now means that you talk about what is going on *right now* between you and the person you are with. Here-and-now conversations often get lost in the organizational world because we focus so often on "there"—everyone and everything else—and "then"—any moment besides now, either the past or the future. Here-and-now conversations have a lot of power because people do not usually get such direct feedback.

Your internal here-and-now reactions in the situation mentioned earlier of the client recounting her successes might be described like this: "So how am I reacting to these stories? I'm not seeing the connection to the topic we are discussing. At first, I resist them and wander off mentally. And now I wonder why she does it."

Once you have identified your internal reactions, you can follow steps 3 and 4 listed above, **telling the client your direct experience and linking it to her work world.** You might say, "I hear you talk about your successes, but I'm not seeing the connection to the topic we're discussing. Frankly I'm starting to wander off. Then I start guessing why you're doing it. Maybe your team tries to second-guess you sometimes too."

Of course, there are risks involved in accessing and using immediacy with a client. You could be way off—or so directly on target that your client gets defensive. You could scare her off by getting too intense too soon. In the best case, however, you command your client's attention in a new way. She may ask you for more of that kind of feedback from you.

Without using immediacy, it is impossible to get to the heart of some issues. Immediacy helps a client identify her knee-jerk patterns and helps her make new choices. It takes tremendous presence to do this as a coach because you must observe patterns of interaction in your client at the same time you are participating and interacting with her.

When you do have the presence to stop your conversation in order to report your observations and reactions, you evoke more presence from your client. The trance of her habitual way of doing things may break long enough for her to see herself in a new way. This can be a tremendous gift to your client. It requires that the coach have the courage to speak directly and that the client have the courage to listen to direct feedback.

I experienced the power of using immediacy with Matt, a prospective client:

Matt

It was early in my coaching career. Matt and I were talking about the successes and challenges he felt as the leader of his department in a large national corporation. I admired his strategic thinking as he applied it to every example he gave. I also saw that he seemed relatively satisfied with his efforts in his department, but he sought some indefinable improvement among the people who worked for him.

After probing in several different ways about the changes and possible outcomes that he wanted, I fell into my own pit. It seemed I had nothing to offer this man, not even a decent diagnosis, because I could not get a handle on what it was that he wanted to be different.

There was a ten-minute stretch when it may have looked as though I was listening to what he was saying, but I was actually berating myself, thinking, "You are so green. You call yourself a consultant and coach? You can't think of a thing to offer him! What business do you have taking up this man's time? How can you gracefully end this appointment?" In other words, I surpassed my tolerance level in my discomfort with his vagueness.

Then I paused to regain my bearings. I began to realize that I already was having a significant experience of this leader and could give him feedback about a pattern I was noticing. It might clarify where he wanted to go next. Giving feedback would be somewhat risky because I did not know him well. It could either end any chance I had of working with him, or catapult us to a higher degree of interaction and productivity in our prospective working relationship. Since I was not currently getting anywhere, I took the risk, and I brought my presence to bear on the next moment with him.

I said, "Matt, I find your strategic thinking quite valuable. It matches much of my own experience, and therefore I trust your instincts about your company and your department. If I were a direct report of yours, I would like your thinking and be ready to follow it. But I also find that throughout the conversation, I am repeatedly having a second reaction to your strategic thinking. You give no goal, no direction, no action to take after you express your opinions. So I find myself ready to follow, but I don't know where to go."

This was a moment of truth. I didn't know whether Matt would bring his own presence to the moment or defend himself against it. In this instance, I was fortunate enough to be with a leader who responded to the invitation to engage on a deeper level.

He hesitated, with a puzzled look on his face. Then he said, "Actually, I probably don't take that next step. It's a bit of a risk, and I don't get around to it with either my boss or my staff." Throughout the rest of the conversation, he was able to engage more specifically about this challenge with his department and his boss. This allowed us to forge ahead into a potential area of coaching work with him to leverage both himself and his department to greater results.

This kind of immediate speaking and listening can foment a daunting yet exhilarating moment. When you do the hard work of bringing your presence to the conversation and the client responds with openness, you break the ground for a strong partnership. When you do not bring your signature self to these moments, you will have the uphill task of trying to leverage change in either stubbornly resistant or overly compliant clients.[6]

> *When you do the hard work of bringing your presence to the conversation and the client responds with openness, you break the ground for a strong partnership.*

Parallel Journeys of Executive and Coach

Besides working on bringing more of your presence through these ways, one of your greatest contributions is helping your client find more of his own signature presence. His presence is the most powerful tool that he brings to his leadership.

Leaders are not immune to losing their effectiveness. When they become reactive in a situation, it can take on a variety of forms:

- Becoming impatient and demanding when people are resistant to dramatic change

- Giving up their agenda whenever a particular staff member challenges their position
- Endlessly seeking more information when facing competing factions
- Vacillating between being a rigid dictator and an overly relaxed observer

A client who exhibits any of these kinds of reactivity has lost the backbone and heart balance between being clear about where he stands and staying connected to those who work with him. When he remains unconscious of this reactivity, he does not seek help but tries the same thing over and over again. If he becomes aware of the futility of his efforts, that is the time that he could learn with a coach.

Your job as a coach is to **help the client strengthen his presence and lessen his reactivity.** To the extent that you struggle to manage your own reactivity and achieve greater presence, you will understand what the client faces in bringing forth his signature presence. You will be familiar with the journey, and its roadblocks and opportunities. The client increases his presence by focusing on the same four approaches to presence that a coach uses: (1) identifying and sustaining a goal, (2) managing himself in ambiguity, (3) increasing his tolerance for anxiety and reactivity, and (4) using immediacy. You can **help your clients assess their strengths and challenges in these four approaches** and incorporate them into their leadership. The next chapter explores executives' reactions to stress and how to help them regain their resilient effectiveness.

Chapter Two Highlights

Signs of Signature Presence

1. Bring yourself to the moment with your client.

2. Increase your tolerance for uncomfortable situations.

Self-Differentiation

1. Work to maintain a balance of backbone and heart in your work.

2. Develop quick recovery from reactivity.

Strengthen Your Presence

1. Identify and sustain a goal for yourself in each coaching session.

   - Choose content and process goals.

   - Know your vulnerability in a reactive system.

   - Remember your goal.

   - Be more committed to your goal than to easing your discomfort in the moment.

2. Manage yourself in the midst of ambiguity.

   - Acknowledge the ambiguity.

   - Distinguish for yourself where you are clear or unclear about the situation.

   - Articulate to others the boundary between your clarity and lack of clarity.

   - Say what it is you want to do, given the situation.

   - Tell others what you need from them, asking them what they need from you.

3. Increase your tolerance for reactivity within you and around you.

   - Identify the triggers to your reactivity.

   - Learn your typical reaction to specific triggers.

   - Choose alternative responses to get you started down a different path.

   - Stay on track with your goals in the session.

4. Bring immediacy to the moment.

   - Scan for parallels between the client's actions in her world and what the client is doing with you.

- Identify your reaction to the client's action.
- Speak directly to the client about your experience of her.
- Make the connection between your experience of the client and how she may be doing the same thing elsewhere.

Parallel Journeys of Executive and Coach

1. Be a resource for the strengthening of the client's presence.

2. Help the client assess his strengths and challenges in these four approaches to presence.

3

SYSTEMS THINKING

Understanding the Executive's Challenges and the Coach's Challenges

This chapter further explores the effects of stressful situations on leaders and the ways those situations elicit reactive responses in them. It instructs the coach in the art of detecting and understanding the impacts of the forces operating in the client's system. As you read, see whether you can detect the systems patterns that work on and through your clients. Also, assess your ability to identify what effects clients have on you and in what ways these forces alter how you work with your clients. Attending closely to the key systems concepts presented here will give you a new way to see the forces that create an impact on you, your clients, and their organizations. Seeing with new eyes gives you greater choices when you face the challenges brought to you by your clients.[1]

Tom and Ben, Executive and Coach

Tom is a senior vice president of finance at a company where he has worked for fifteen years. The company, part of an industry that has remained pretty staid over the past forty years, has made money without a lot of effort. Now the industry is rapidly changing and requires aggressive entrepreneurship, but this company is unprepared for the adjustment. A new chief executive officer, Susan, has been hired from the outside and has the vision and energy that the board knows it needs to move forward.

> Susan tells Tom that the lackadaisical way in which he has run finance is no longer acceptable: the monthly accounting report dates have to be moved up by a week, and the department must reduce operating costs by 30 percent. She expects Tom to generate the plan to get there.
>
> Tom is anxious about the demands in these mandates because he has never pushed his people before. In fact, he avoids conflict at all costs. Tom seeks help from Ben, an internal organizational development specialist for the company.

Tom, rather unexpectedly, has found himself in hot water and off balance. Everything is changing around him: the business environment, his boss, and his boss's expectations.

How can Ben coach Tom effectively? If you were Ben, what would you do? How does Ben approach an anxious executive who feels he is under siege? What framework can Ben bring to this coaching relationship so that he can stay on course himself?

Ben can benefit from using a systems perspective, the second principle from Chapter One. Using this perspective keeps executive coaches focused on the fundamental forces promoting or impeding their work with clients.

Specifically, I adapt the systems perspective from the family systems field and apply it to organizations. I find it to be one of the most powerful lenses to use in assessing business issues. Although I neither use the specific techniques of that field nor attempt to make therapeutic interventions, I apply this way of *thinking* to organizations because it is so relevant to how executives and their work groups interact together.

A systems perspective resists identifying a single element or person in a system as the root cause of a problem. A system can guide the actions of individuals and tends to have greater staying power than the personalities of individuals or the mission and goals of the organization. Following are a handful of concepts from this world of systems. (These concepts, and those in Chapter Four, drive the methodology in Chapters Five through Eight.)

A systems perspective resists identifying a single element or person in a system as the root cause of a problem.

The Interactional Force Field

When any two or ten or one hundred people interact with one another over time, they create a **social interactional field.**[2] It operates through the relationships of those involved, but it develops a character, shape, and set of rules transcending any of the individuals who contributed energy to its creation.

A spider web is a good metaphor to describe an interactional force field. When anything comes in contact with a spider web, anywhere on its surface, the whole web moves. If anything shakes or disrupts the attachment points of the web, the web moves. Yet a spider web has amazing tensile strength and can withstand strain on its strands many times greater than its weight. The spider web's resiliency, the ability to be strong yet flexible, allows it to maintain its integrity through wind, rain, flying insects, and other disruptions. Spider webs are often invisible to the observer, yet they go on functioning in their interplay of movement and stability. A web, however, also has a breaking point and can be disturbed or torn to such an extent that it is destroyed, losing its integrity, strength, and beauty.

So it is with an interactional field established between two or more people. It has its own anchor points, resiliency, and breaking point, and it is most often invisible to the members within it. **When anyone within the field moves, all members feel the effect, though differently, based on their positions.** Other metaphors for the interactional field are the gravitational and magnetic fields. We are immersed within their invisible forces and we feel their influence, though most often that influence is unconsciously experienced.

Say three people are meeting with their boss. Person A reports on his week's activities, while Person B gazes out the window, and Person C writes notes in her binder. Person D, the boss, asks questions of Person A.

Before I continue, choose one of the people in this scenario whose actions you are most likely to duplicate in a similar circumstance. In the setting of a routine business meeting, do you identify with: Person A, B, C, or D? Is this because you are by nature conscientious (A), bored at meetings (B), able to do multiple tasks (C), or show interest in the topic at hand (D)?

Now imagine that the boss's boss, Person E, walks into the room unannounced. How are the players likely to react? How is your character likely to react? Do they continue doing exactly what they were doing before? Usually the answer is no. Every person in the room gets organized in a new way because of the introduction of another variable, Person E, the boss's boss. No one stopped the meeting or changed the agenda. No one's personality was suddenly altered. Yet all kinds of things have perceptibly shifted.

Let's say that note-taking Person C is a new employee who started just that day. She has never met Person E and does not know he is the boss's boss, but she experiences the invisible interactional force field by witnessing the change in behavior of the other three people. Like the needle of a compass pointing north, the new employee is starting to shift toward the direction of the others' change in behavior, feeling the magnetic pull. The members of the meeting reorganize themselves without explaining any new rules to her or to each other. Yet the effect is immediate and obvious.

Interactional fields take on a life of their own, even as individuals in an organization come and go. I once worked for a restaurant that maintained the same level of service and quality through several years. It aspired to be world class, and it was indeed good but not exceptional. Over those years, 100 percent of the managers and 70 percent of the staff left, and newcomers took their places. However, the social interactional field remained the same: good but not excellent. There were factors in place affecting the system that were more enduring than the individuals within it.

Seeing the Force Field

You may be thinking, *How do I learn about the social interactional field? How can I begin to see it?* You can become aware of the different ways in which you show up in various groups and the effect that the system has on you. Say, for example, you fly from Chicago to Boston with Cattle Call Airlines. Just flying with CCA sets your teeth on edge because, among other things, the employees do not smile and never look you in the eye but rather just go through the motions, and the beverage service is slow. By the time you get to Boston, you are crabby and tired.

The Chicago-to-Boston flight of Peak Service Airlines is completely different. PSA employees smile, act as though they like their coworkers, and deliver service efficiently, on time, and with warm friendliness. You leave the flight calm and contented. You had the same flight time and the same kind of airplane, but the web created by each of these systems elicits different responses in you.

When people talk about the "feel" of the place, they are noticing the web created by the system's interactional force field. When you notice that you are having distinctly different feelings, thoughts, and motivations just by virtue of being in two different organizations, you are experiencing the unique interactional fields of each of those organizations.

Yes, you may say, *I can see what you're saying, especially when I am a customer, but often I have the same experiences no matter where I go! For instance, no matter what organization I work for, I always wind up being the unsung hero who works too hard, saves the day at the last minute, and feels burned out afterward. My experience is that all work systems are alike.*

In an uncanny way, organizations seek individuals to fulfill the same roles they have always had for certain positions or in particular departments (unsung hero, watchdog, cheerleader, underachiever, and so forth). You may be selected for your ability to be an unsung hero over and over again because the systems employing you know a hero when they see one. Also in an uncanny way, you seek out organizations that have vacancies in the role that you naturally take on.

You probably learned to be an unsung hero from your first organization, your family. Families develop their own social interactional fields that shape the experiences of those within them. Consequently systems interlock with each other. You take the interactional field from your family with you when you step inside your work organization. This can lead you to the same experiences everywhere you go because the different systems bring forth the same response from you—the one you have been trained to give.

What do these interactional webs have to do with coaching? Practically everything! First, it is critical to **recognize how organizational systems affect you, including the ones you are in and those that you co-create.** Your reactivity (see Chapter Two) to a system also shows where you are particularly vulnerable in a system because you may respond with knee-jerk habits. When you maintain a self-differentiated presence, you can feel the effects of a system but avoid reacting automatically. Developing the four approaches to presence will improve your effectiveness in maintaining your equilibrium in the system's force field.[3]

Second, it is equally important to **attend to the system co-created between you and your client.** Within interactional fields, people establish ways of relating that become like choreographed dance steps over time. These patterns can be either useful or counterproductive. Typical client-coach patterns include a wide variety of behaviors. Here is a sample of them (the first two are useful, the second two less effective):

- Client seeks advice: coach fosters independent thinking.
- Client seeks tough feedback: coach gives it.
- Client vents: coach placates.
- Client is continually late for appointments: coach tolerates it.

Every relationship develops a system "dance," and the coach-client relationship is no different. It is important to take an inventory and figure out the types of dances in which you engage with different kinds of clients. Can you name the typical patterns of interrelating that you and your clients develop over time? Are these patterns effective for your clients and your coaching?

Third, it is important to begin to **see the system within which your client operates.** Often the very pattern developing between you and the executive is a living sample of the system the client is in with his own organization. Systems have a way of extending themselves out to their furthest boundaries and pulling anyone who comes close to them into their interactional vortex. In that way, they act very much like the pull of gravity.

In the following example, I learned about my client's system by paying attention to how she interacted with me.

Joanne

Joanne was like two different people. Part of the time she seemed relaxed and unhurried. In fact, she was not focused enough to make any progress. Although she never said it, her attitude seemed to be, "Don't worry about it; it'll take care of itself." When we had our sessions, she treated them like friendly chats. But then she would call out of the blue, harried and tense, insisting that she needed to see me immediately to settle an emerging crisis. She wanted to resolve the issue, and she asked (and sometimes insisted) that I make sessions with her a priority in my work life.

Like Joanne, the organization in which she worked exhibited the two states, from a laid-back atmosphere of high sociability to a five-alarm-fire response. My client was one of the high-ranking executives who perpetuated this dichotomy of energy. Although the project she was addressing with me did not require these two energies, they seeped through anyway. **The more you take your working relationship with your client as a learning lab for the greater system, the more you can help your client see the system's pull on her and her influence on it.**

It is not surprising that **as a coach, you get pulled into the client system's self-perpetuating patterns. This is both a blessing and a curse.** The benefit is that you get firsthand knowledge of what it is like for your client to live in that system. You start experiencing the same gut reactions that the people within that system do. The problem is that you have the same gut reactions that people within the system do. The larger perspective you bring to your client can begin to diminish. This is why understanding how systems work, identifying their force fields, and breaking out of counterproductive patterns are essential for coaches.

> *As a coach, you get pulled into the client system's self-perpetuating patterns. This is both a blessing and a curse.*

In summary, you can learn to see the interactional field's effect on your coaching by:

- **Getting to know your vulnerability to a system, where and when you get reactive.**
- **Identifying the client-coach dances you co-create.**
- **Discovering the system's pull on the client by observing how she is reacting to you.**

The Effect of Anxiety in the Workplace

When a stable interactional force field (whether it is a work team, a family, or an entire organization) encounters a challenge or disruption too large for its own resiliency, the people within it experience heightened anxiety. Some examples of major disruptions include:

- The company is being sold to another company.
- A boss is leaving, and another is replacing him.
- Market forces are signaling a shift.

Anxiety jams the normal comfortable way of interacting within a system and causes a variety of reactions:

- Resistance
- Blame
- Reorganization
- Self-protection
- Loss of creativity
- Heroic efforts

Moments of anxiety seriously challenge the client's ability to bring her presence and creativity to a business situation.

The use of the term *anxiety* does not refer to its everyday use—the kind of natural anxiety people get when they try out a new skill or the nervousness that comes with giving a presentation. In fact, some anxiety is productive for learning because it indicates that we are on the edge of our known skills and are about to launch into new territory.

I am using *anxiety* more technically to refer to the response people or systems have to forces that stretch them toward a potential, or perceived, breaking point. **Anxiety is the early-warning device that alerts the system to counter with a self-preserving reaction, often a variation on fight or flight.**

This anxiety throws people off balance, and they become reactive, an unproductive automatic response to forces around them. They lose their creative response. It is like overturning a boat while whitewater rafting rather than successfully navigating through the rapids.

In addition to anxiety, several other major variables affect leaders and systems: the skills, capabilities, motivations, and contributions of people in the organization. These variables must be assessed when evaluating how well an organization or leader can achieve business goals. However, even the most skilled, capable, motivated, and insightful people become less effective if they do not acknowledge and face the power of the system and their unique vulnerability to the system's pull on them.

The Leader's Challenge

In low-stress situations, a talented executive whose anxiety is low meets challenges well and can accomplish the two critical activities of leadership: (1) leading with backbone (taking clear positions on issues) while at the same time (2) leading with heart (staying connected to the people who work with her) (see Figure 3.1).

When the external challenge escalates and, more important, the leader's reactivity to the situation increases, it creates internal tension. Her anxiety reaches a level that floods her normal responses and diminishes her ability to take clear positions, stay connected to her staff, or both (Figure 3.2).

Figure 3.1 The Leader's Response in Low-Stress Situations

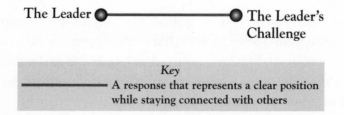

Figure 3.2 The Leader's Anxiety While Under Increased Stress

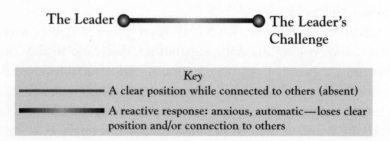

How can you determine if the executive with whom you are working is falling into her knee-jerk reaction? The symptoms can vary widely. A mixture of thoughts, feelings, and desires hold sway when someone experiences reactive anxiety. Here are a few possibilities, some of which you may have heard from your clients:

The Executive's Internal Voices While Anxious

- I don't have a clue what to do now.
- Why don't they just do what I want them to do?
- I have lost track of how to prioritize all the variables.
- I'll do the first thing that comes to mind.
- If they understood how complex this is, they'd stop whining about it.
- Maybe someone else will know what to do.
- I'll look for a magic bullet.
- I'm so mad I just want to lash out.
- How did I get into this mess in the first place?
- They let me down again. I can never depend on them.
- I'll probably lose my job over this.
- I always have to go it alone.

Catastrophic either-or thinking, with "always" and "never" thrown in for good measure, is a sure sign that the executive is in the throes of reactive thinking–action patterns. Essentially she has lost access to her internal resources and resilience. She unconsciously disengages from herself, a sign of the depth of the problem but also a key to its resolution. She can regain her presence by rebalancing backbone and heart (the key). But she has difficulty locating the key because it is buried under all her reactivity and her actions to avoid facing her anxiety.

Triangles: Whose Stress Is This, Anyway?

One response to anxiety is to turn to a third person, hoping that conversations with a third party will relieve some of the pressure between the first individual and the challenge he feels (from a person, an issue, or a group of people). This creates a triangle of involvement between the initial person, his challenge, and the third person. Triangles are often created unconsciously to lower stress. Sometimes turning to a third person is a good tactic because it helps the anxious person collect his thoughts and revisit the challenge with renewed energy. More often, however, reliance on a third person prolongs the unresolved situation.

There are many triangles in life. Some of the stereotypical ones are:

Anxious Person	Is Challenged By	And Turns To
husband	wife	work
parent	child	teacher
wife	husband	friends
manager	employee	human resource department
customer service rep	customer	salesperson
vendor	inventory supervisor	production manager

Leaders may form such triangles under stress. An example of triangulation occurs in the story at the beginning of this chapter. Tom, the senior vice president of finance, is anxious because he feels challenged by Susan, the new CEO. Tom becomes disturbed about the relationship he has with Susan and the demands she places on him. To relieve his anxiety, Tom turns to Ben, the internal organizational development specialist, and involves him in the work relationship between Tom and Susan (Figure 3.3).

Figure 3.3 Triangulation

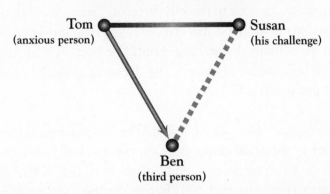

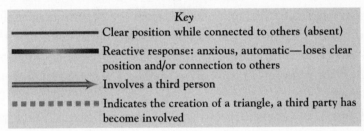

Key
Clear position while connected to others (absent)
Reactive response: anxious, automatic—loses clear position and/or connection to others
Involves a third person
Indicates the creation of a triangle, a third party has become involved

You have probably witnessed clients doing this with their work relationships. There are many ways that Tom could triangle someone else into his relationship with Susan. Some of the possibilities follow (the first two perpetuate anxiety; the third one addresses it productively):

- Tom could use one of his staff members to vent about Susan. He says to the staff person: "Can you believe what Susan did in the meeting this morning? It just shows you how out of it she is about our situation."

- Tom could create an alliance with Susan by turning another senior vice president into a common adversary. He says to Susan: "Last spring, Jack's audit of my department said I was running at peak efficiency. If I had known how far off he was, I would have come to you as soon as you took the job to see how we could solve the problem."

- Tom could go to human resources (HR) to help him work with Susan. He says to the HR director: "Susan and I don't see eye to eye at all on this one. Can you help me figure out what we're really disagreeing about? I've been over and over it with her, and we keep covering the same ground. I need a fresh perspective."

Do these reactions sound familiar? The first two examples show how we try to throw off our anxiety, get rid of it, build walls around it, pass it on to someone else, and hide from it. It is as though we are allergic to our own anxiety. When in the throes of stress, we go to great lengths to distract ourselves from the very anxiety fueling our distress. That approach is about as effective as dealing with a gas line fire by turning away from the source of the leak ("If I don't see it, it's not there.") rather than finding a way to deal with the gas line leak.

Even Tom's own internal voices, anger, worries, fears, and disappointments are distractions that keep him from focusing on the monumental task of the external challenge. These voices are like internal triangles that lock up or siphon off the executive's energy rather than allow him to focus on the challenge at hand. The real challenge is summoning up the courage to face the situation and discover what is required from him in terms of a response.

Signs That Triangles Are Distracting Leaders

The leader's reactivity often involves multiple parties and creates multiple triangles in an attempt to lower anxiety. Reactivity can cascade throughout a system through requests, new rules, demands, or gossip. These reactions drain the system of creative resources to solve the problem. Here is what happens with Tom (Figure 3.4):

Figure 3.4 Cascading, Interlocking Triangles

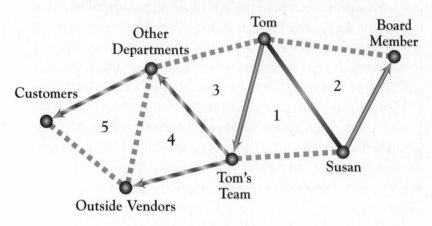

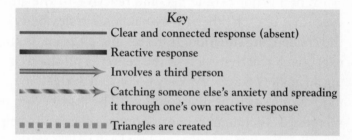

Key

————————— Clear and connected response (absent)

▬▬▬▬▬▬▬ Reactive response

————————▷ Involves a third person

◄▬▬▬▬▬▬▶ Catching someone else's anxiety and spreading it through one's own reactive response

▪▪▪▪▪▪▪▪▪ Triangles are created

Tom and Ben, continued

Before talking with Ben, Tom tells his team what Susan has said. He paints an image of Susan as the evil disruptive force from outside (triangle 1). Members of the department become very upset and talk about the company's letting them down. They sympathize with Tom and cite the terrible pressure he must be under. After the meeting, the department's gossip grapevine feeds the team's anxiety about their job security, fuels resentment about having to change procedures, and foments speculation that Tom probably is not standing up for their interests with Susan (triangles are multiplying).

In senior vice president team meetings with Susan, Tom is silent during the brainstorming discussions on models for restructuring. Susan becomes irritated with Tom's lack of action and starts talking to a board member about the possibility of replacing Tom (triangle 2). Tom's team, distracted by the turmoil in their department, starts missing deadlines with other departments (triangle 3) and outside vendors (triangle 4), thus affecting the service the company's customers are receiving (triangle 5).

When other people become reactive to the situation, the executive, or each other, the system loses its flexibility to deal with the challenging situation. It freezes and locks up. In this case, the executive's reactivity acts as the center of all the triangles, creating an anxiety vortex. Anxiety becomes a distraction rather than a motivator to seek creative solutions. The leader's own resilience is suppressed. Your number one priority as a coach is to help the executive face his own reactions and get back to his creative center.

> *Your number one priority as a coach is to help the executive face his own reactions and get back to his creative center.*

Enter the Coach

When leaders become reactive to their own challenges, they can turn to a coach to help them out of their quagmire. This client-coach relationship can create a healthy triangle between the leader and his dilemma. There actually *are* such things as healthy triangles. They are healthy when they are used not to flee anxiety, but to face it and return to the challenge at hand. It helps the client work toward regaining balance and returning to more constructive work relationships (Figure 3.5).

Figure 3.5 The Triangled Coach

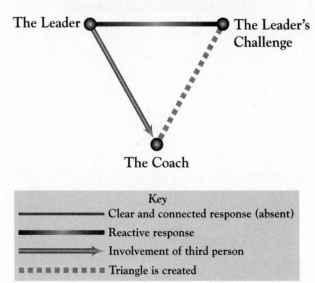

The Leader

The Leader's Challenge

The Coach

Key
——————— Clear and connected response (absent)
━━━━━━━ Reactive response
═══════⟶ Involvement of third person
▪ ▪ ▪ ▪ ▪ ▪ ▪ ▪ ▪ Triangle is created

Let's look at what Tom does. He feels so much anxiety that he approaches Ben for help. Triangles can have either a creative effect on a system or a debilitating one. If used creatively, a triangle gives anxiety a temporary place to reside while the client chooses a thoughtful next step. If Tom does this to clear his own thinking so he can choose a course of action, turning to Ben is a healthy use of a triangle. If Tom goes to Ben in an attempt to avoid his situation, he will remain reactive and get less out of his sessions with Ben.

Who has not first tried to get out of a tough situation before truly dealing with it? A coach's beginning relationship with clients often involves the client's wanting to offload the problem rather than face it, and coaches need to watch for this propensity in their clients when entering the coaching triangle.

Your position as an executive coach within the multiple triangles is a powerful one, and you can use it to help thaw the frozen system. But you do not want the client to siphon off his energy by turning to you so that you will face his dilemma for him. Paradoxically, you enter the triangle in such a way that you stay out of the way of the client so that he can face his own dilemma.

Tom and Ben, continued

Ben is thinking, "Tom is spawning triangles throughout his entire system. They're just digging him further into his hole. And he's got his eye out for Susan like a rabbit has its eye out for roving dogs. What he needs is to become more the master of his destiny rather than a victim of it." Ben believes that what may be most useful to Tom is refocusing him on his goals and how Susan's mandates fit into those goals. That would be the place to start, with a close second being increasing Tom's ability to manage himself in the midst of all this ambiguity.

This is easier said than done. When an executive under stress turns to a coach for help, one of several **common patterns** emerges between client and coach:

1. The executive retains ownership of her challenge and uses the coach as a sounding board to clear her thinking and set some goals.
2. The executive attempts to offload her anxiety onto the coach, but the coach refuses to take responsibility for the problem.
3. The executive offloads her anxiety onto the coach, and the coach works harder than the client to solve the client's situation.

The first option is a great experience with a mature client. The second is effective when the coach can stay firm and compassionate with the client. As for the third, interactions between a client and a coach can be off and running and well down the road before either realizes they have both been enabling the client to avoid her dilemma. This pattern temporarily relieves the client of stress but does not empower her to surmount her own challenges.

The third path happens more times than coaches, myself included, would like to admit. Goodness knows how often I have done this in the past (who am I kidding? I can still get caught up in it!). Therefore, the task at hand is learning the patterns you play out when you get stressed by anxious clients. You need to ask yourself, "How does this dance get started? Why didn't I see it coming in the first place?" You cannot take effective action until you discover your contribution to the pattern.

Patterns: Shall We Dance?

Patterns are either useful or counterproductive depending on whether they help people face what scares them so that they can achieve their goals.[4] Patterns are suprarational, meaning they exist beyond a logical process of how people plan to relate. This unconscious system reinforces itself and calls on both parties to adapt to it and perpetuate it.

It is difficult not to attribute these patterns to the intrapsychic (internal) process of one individual. Actually they are snapshots of the system as a whole. It is truly a dance—the constant moving and adapting together that makes or breaks graceful movement. There are endless variations of two-person dance patterns. Here is a representative sample:

- One pursues and the other distances.
- One attacks and the other defends.
- One underachieves and the other overachieves.
- One initiates and the other follows.

Both partners contribute equally to creating the seamless (though sometimes stormy) flow of their relationship.

Key questions can help you discover patterns you are in with your clients:

- What dances do you develop with which kinds of clients?
- Can you give them names that would help you recognize them sooner when you are in them?

- To what extent can you acknowledge your own dance repertoire of patterns that determines how you relate to clients when you are not at your best?

Say you find yourself recognizing the response mentioned earlier: taking on the client's burden (overachieving while she underachieves) with some of your coaching clients. Sometimes it happens subtly. It takes courage to admit to being a co-creator of this pattern. One way of testing for it is to ask the following questions:

- Who is working harder to figure out and solve the problem: you or the client?
- Who's sleeping better at night: you or your client? (You're in trouble if it's your client.)
- Which calls from clients do you dread?
- Who requires a higher level of energy from you because being with them takes a lot out of you?

> *Who's sleeping better at night: you or your client?*
> *(You're in trouble if it's your client.)*

When you answer these questions, you may realize that you are taking more ownership for your client's stress than is useful for either of you. To understand these dances, let's take a closer look at how anxiety in a system affects the interaction between client and coach.

The Coach's Challenge

Remember the strength of a social interactional field: systems extend themselves out to their edges, pulling you into their vortex. As I mentioned before, coaches can catch the system's anxiety.

As a coach, you can lose command of your own strengths and resources just as the client has lost hers.

Coaches are not immune to becoming anxious, especially while facing the anxiety and reactivity of their clients. This is why it takes courage to work with an anxious client. If you sit long enough with someone who is anxious, it will eventually get on your nerves (after, say, twenty minutes or, whatever your limit is). Anxiety, left to its own devices, spreads and multiplies quickly through a system. Clients do not need coaches to act as anxiety step-up transformers. They are surrounded by enough people who do that already.

No one is immune. There will always be a cluster of anxiety-producing circumstances that will cause you to become reactive and lose your bearings. To be a better coach, you have to recognize your unique propensities. To which of these circumstances are you most susceptible?

1. You enter the client's interactional field, which has all the hallmarks of high anxiety and reactivity.

2. The client has become rudderless.

3. The client is looking to you to save her and believes that you have the resources she wishes she had.

4. You have bought into the anxious belief that it is your responsibility to rescue her.

The last circumstance is the avalanche created by the combined weight of the first three. When I get caught in the interactional field of my client's anxiety, I distract myself and my client away from her challenges. I adopt her challenges as my dilemmas to solve because I've caught the "flu" of my client's anxiety. When anxious, coaches become less available to themselves and therefore lose their creative thinking with the client.

Sometimes the thoughts I have are tip-offs to this anxious state. Here are a few of my personal favorites. You may have some of your own.

The Coach's Internal Voices While Anxious

- The client looks to me for help, and I haven't a clue what to offer.
- Advice comes out of my mouth, and even I don't buy it.
- She just doesn't get it.
- She isn't taking my advice.
- I'll do the first thing that comes to mind.
- I'll just prioritize these items for her.
- I'm intimidated by this kind of leader.
- I'm not giving my client her money's worth.
- I'm working with a client who doesn't have what it takes.
- How did I get into this situation in the first place?
- I'm taking sides between the client and her team.
- I can't stand the discomfort she is in. Maybe Herculean efforts on my part will save her from her dilemma.

Have you ever had one of those days when a client pours out his troubles to you, and they are huge? They are real problems that could challenge the wisdom of King Solomon himself. Then, with his big eyes staring at you, he pauses, waiting for a response from you. Sometimes clients' hand-wringing over their dilemmas can be contagious, and we feel pressured to come up with the answer. When I am in the throes of my own anxiety, I grasp at giving advice, using techniques on them, or cheerleading them out of it. Though I do not admit it, I do this to lower my own anxiety, or at least to distract myself from my own discomfort. Worse still, I rationalize to myself that I am being useful to my client.

These internal voices can distract you from the central task of being in relationship to an anxious client in such a way that he is able to regain his resources. If you are not careful, you can become a substitute player for the client in his own organization, where suddenly you act as the organizing principle in the system. That is what happens with Ben as he works with Tom.

Tom and Ben, continued

Ben is taken aback when Tom, in their next session, tells him not to tell anyone that he (Ben) is coaching him on this problem (secrets are another form of triangulating). Tom is embarrassed about needing help and doesn't want to appear weak in front of the other senior vice presidents and, especially, Susan. His job may be on the line if he doesn't pull this off well and soon.

Tom's request for secrecy increases Ben's anxiety because Ben has his own stake in this. He wants Susan to respect him for the help he can offer in resolving business challenges. She doesn't have a lot of patience for team processes that go on and on with few results. Since Susan is new, she has yet to see what value Ben brings to organizational issues.

Ben feels as pressured as Tom does to produce results. He's torn and finds it difficult to identify his first priority and his primary client. He figures he can either coach Tom in his development, or get on Susan's reorganization train (his growing reactivity presents these two options as polarized). His response to Tom is, "Hey, don't worry about it. Let's get right down to business and figure out a reorganization plan for your department."

Ben alleviates some of Tom's anxiety by managing the reorganization strategy, although this is not officially his responsibility. Tom is the up-front lead, of course, but Ben is in essence supervising Tom's efforts. Ben tells Tom to schedule team meetings. During the meetings, Ben gathers the team's ideas and collates the information for Tom.

When Susan requests that Tom furnish a revised organization chart in two weeks, Ben sets up a time line of activities for Tom to follow so he will meet the deadline. Team members individually approach Ben (more triangles) with their concerns about the new structure, as well as concerns about Tom's ability to manage the new structure. Ben works harder to find a structure that suits Tom's abilities and the interests of the team while still satisfying Susan's parameters.

This story shows how something insidious happens when the coach takes on the executive's burden. This coach's actions betray that he no longer believes the client is capable. One of the core tenets of coaching is the belief that a client has his own resourcefulness to face his dilemmas. That resourcefulness can include seeking assistance from a coach. The help, however, should support the executive as *the executive* faces the issue and sees it through.

When you lose faith in your client's ability to lead, you have also lost faith in your own ability to coach an anxious client. True coaching requires standing in the uncomfortable crucible of the client's anxiety without stepping in and doing his job for him. The vacuum you create by a loss of faith in yourself and in the client draws a kind of pseudo-help out of you. It may have short-term benefits but does not cultivate a more resilient executive in the long run.

> *When you lose faith in your client's ability to lead, you have also lost faith in your own ability to coach an anxious client.*

Once you identify your susceptibility to taking on the challenges of your client, the next step is to think through your role in the triangle. Once you see how you can act powerfully within it, you will unlock your own ability and creativity to generate effective interventions. Chapter Four offers just such a model.

Chapter Three Highlights

Systems Perspective Useful to Coaches

1. Learn to see interactional fields and your vulnerability within them.

2. Identify the coach-client dances you co-create.

3. See the system that surrounds and is co-created by the client.

The Effect of Anxiety in the Workplace

1. Learn to distinguish productive anxiety from a reactive response to system challenges.

2. Look for triangles the client creates.

3. Learn to identify the cascading effects of triangles throughout a system.

4. Anticipate being triangled by the client into his dilemma.

The Coach's Challenge

1. Help the executive recover her resilience.

2. Work to keep from taking on the client's burden.

4

THE TRIANGLED COACH

Being Effective in the Middle

If you have ever found yourself working harder than your client on her problem, you know viscerally what it is like to take on more than you should. Putting in more effort than the client, as Ben is doing with Tom, does little to build the client's ability to face challenges. Executive coaches need a way to work successfully in the triangle of client–client's challenge–coach.

The following contrasting models outline substantially different paths that coaches take while functioning within this triangle. I invite you to avoid the Rescue Model and use the Client Responsibility Model. The latter keeps you on track even while the client's anxiety buffets you. When you start questioning your actions, this model can help you return to home base, where you can make better choices.

The Rescue Model and the Client Responsibility Model of Coaching

In the **Rescue Model** the coach takes on the client's burden and becomes the pseudo leader of the situation. This can temporarily ease the anxiety of the executive. As a Rescue Model coach, you develop relationships not only with the client but also the client's

---

The juxtaposition and contrast of models for coaching in the business environment (named here the Rescue Model and the Client Responsibility Model) are the invention of Rob Schachter, a senior consultant and colleague. Schachter bases his approach on the seminal theory of Murray Bowen and the expansion of Bowen's work by Edwin Friedman.

Figure 4.1 Rescue Model of Coaching

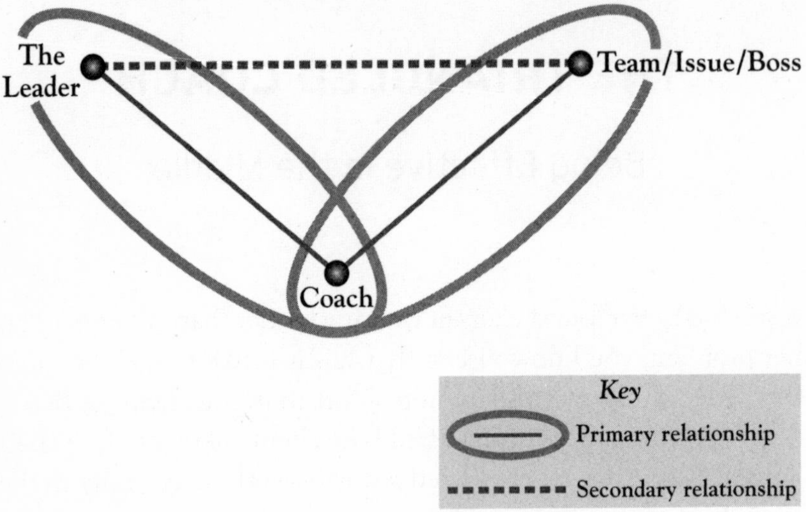

Key

Primary relationship

Secondary relationship

team, the issue itself, or the client's boss that foster dependency on you for the solution. You can become so central that the client's own relationship to her issue is weakened and takes a back seat (Figure 4.1). When you take ownership of the client's problem and lead the process to solution, including facilitating, training, setting guidelines, advising, and making decisions (for example, Ben's "supervising" of Tom), you also develop strong relationships with both the client and the team (if you are also working with them). The result is that the client and her team stop developing their relationships with each other and focus more on relating to you.

In contrast, as a **Client Responsibility** coach, you use your position in the triangle to uncover information about the system that the client can use to resolve her problem. Then the client and the rest of the system can regain use of their own resources and continue to relate more strongly to each other than they relate to you. You take a back seat and do not come between the client and her team, problem, or boss. Your actions ensure that the integrity of those relationships remains intact (Figure 4.2).

Figure 4.2 Client Responsibility Model of Coaching

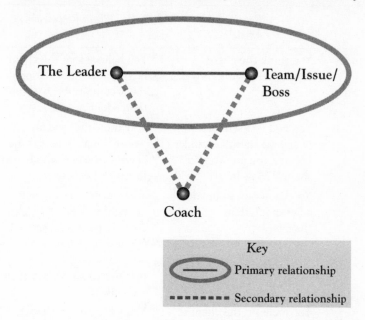

As a coach you may still include activities of facilitating, training, and advising, but the client owns the process, the solution, and the decisions. The Client Responsibility Model respects the fact that the coach is secondary to the situation rather than a primary player. You work alongside and in partnership with your client.

In the Rescue Model, the same problems resurface when you leave. In the Client Responsibility Model, the client and the team strengthen their capacity to move through their work issues when you are not there. It may seem obvious that the Client Responsibility Model is more effective for the client. However, we consultants and coaches fall into the Rescue Model when we succumb to the system's forces and to our own anxiety in the face of the client's distress.

How do I know I am in one mode as opposed to the other? Two areas to watch out for are your attitude and your actions toward the client. Note in Table 4.1 the contrast in attitudes and behaviors between the two models.

Table 4.1 Contrasts Between Coaching Models

	Rescue Model	Client Responsibility Model
Attitudes	You think the client cannot do it without you.	You believe that the client has to come up with approaches she is comfortable with rather than adopting yours.
	You find yourself looking over your client's shoulder because you are worried she will blow it.	You know that you are a "short-timer" here and the client is the one who has to live with her results.
	You know you would do a better job than the client.	You accept that a "good enough" action by a highly committed and motivated client is ten times better than an outstanding action on your part that creates passivity in your client.
	You focus on the client's weaknesses.	You focus on the client's strengths.
Behaviors	You give answers rather than offer clarifying questions.	You stimulate your client's thinking so that she learns more about her own position.
	You make decisions for the client.	You seek opportunities to invite your client to be decisive and clearly articulate her decisions to others.
	You consistently take up more airtime than your client when you are with her and her team. They learn more about you instead of learning more about each other.	You invite your client to keep tuned in and relating to her team, so she creates more productive work relationships with them.

The Client Responsibility Model can help you work within the triangle effectively. The goal is to use your signature presence to keep the client focused on her challenge in a productive way.

Let's check back with Ben and backtrack to the moment before he lost his balance and fell into the Rescue Model of coaching. It happened when Tom asked him to keep a secret, which triggered Ben's anxiety. If Ben had stayed grounded in the Client Responsibility Model, he could have helped Tom get back to or develop his own problem-solving skills. Ben's use of the Client Responsibility Model with Tom could look something like this:

Tom and Ben, continued

Ben says to Tom, "Tom, you are in trouble. But spending your time and my time hiding from this fact isn't going to do you any good. What I could do is help you think through a number of serious questions you need to answer for yourself, like, have you decided to stay and meet this challenge, or are you thinking of leaving because of it? Are you up for this big of a change in how you do things? If you decide to stay, how does this challenge fit into your goals? What does successfully fulfilling those goals look like?"

These questions accomplish two things: they keep Ben from taking Tom's challenge out of Tom's hands where it belongs. And the questions help Tom squarely face what he is up against. If Tom opens himself to the challenge embedded in these questions, he has a chance to choose his response rather than avoiding his dilemma and looking for Ben to give him the answers. If Tom chooses to face this challenge, and given more coaching sessions, Ben can ask Tom more questions to stimulate his thinking and creativity:

- How can you talk to your team so they understand that you stand behind this challenge?
- What parameters can you give your team for a new organization? What information can you share with them?
- What information do you require from them?

- What other resources do you need from Susan, your peers, and me as your coach to get the results you want?
- What changes in your management style do you need to make so this change will work well?
- What strengths in your management style and in your team do you want to preserve?

These are the beginning conversations that would put Tom on the path to becoming more self-directed. When you remain in the Client Responsibility Model, you strengthen the client's ability to use the four approaches to presence I covered in Chapter Two: staying focused on specific goals for each meeting, managing ambiguity, dealing with reactivity, and becoming more immediate with the staff.

One of the occupational hazards of coaching from the middle of the triangle between a client and his challenge is to get into the kind of difficulty that Ben did with his Rescue Model coaching of Tom when he stepped in and managed his client. I have been in Ben's shoes more times than I care to admit. In order to counter the pull to pseudo manage your client, you must remain focused on your goal with the client. Stay grounded in your goal, even given the system's pull on you, so that you can withstand your client's anxiety rather than catch it from him. You should not abandon him in his anxiety or be thrown off course when your approach may not appear to be help to him at the moment. This kind of calm presence in the middle of a triangle with an anxious client and his challenge can help clients find answers to their organizational dilemmas.

Sometimes, however, a coach's anxiety can cause her to use the Client Responsibility Model in a way that is not helpful to her client. Not pacing with your client because of your own anxiety can be jarring to a highly anxious client, even when you are using the Client Responsibility Model. This happened to me with one of my clients (for an organization chart to the story, see Figure 4.3). I almost used it as a hit-and-run tool before I went fleeing from the scene.

Figure 4.3 Organizational Roles in the Case of Jill

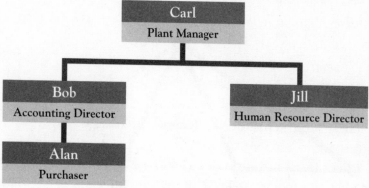

Jill

Jill, the director of human resources, came into our meeting quite harried about an emerging situation with Alan, the purchaser for the production plant, and his boss, Bob, the accounting director. Bob had set some stringent guidelines for Alan that Alan did not like. Alan went to Bob's boss, Carl, the plant manager, and complained bitterly about Bob. Carl had his own doubts about Bob's ability to manage his people. Then Carl came to Jill, hoping she could be a mediator between Alan and Alan's boss, Bob. Jill breathlessly came to me to ask whether I would be willing to mediate a conversation between the two.

Here is another example of cascading, interlocking triangles that multiply because of people's anxiety about their relationships with each other (see Figure 4.4). Alan is upset with his working relationship with his boss, Bob. Alan triangles Bob's boss, Carl, into Alan's relationship with Bob. Carl has his own issues with Bob, which he has not directly addressed with Bob. Carl triangles Jill into his relationship to Bob and Bob's relationship with Alan. Jill is nervous about the way Carl uses her in these situations, and so she triangles me (as her coach) into her relationship to Carl,

Figure 4.4 The Multiplying Triangles Entangling Jill

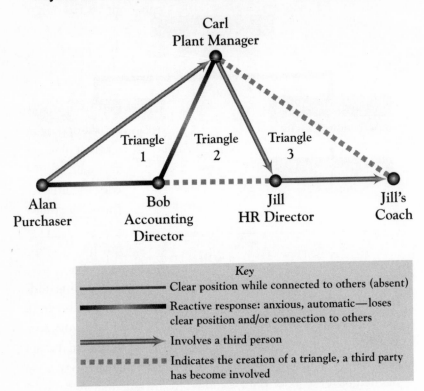

which could ricochet me into the middle of the originating triangle among Alan, Bob, and Carl. Talk about the slippery slope—you can find yourself sliding into other people's triangles in no time!

Spreading triangles often throw a smokescreen over issues of accountability and authority. Carl needs to deal with Bob directly about Carl's issues with Bob's leadership. Bob has to act on the legitimate expectations he has of Alan. Instinctively I knew that the last thing this system needed was for me to join the long chain of triangles.

Jill, continued

With the best of intentions but with a tight, anxious tone, I said (matching Jill's breathlessness), "Getting someone from the outside doesn't make any sense. Let's look at how you could be a resource."

It sounds logical and helpful and comes out of the Client Responsibility Model of coaching. However, my own anxiety about getting caught in the middle caused me to drop Jill's request without staying connected to her. I was in fact fleeing from her. She probably felt abandoned by my response.

Jill must have smelled my skittishness. She said that she was irritated with me because it seemed as though I was dropping her like a hot potato. My own anxiety was rebuffing her anxious request too quickly. If she were in touch with her own resourcefulness at the time she asked me, she would not have needed to turn to me in the first place. Actually, this would have been the perfect time to decisively give her what she wants and in the process hand her own leadership back to her. That would look something like this: "Jill, I would be happy to be a mediator if that is what you most need. But first let's take a look at the whole picture and talk through the best course of action."

Jill was able to tell me that she was not feeling confident or resourceful about being the mediator. We slowed down and took a look at the situation more neutrally, talking through the triangles (see Figure 4.5). As her coach, I was able to direct her focus to how she could first work on her approach to Carl (action 1: Jill coaches Carl) to help realign his relationship with Bob (action 2: Carl talks to Bob about Carl's expectations of Bob), which had implications for how Carl would more immediately respond to Alan (action 3: Carl is not the one to talk to Alan about expectations, Carl coaches Bob on how to talk to Alan). By the end of the session, Jill did not feel a need for an outside mediator. And neither was she going to mediate as her first course of action. She was going to work with Carl to help him address the performance issues he had been avoiding.

Jill calmed down enough in our conversation to regain her clarity regarding the situation. She felt much more grounded, found her backbone, and saw what her position should be with Carl (that a mediator was not necessary for Alan and Bob if Carl communicated his expectations to Bob about Bob's leadership,

Figure 4.5 Client Responsibility Approach: Actions to Take in Sequence

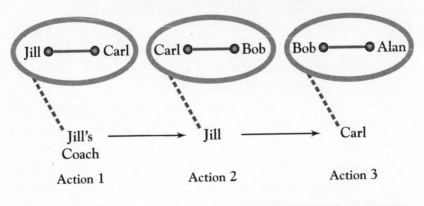

Jill ●——● Carl   Carl ●——● Bob   Bob ●——● Alan

Jill's Coach ——→ Jill ——→ Carl

Action 1   Action 2   Action 3

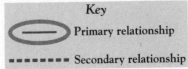

Key

—— Primary relationship

▪▪▪▪▪▪▪ Secondary relationship

and Carl communicated to Alan that he needed to go back to Bob and work out their conflict). As a result of using the Client Responsibility Model, finally in a way that paced with my client, I helped her calm down and get clear about her position and action plan.

In summary, here are the actions you can take as a coach to remain most effective with your clients when you are brought into the middle of the triangle of their troubled relationships to others:

- Identify and avoid Rescue Model attitudes and behaviors.
- Use the attitudes and behaviors of the Client Responsibility Model—sustain a belief in your client's resourcefulness.
- Support the primary relationship between the executive and her challenge, whatever or whoever that challenge may be. With heart and backbone (being both compassionate and firm), keep turning your client back to face her own challenge.

> *Support the primary relationship between the executive and her challenge, whatever or whoever that challenge may be. With heart and backbone (being both compassionate and firm), keep turning your client back to face her own challenge.*

Coaching from the Middle

Once you enter into the executive's triangle of anxiety, there are some systems lenses you can use to help you adhere to the Client Responsibility Model. The more you understand patterns, homeostasis, boundaries, and the distinct change management roles in a system, the more you can leverage them as you work from your middle position in the triangle. Then you will help a client make real choices in the system rather than act solely from avoidance of his anxiety. You can also watch out for his tendency to call on you to be his replacement in his work relationships rather than meeting his work relationship challenges himself.

Patterns in the Client's System

For the most part we have been using pattern thinking to identify the dance between you and your client. You can also use it to help your client to see and address the patterns within her organization that she co-creates. You can detect established patterns of interaction within groups that create and reinforce their results, whether the group performs at a high level or flounders. **You are an invaluable resource to your clients when you teach them to identify the patterns in which they are immersed.**

Following is an example of a powerful pattern that one of my clients and her team co-created.

Barbara

Barbara was a driving, excellence-oriented executive. However, her team seemed to be drifting into mediocrity, unable to find a way out. She spent quite a bit of time worrying about their performance, both silently and aloud at team meetings, and wondered why they couldn't increase their plateau of performance. I talked with Barbara and asked about the kinds of interactions she had with her direct reports, both one-on-one and together as a group. I also spoke with each team member and sat in on a meeting. Although there was a lot of discussion—each person talking both privately and publicly about his or her desire to excel—there was a central pattern impeding their progress, best described as "avoid-avoid." Although Barbara talked about excellence, she did not insist on behaviors that would get them there or challenge the actions (or inactions) of team members that were leading to their mediocrity. That was her side of the avoiding. For their part, the team members avoided challenging each other to higher performance and neglected to tell Barbara what they needed from her to break through to a higher level. The avoid-avoid pattern was choking off performance from a talented and well-intentioned team.

Dysfunctional patterns can be the side effect of a triangle at work. When anyone avoids the challenge in a relationship and does something else, that something else can become a pattern. The pattern is reinforced every time the person actively avoids her challenge. The other person in the relationship responds in a way that enables the first person to avoid whatever challenge she had with that other person in the first place. Thus, everyone plays out the pattern they co-created rather than facing the challenge to relate more directly to each other. Barbara and her team were playing out such a triangle using the avoid-avoid pattern, which meant that they talked about everything but the needs they had of each other and the consequences of not getting those needs met.

Addressing a pattern when coaching a client can get tricky, particularly if, as the coach, you see it before the executive or the team does. It is usually easier for the third person in the triangle to see a pattern than for the two primary players to see it. The third person in the middle (in this case, the coach) can have just enough distance to gain a clearer perspective.

To help the client identify patterns without getting resistance from her when she cannot see them, **asking the following questions can be useful:**[1]

- What does Person A do that seems to trigger Person B's response? What does B do or not do that starts A down that path in the first place?

- Does this interaction have a familiar ring to it? If you were a betting person, could you count on these two people or this group to react in these predictable ways?

- Does this recur so often that you could even give a title to the pattern? How would this be identified as a news headline? For example, it might be "Attack/Counterattack," or "Bully Finds Placater," or "Rescuer Saves the Day," or "Avoid/Avoid," or "Pursuer Chases a Distancer." In the case of the last example, the pursuer does something to help people retreat. At the same time, those who keep their distance continue to draw out the pursuer to chase them. No one is innocent.

Pattern identification needs to be offered respectfully and provisionally. The more tightly you hang on to your way of seeing your client's pattern, the more resistance you are likely to get. An occupational hazard of the middle position in a triangle is that your point of view may receive a lackluster or even a hostile reception from the primary parties.

There is no objective truth to the name you give to a pattern. It is only important that the primary players see their circular self-reinforcing dance. **Once they acknowledge that there is a** repetitive, predictably familiar tone to their interaction, you can invite them to name the pattern for themselves.

Since patterns are self-reinforcing, they are hard to break. Once we realize this, we can proceed to help clients break through some of the patterns they perpetuate.

Homeostasis

Homeostasis refers to the forces that keep a system at its current level of functioning, thereby preserving the established patterns. Members of the group may find the current level to be highly unstable or chaotic, but there is a sameness to this instability. The group consistently fails to reach a more stable plateau. Homeostasis is like a well-functioning thermostat on a specific setting that resists change. It naturally has a low tolerance for any change in the temperature.

Neither good nor bad, homeostasis is a natural part of the self-preservation of any system. Organizations, ecological niches, even single-cell amoebas rely on homeostasis for survival. Homeostasis preserves inner stability so that a system can remain at its current level of functioning, which may be highly effective. However, it may cause a system to resist a change that may actually prove advantageous. Sometimes a system can be too slow to adapt to a change required for its survival.

People within groups can resist even changes that they intellectually know will benefit them. These "don't-change" or "push-back" impulses in a system have undone many executives. Homeostatic resistance has undone many coaches too, because coaches are vulnerable to such resistance by being in the middle of the triangle of the client and his challenge.

The coach needs to attend to this natural, unintentional resistance in order to help a client significantly alter a system's way of operating. Otherwise a client's best intentions unravel. Understanding the power of homeostasis helps both the coach and the client take the situation less personally and avoid thinking, "They're doing this to *me*."

Understanding the power of homeostasis helps both the coach and the client take the situation less personally and avoid thinking, "They're doing this to me."

At first, it is easy to feel gloomy about systems and think, "This thing is bigger than all of us!" However, there is a common proverb of systemic thinking: "The focus for change is the system, but the agent of change is the individual." Systems change when individuals have the courage to do something different and the stamina to withstand the resistance to the change they are creating.

The coach's reaction to a client system's homeostasis can get tricky too, and the weakness of the Rescue Model comes into full play. Coaches get distracted by a system's push-back response and start to believe it is up to them to break through the system's resistance. If, in your middle position in the triangle between your client and his challenge, you take on your client's job of dealing with his system's homeostasis, you will undertake the mythical job of Sisyphus. He had to roll the rock up the hill, only to see it fall back down, only to roll it back up, then have it slide back down again—repeatedly and forever. In fact, this is one of the chief reasons coaches and consultants burn out. They take too much responsibility for fighting the push-back responses in a system.

You serve your clients better when you help them face the homeostasis of the system instead of taking on the burden yourself. **It is essential to educate clients about the natural occurrence of homeostatic resistance to their changes.** Once they see it, this understanding can free them up when they learn to anticipate a team's push back. **They are less likely to take the resistance personally.** Clients must be willing, however, to withstand this predictable reaction.

Barbara, continued

Barbara and her team took quite readily to seeing themselves in the avoid-avoid pattern. They were relieved when they could finally name the dynamic. Then Barbara went after it with a vengeance when the team were in meetings. She recognized the moments when members retreated into their silos, and she challenged them to do more interdisciplinary work together to reach a higher level of interaction. Members of the team said that they liked it. They had been neglected as a working group, so any attention in that area seemed right to them.

Although the meetings were much more stimulating than they had been, the results did not improve. Actually Barbara was still dealing with her own internal thermostat because she talked big at the meetings but did not follow through with the challenge when she managed her direct reports on a one-on-one basis. The staff lapsed into their old ways of working when they perceived that Barbara's pressure to change was intermittent.

When we discussed the natural slide back into the old pattern, Barbara was faced with a decision: Was she going to keep the pressure on herself and her team so they could break through to higher results? Yes, she decided. She pulled it off only because she was vigilant in looking out for the recurrence of the old pattern in herself and in others. She learned that it wasn't so much that they were conspiring to resist the change, but that the old pattern came so naturally.

Raising their internal tolerance for homeostatic resistance serves clients well. You can help your clients anticipate this resistance to change, which prepares them for the reactions they are likely to encounter when they challenge a long-standing pattern.

Boundaries

Systems maintain health when they have strong yet permeable boundaries around them. Boundaries that help create a group's identity are sometimes established through rules: who is in and who is out or the expectations of members' behavior. Subgroups clarify their roles and find ways to be open to receive communication and feedback from other parts of the system. Boundaries hold a group together so they do not lose their identity in the crowd (the larger organization). They need to be loose enough, however, to allow information and visitors from other subgroups to flow in and out, enhancing rather than disrupting the group as it pursues its goals.

Boundaries become invisible to those within the system. You can help clients see which organizational activities contribute to building healthy boundaries. These issues are relevant for looking at boundaries both *within* organizations and *between* an organization and other systems.[2] Some examples of clarifying boundaries within organizations include the following:

- Developing job expectations
- Enrolling new employees in orientation processes
- Defining what information is confidential and who can know it
- Deciding when to say yes to certain projects and no to others
- Clarifying territories of customers and prospects
- Defining protocols

When a coach enters into the middle of the triangle between her client and that client's challenge, the client often hopes the coach will step over established role boundaries and act on the client's behalf so he will not have to. It is critical for coaches to respect and honor the role boundaries of the client and coach relationship so that the client maintains responsibility for the duties of his role.

Many ineffective patterns result from the violation of appropriate boundaries. For example, when people are not clear about who has legitimate authority in a system, the pattern of unproductive arguments can derail a major project. Constantly revisiting the same decisions can significantly slow the manufacture of a product or the delivery of a service. If members of a system know who plays what roles and who possesses what information, they can operate much more effectively.

Coaches can help clients review the boundaries of their system. One way is asking their clients questions to increase their clarity about appropriate roles and boundaries. Here are a few:

- Do people know what is expected of them?
- What are the boundaries of this system?
- Are they frequently compromised so that work is difficult to do?
- Are they so rigid that people do not get essential information from other parts of the organization?

Barbara, continued

One of the discoveries Barbara made was that the boundaries in her organization could not support the change she wanted. In many places they were too rigid, shutting out information from those who needed it. For example, team members did not habitually share information with other team members or ask for help across the disciplines. This created too many barriers between them; it was hard to overcome the distance when a need arose for them to put their heads together to solve a productivity problem. Barbara also realized that she was protecting the team too much from the mandates of her boss. In trying to save them anxiety about the state of the business, she was lulling them into too low a sense of urgency.

Know the Roles That You and Others Play

The concepts of triangles, patterns, homeostasis, and boundaries have their roots in family systems theory. To link this approach more deeply to the organizational world, I have used the work of Daryl Conner (1993), who applies systems thinking to organizations as they undergo change initiatives.[3] Assume that you will deal with clients who are either on the brink of or in the middle of these initiatives. Barbara's case is but one example of such a change.

Conner's research identified four key roles necessary for successful and sustained change efforts in organizations: sponsor (and sustaining sponsor), target, advocate, and agent. Although individuals can play more than one role, it is critical that they are clear about which role they are in at any one time and that they work within the appropriate boundaries of that role. Often change fails because these roles are not aligned with each other and the boundaries of each role are not respected. In those cases, the team is not likely to break through natural homeostasis to change the status quo in the direction that the executive is working to steer the organization.

These roles are central for executives leading changes in their organization, and so coaches must encourage clients to think through these roles carefully. They are simple and obvious in their definition, yet they are hard to enact with integrity because of the ingrained patterns present in any organization. (According to Conner's perspective, the coaching role itself is synonymous with the position of change agent.)

Another reason these roles often are not successfully cast is due, again, to the dynamic of triangles. It takes backbone and heart (clear positions and staying tuned in to others) to fulfill each of Conner's roles effectively. When people are under stress, they avoid the job of these roles and triangle with someone else (sometimes a coach!) through a variety of actions: gossiping about others and their roles, trying to off-load their role duties onto someone else (sometimes the coach!), or sloughing off the responsibilities by verbally complying but not following through with action.

One of your greatest contributions in coaching a client can be to help him look at the roles everyone is playing (including him), weigh whether they are fulfilling these roles productively, and decide on an action plan to correct any misalignments in these roles. Here is a definition of each of the roles crucial for successful change to occur.

The **sponsor** has the authority to make a change happen. She legitimizes and sanctions the change (for example, Susan, the CEO from the vignette, and Barbara, my client from the story). A sponsor is a sponsor only if she has line authority over the people who will implement the change. She also has control over necessary resources, for example, money, time, and people. Good sponsors have a clear vision for the path of change, including goals and measurable outcomes for the initiative.

Sustaining sponsors (for example, Tom, the vice president from the vignette) are those responsible for facilitating the change in their own area, a change that may have started with an executive initiating sponsor higher up in the organization.

Conner (1993) defines the **targets** (I prefer the term *implementers*) as the people "who must actually change" (p. 106). I think of them as the people who must implement the change (for example, a member in Tom's finance department or a member of Barbara's team). They have direct report accountabilities to their sponsor and are most effective when they listen, inquire, and clarify their questions and concerns with their sponsor at the beginning of a transition. This way, they can commit to the effort rather than falsely complying and later sabotaging the change. Their job is to continue to provide information about their experience of the implementation, thus providing an essential feedback loop in the system.

Excellent implementers can save sponsors from tunnel vision or from being surprised by obstacles that those closest to the change may notice first. Every sustaining sponsor needs first to be an excellent target with his own sponsor. The sustaining sponsor should make sure he knows what is expected and commit himself to the change. That way, he gets on board with the change goals rather than telegraphing a lack of ownership to the team (as Tom did to his department).

An **advocate** develops an idea about how a change can happen but needs a sponsor for her idea to be implemented. An advocate could have any number of reasons for promoting her idea. She may have noticed something in the system that inherently blocks the effectiveness of the implementers, may be passionate about the change idea itself, or may want something different for herself and her work in the organization. Any of these motivations is legitimate.

Advocates often become frustrated and demoralized when they cannot seem to get anyone to implement their idea. They are missing the key requirement: a sponsor to own their idea. Savvy advocates promote ideas by showing their compatibility with issues near and dear to a sponsor's change projects and goals.

Conner says that a **change agent** actually makes the change. That description can be misleading and lure would-be change agents into the trap of the Rescue Model. I believe a change agent is the facilitator of the change (as Ben was) by helping the sponsor and the implementers stay aligned with each other.

To increase your effectiveness as a coach, you have to understand the change agent role and its crucial interplay with the other three roles. The change agent can work with both the sponsor and the implementers and can be internal or external to an organization. He can play a number of roles: data gatherer, educator, adviser, meeting facilitator, or coach. He most often has no direct line authority over the implementers and is therefore situated in a naturally occurring triangle of sponsor–implementer–agent. Conner believes that this triangle (when the implementers do not report to the agents or the implementers and agents do not have the same boss) is most often doomed to fail. In my experience, organizations change more successfully *if the sponsor retains the role of sponsor and does not abandon the agent to work with the implementers* as a substitute for the sponsor.

> To increase your effectiveness as a coach, you have to understand the change agent role and its crucial interplay with the other three roles.

The goal for a change agent is to use the role in the triangle to help all parties function effectively. That means the sponsor focuses on the tasks of sponsoring, and the implementers perform

the tasks necessary for change. The change agent facilitates, without taking on the roles of either of the other two parties.

The natural triangle of sponsor–implementer–agent can easily get out of alignment. Since executive coaches are change agents in the middle of this triangle, they must look out for possible role malfunctions. Sponsors often drop the ball, and implementers can get disconnected from the sponsor and the change effort. When this happens, **a change agent can often overfunction, filling in gaps left by the sponsor.** This is pseudo sponsoring, akin to the Rescue Model, and perpetuates a pattern in the triangle that can keep the system ineffective.

The coach can work overtime trying to infuse her client, the sponsor, with a sense of urgency. And she can overfunction by begging, pleading, threatening, managing, or cajoling the implementers. From what you now know about systems, this should sound a warning for you that the coach has misaligned her own role in the triangle and the change effort is in danger of unraveling.

It is critical for a coach to work with her client from the perspective of a change agent and work for alignment of these roles within a change initiative. Although your clients are leaders, the change management role they play needs assessment for each situation they face, and possible alteration. If your client has an issue with her boss, your client is an implementer for that moment. Or she may be advocating for a change with a peer in another department. Or her boss may expect her to act as a change agent, which means she has multiple roles and needs to maintain the clarity of each role.

Barbara, continued

Barbara and I reviewed her roles and those of her team. It did not take her long to see that their roles were misaligned. Because she was at a high level in the organization, all of Barbara's direct reports were executives themselves and therefore sustaining sponsors of her change initiatives. However, they did not act like sustaining sponsors because they did not foster the change initiatives vigorously in their own areas. They seemed to leave that up to Barbara. No wonder she was burning herself out.

Barbara discovered another misalignment once she understood these roles better: two of her direct reports were going to her human resource director to find out what Barbara meant in the team meetings. Previously she would have figured their actions saved her time explaining things to them (of course, it also perpetuated the avoid-avoid pattern). Now Barbara saw that her direct reports were asking the HR director (Barbara's change agent) to fill in for Barbara (which perpetuated an ineffective triangle and a boundary violation). Only Barbara could convey the urgency and clarity of her message to her direct reports. She told the human resource director to stop speaking on her behalf, a habit that was well intentioned but in fact diluted the effort.

You can help a client dramatically increase her effectiveness by helping her enact her specific change role fully and assisting her in keeping the boundaries of that role clear. You can help the client clarify what she can expect from others, based on their roles. Just as important, you need to stay within the boundaries of the change agent's role as a coach. **Aiding clients in defining role boundaries and responsibilities and keeping them clear, strong, and flexible are some of the most rewarding contributions you can provide as a coach.** And it creates a big payoff in organizational change efforts that executives lead all the time.

Understanding the systems concepts of patterns, boundaries, and change roles helps you diagnose your clients' issues in their organization as well as work relationship challenges. Everything does not always boil down to personality traits or solely interpersonal conflicts. Executives need to learn to see the signs of traits and conflicts as potentially the symptoms of an ingrained pattern that is not working, or boundaries that are not well maintained, or change roles that are being neglected. Developing your ability to help them see this broader world in their work is one of your essential jobs as their coach.

The systems perspective of coaching from the middle of the triangle between a client and her challenge fuels the four phases of coaching outlined in Part Two of this book. Carry the Client Responsibility Model forward with you as you explore the phases outlined in the following chapters. It underlies the reasoning behind the specific actions suggested in each step of the coaching process.

Chapter Four Highlights

The Client Responsibility Model Versus the Rescue Model of Coaching
1. Identify and avoid Rescue Model attitudes and behaviors.
2. Use the attitudes and behaviors of the Client Responsibility Model. Sustain a belief in your client's resourcefulness.
3. Support the primary relationship between the client and her challenge, whatever or whoever that challenge may be. With heart and backbone (being compassionate and firm), keep turning your client back to face her own challenge.

Patterns in the Client's System
1. Help the client identify the patterns in which he is immersed.
2. Ask the client questions to reveal the central "dance."
3. Offer your identification of the pattern respectfully and provisionally.
4. Invite the client to name the pattern himself.

Homeostasis
1. Help the client anticipate and prepare for inevitable resistance.
2. Help the client learn not to take resistance personally.

Boundaries

1. Learn to see organizational activities that promote healthy boundaries.

2. Inquire about the boundary-making activities in the client's system.

Know the Roles You and Others Play

1. Understand the roles of sponsor, implementer, advocate, and agent.

2. Learn how the triangle of sponsor–implementer–agent can function well or create problems.

3. Help the client define the boundaries and responsibilities of her role and the roles of those around her for improved alignment.

Part Two

METHODOLOGY

The Four Phases of Coaching

5

PHASE 1–CONTRACTING

Find a Way to Be a Partner

If you are familiar with the action research methodology from the organizational development field, you will recognize the four phases of executive coaching I outline here.[1] They come directly from that tradition.

The Roots of the Coaching Phases

The five classic phases of action research are (1) entry and contracting, (2) data collection and feedback, (3) action planning, (4) implementation and follow-through, and (5) evaluation, including either termination of the contract or recycling through the steps. The four phases of executive coaching I cover here—contracting, planning, live action coaching, and debriefing—constitute a form of action research.[2]

I combine the action research model with the systems perspective because each leverages the other for greater results. As I discuss these phases, I highlight areas of systems assessment and intervention. The systems approach—noticing and changing patterns—supports action research methodology. Action research is based on the concept that intervention in any phase, not just during the implementation step alone, can create change. As soon as an organization begins to engage in action research, it creates a heightened self-awareness that readies it for change.

In these four phases, I highlight the critical issues that are often underemphasized in the coaching literature. These include a focus on specific business results and the leader's need to create organizational alignment.

Contracting

In many ways, contracting is the most important phase. Both parties, the coach and the client, need to build a relationship, and the coach needs to establish credibility. The client wonders, "Can the coach help me?" The coach asks herself, "Is this executive open to feedback?" Together they must establish the goals and parameters for the coaching relationship and set expectations that drive the remaining phases. At this stage, coaches offer clients a sense of what working together will be like.

An executive coaching contract works for two kinds of clients: the new client who wants just executive coaching services and the new or existing client with whom you will work on a large organizational intervention where the one-to-one coaching is only one part of the overall work.

Regardless of type of client, there are a number of important steps in contracting:

- Join with the client.
- Familiarize yourself with your client's challenge.
- Test the client's ability to own his part of the issue.
- Give immediate feedback to the client.
- Take a systems view of your client's issue.
- Establish a contract.
- Encourage the executive to set measurable goals.
- Involve the boss.

The contracting conversation allows you to launch a productive partnership and build elements into it that will keep the other phases on track.

Join with the Client

There is no getting around good old-fashioned social skills on the front end of contracting: friendliness and approachability, a sense of humor, and a sincere interest in the other person. The ease, flow, and even fun in your conversations build strength for the tougher times that will later stress the fabric of your relationship.

A new client needs answers to the following questions: "How quickly can you get on board with me? Do you get what I'm talking about? Are you practical, effective? Do you have some depth to your experience?" She wants to know whether you will really help. She may not explicitly voice these questions. Nonetheless, you must pass the client's test.

You need to qualify your client as well. This kind of executive coaching requires clients to explore their strengths and drawbacks willingly. Wise executives see themselves not only as an individual but also as a deeply embedded factor in the success and disappointments of an organizational effort. When they readily look at themselves, energy-draining homeostasis is less likely to keep the system from productive change.

Familiarize Yourself with Your Client's Challenge

The partnership begins when your client talks about the specific issue by which she is currently stymied. The problem could be with one other person (an employee, boss, or peer), or it could be a work group or larger organizational issue (lack of resources, a visioning effort, downsizing, or work redesign). Often just **listening, following your curiosity about the issue, and constantly restating for clarity** can help the client define the central issue and her opportunities and challenges within that issue.

Use specific listening skills. A whole host of listening skills enhances the early part of the coaching conversation. I highlight four here that I use most often at this stage: **concreteness, empathy, confrontation, and respect.**[3]

Concreteness **means inviting the client to get more specific about the issue.** Executives often speak in global terms and have little patience for details. Do not get intimidated by this impatience. You are not asking details for details' sake but inviting the client to describe actual behaviors and circumstances so you both can see what she really means by her global terms. Many clients articulate global dissatisfaction, but have been unclear with their staffs about their expectations. By pushing for greater specificity from clients, you do an enormous favor for organizations.

Some questions that elicit a specific concrete response include the following:

- What specifically frustrates you about the situation?
- Can you give me an example?
- What do you mean?
- When did this happen?
- What specifically do you expect from them?

Empathy **is your effort to show that you understand your client's concerns.** The more you can express the client's message in your own words, the more she will think, "Okay, he knows what I'm talking about!" When you nail down the client's core concern, you address her real issue—not the issue you think she means. Following are some examples of using empathy in a coaching conversation:

"You seem most concerned about the expanding demands of the business and whether you have the staff to cover those demands."

"Do you mean you are caught between being loyal to the employees who built this company with you and at the same time wanting to take advantage of the hot new stars in the business?"

"It seems you are struggling with giving hard feedback to a couple of long-term employees, and they may be unaware that their performance no longer meets the demands of their positions."

Showing empathy can help a client sift and weigh her concerns. She can either say, "Yeah, I guess this is a big issue for me," or she can say, "You know, when I hear you put it that way, I'm actually more troubled about something else."

Confrontation does not mean inciting a conflict with the client. In this context, **confrontation means pointing out discrepancies between what the client is saying and what she actually does.** It could be a mismatch between what she said twenty minutes ago and what she is saying now or between her words and her actions. You bring forth the discrepancy in a neutral tone, not with a "gotcha" attitude. You simply hold up a mirror so the client can make her own judgments about her incongruence.

The more neutral you are about showing the mismatch, the more powerful this intervention will be for the client. Neutrality means being descriptive rather than critical or judgmental about the client's behavior. Here are some ways of using confrontation in a coaching conversation:

"You say excellence is your number one concern, yet you report that you haven't set competitive standards that are up-to-date in your market."

"In the past ten minutes, you have given arguments both for and against creating the new position."

"This is the first time I have heard you question the CEO's direction and lay out a thorough alternative strategy."

Spending time on a client's discrepancies in behavior helps her finally deal with contradictions that she has been living with for months or even years. It helps her get ready to change them rather than chronically tolerate them.

Respect goes beyond holding the client in high regard or admiring her qualities. Actually, **it has to do with having a deep**

belief that she has the capacity and the resources to handle and resolve the situation. You believe and show that the client ultimately has the resilience she needs to address her issues. Respect keeps you in the Client Responsibility Model. The Rescue Model ultimately disrespects your client because the coach takes on the client's problem-solving accountability. You can use respect in a coaching conversation in these ways:

> "You have successfully dealt with challenges like this before."
>
> "You actually show more knowledge in this area than you give yourself credit."
>
> "The combination of traits you bring to the issue—practical savvy along with keeping an eye on the larger goal—is what the situation calls for."
>
> "You have a way of using your sense of humor to keep perspective while you wade through the toughest phases of the project."

Once you have engaged your client using these four listening skills (concreteness, empathy, confrontation, and respect), she is equipped to better understand her situation. You both will know more about what is at stake and understand the context surrounding your client's dilemma.

Test the Client's Ability to Own His Part of the Issue

When entering into a contracting conversation with a client, I determine whether he is willing to explore the possibility that he simultaneously enhances and detracts from his ability to achieve his goals. A client can use coaching as an effective tool only when he is willing to focus on his own performance. Coaching is not effective without this willingness.

At the beginning of your partnership, your client learns that you probe not only for the external factors in the situation, but also for the ways in which he contributes to them. The guiding principle of this kind of coaching is to **keep the client's habitual response to the issue the central focus,** even while the goal is creating a change in the environment. There may be many other venues for the client to find the answers outside, such as new techniques or training programs. Clients need to find a coaching partner who helps them develop their own leadership as a way to effect change in the organization.

> *Keep the client's habitual response to the issue the central focus, even while the goal is creating a change in the environment.*

This is not therapy or esoteric wisdom but the realization that the client's greatest leverage for change is his own response to the issue. Your contribution is to help him identify his part of the co-created system. You can test the client's willingness to scrutinize his role by asking the following questions or questions like these. If the client welcomes this kind of self-reflection, you have potentially a good client.

- What recurring patterns or habitual responses are present in your situation?
- Which patterns work well, and which ones detract from what you're trying to accomplish?
- How have you responded to this issue before?
- What part of this pattern results from your own knee-jerk reactions? For example, are you often the overachiever, the blamer, the pursuer, the victim, the helper, the avoider, the parent?
- Can you imagine a different pattern resulting from a different response on your part?
- How much stamina do you have to eliminate part of the pattern that is no longer effective?

- How will this help you get to your goal?
- How can I be useful to you moving to that new behavior?

Give Immediate Feedback to the Client

Find a time early in your relationship to give your own feedback and observations to the client. Even if you have just met, you have your own experience of her up to this point. From a systems view, this brief experience with her gives you a picture of her functioning in the organization with regard to the issue.

As I discussed in Chapter Two, the use of immediacy is a potent tool for the coach. Your own interaction with the client opens a window into her characteristic patterns. I encourage you, particularly in the contracting phase, to feed back your own impressions of the client. What follows in the immediacy of this moment should help you ascertain what happens in the client's work world. The feedback needs to be delivered with backbone and heart. It must be frank, specific, and collaborative without being overly protective.

Ned

Ned, a prospective client, called to ask me to do a team-building retreat because there was a lot of dissent among his staff. As we talked and explored the issues, I declined the offer. I thought the one-day event that he planned would not address the issues. He later called to say his staff was doing a survey feedback process instead and asked whether I would submit a proposal. We talked more, and although I believe in the effectiveness of feedback action planning projects, I judged that he had abdicated his authority in the process, and that would undercut the effort. I told him as much and said that I would include a coaching contract with him as part of my proposal. At the end of the conversation, he declined my offer but said, "I think I just got some of the best consulting I've ever had, and it was for free."

A month later, he hired me to coach him. At the contracting meeting, he talked about the challenges he faced with his team. And he talked. And talked. And talked. I started to have a queasy feeling imagining enduring his verbose style. I knew I either had to give him my immediate feedback and potentially lose him as a client again, or pay for my silence by being a victim of his talking.

I interrupted him after about fifteen minutes, and said, "You know, as I'm listening to you, I find it hard to concentrate on what you're saying. I get a breathless feeling, and it's hard to know when I can break in. I also wonder if that's how your staff experiences you."

Ned stopped dead in his tracks and burst out, "That's exactly what I deal with! I'm making so many connections when I'm talking that I lose sight of the conversation." It was in that moment that he knew he would get the real stuff from me, and I knew that he was open and resilient enough to let it in.

Clients receive this kind of immediate feedback so rarely that it gets their attention and tests the cliché they often say but do not tolerate: "I don't want just another yes-man." I call it the stick-my-finger-in-their-chest moment. It can be delivered boldly and respectfully by directly engaging the presence of the client. He may step into the moment, seeking more information and learning about himself. When this happens, he might say, "This is the kind of feedback I can do something about." Or he could retreat from the frankness, which helps you to decide whether you want to pursue this contract.

A former mentor and coach of mine, John Runyan, called this kind of experience "consumer education." He recommended finding an opportunity early in the contracting phase to use the immediacy of feedback with the prospective client in order to show the client how you coach. The prospective client then decides if he wants this kind of coaching.

The three necessary conditions for a successful coaching contract are the willingness of the client to (1) see himself

honestly, (2) own his part in the patterns at play, and (3) be receptive to immediate feedback making changes in his behavior. For you to say yes or no to the contract depends on whether you have this critical cluster of conditions.

Take a Systems View of Your Client's Issue

You can pick up information about the patterns in the system very early in the interaction, such as the possible effect of Ned's speaking style on the team. **With systems thinking, you can also wonder about the other elements of the pattern.** This client is not operating in a vacuum; he has help from under involved members of his team. To maintain a systems view, you must develop positional neutrality toward the players: there are no pure good guys or bad guys. Everyone is a co-creator. To be effective, you cannot side with one member over another in the system.

A word about neutrality: try as you might to maintain this stance, you can count on being drawn into the system. That is, **you will feel the pulls of anxiety the same way the members of the system do.** It is not a matter of *if* you get inducted but *when*.

The beauty of being pulled in is that you can learn more about what it is like to be a member of that system. The trick is to recognize this response and **find your way back out.** For example, when the client talks about his situation, you need to watch for the emotional pull in you to take sides between the client and his team as you listen. The questions you ask the client to help him identify his part in the web are beneficial to you as well (for example, "What recurring patterns are present in this situation? What is your contribution?"). They remind you that everyone contributes to co-create the situation.

The identified problem is usually not the real issue. Difficulties stem from how the client addresses the problem. Here is another reason to refrain from taking sides or identifying villains. Instead, you help the system use dormant abilities in all the players—abilities suppressed by their prevailing responses.

The identified problem is usually not the real issue.
Difficulties stem from how the client addresses the
problem.

Establish a Contract

For the external coach, establishing an explicit contract moves the conversation along to specific goal setting. For internal change agents in an organization, the explicit offer to coach is equally essential. As an internal organizational coach, I learned that I got into more trouble when I did not make an explicit offer to coach the executive. Without it, I entered into conversations to which I was not invited and assumed learning contracts with leaders that I did not have. And I wondered why they weren't using my wisdom! These situations led to either active resistance or eyes-glazed-over passivity. When it comes time to negotiate how you will work together, make sure to define any requirements you may have in the coaching contract (Table 5.1 gives you some ideas for categories). To the extent that you have expectations essential to the coaching partnership, it pays to mention them up front rather than trying to bargain or plead for them later. These are just a few of the ways to include mutual responsibility as an explicit part of the contract. (For more ideas, see Whitworth, Kimsey-House, and Sandahl, 1998.)

The offer to coach includes the ability to **describe the options** within the role in a simple way. There are two options, which may be pursued either separately or together. The more common option is **behind-the-scenes coaching.** This includes a planning stage (Chapter Six) that helps the client clarify how she will face a particular situation and a debriefing stage (Chapter Eight) in which she thinks through how she did, celebrates her success, and plans steps for improvement for the next time.

Table 5.1 Topics of a Contracting Conversation

Scheduling of meetings	How long, how often
Agenda management	Who plans the agenda for a meeting; who manages the agenda during the meeting
Confidentiality	Who else knows, who tells them, functionally working the triangles in the contract
Contracts	Whether a written legal document, a letter of agreement, or a verbal agreement, identify the focus of the work
Reports	Written or verbal, generated and distributed by whom
Fees	Including payment and cancellation terms
Expenses	What is covered by the client, what is covered by the coach
Logistics	Where to meet (on-site or off-site), who secures the place, who provides needed materials
Contact person	The client or someone else (for example, executive assistant, HR, sustaining sponsor)
Accessibility	Expectations around frequency and timeliness of contacts in between business meetings
Debriefs and follow-ups	Frequency and scheduling
Recontracting	When things "go south," when the work shifts, when it is time to end the work together

The second option is what I call **live-action coaching** or **live team coaching** (Chapter Seven). In this approach, the coach is present in the room while the client deals with her issue in real time, whether that entails a meeting with an employee or a group, or a coworker.

Encourage the Client
to Set Measurable Goals

Once you and the client have settled on a coaching contract, you need to clarify **goals and expected outcomes for the project.**[4]

Executive coaching involves working with clients on their own leadership issues and many of the issues that revolve around how they work with others. By the time a coach arrives on the scene, a client may have been mired in a problem for a long time. Sometimes he and his team start focusing only on interpersonal issues or personality traits and lose sight of the business issues.

Less experienced coaches can let actual business results get lost in the process. They get distracted by the client's interior focus and lack of attention to measurable results. Out of desperation, the client may say, "I need to get along with my team better," or "I need to be more patient," or "I need an open door policy." The coach must help the client determine which of the client's stated goals will yield the greatest results.

Focusing on specific outcomes is essential. How will the organization benefit if the client becomes more collaborative, more approachable, more decisive, or clearer? People assume these changes improve productivity in the organization, but becoming more collaborative, more approachable, more decisive, or clearer may not lead to specific business outcomes. **It is important that the executive coach not confuse work relationship goals with business outcomes, because clients do it all the time.**

Use the Three Key Factors Methodology

You can set up a coaching contract for success by helping a client identify the **Three Key Factors** around a specific business challenge she faces: (1) **the business results** that leaders need to achieve, (2) **the leader interpersonal behaviors** they need to exhibit in their key work relationships, and (3) **the team interactions** necessary to attain the desired business results (Figure 5.1). These key

Figure 5.1 Three Key Factors for Leaders

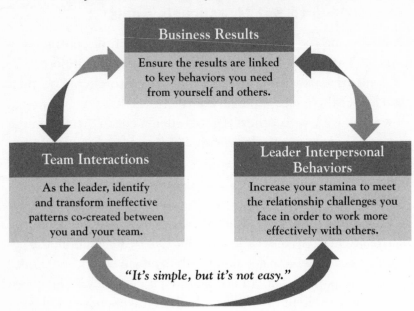

© 2003–2006 Mary Beth O'Neill.

factors are areas executives manage every day but whose potential is underused.

My motto for identifying and using these Three Key Factors is, "It's simple, but it's not easy." Every executive knows that these three categories are important, but very few executives working under pressure manage all Three Key Factors simultaneously. One or two of the key factors escape the leader's attention. Inability to manage all Three Key Factors is often the trigger that prompts a call to a coach in the first place.[5]

The real challenge for leaders and coaches is to ensure that the Three Key Factors are linked and interrelated to each other. They must also incorporate the key factors into the choices the leader makes daily. **Identifying and customizing the Three Key Factors to their situation (1) launches the coaching process and (2) produces interrelated categories that can be assessed for the value of the executive coaching work** (see Chapter Nine).

Look at the guiding principles under each of the Three Key Factors in Figure 5.1. You will find a three-pronged approach that builds the synergy your clients need to achieve outstanding results on tough business issues. Here is a quick overview of each factor with its guiding principle:

- **Business results: "Ensure the results are linked to key behaviors you need from yourself and others."** The coach and the client are like detectives working to put the intricate pieces of a mystery together. The logical discovery process requires that you encourage your client to identify goals that are customized, specific, and measurable. That includes business results, leader interpersonal behaviors, and the team interactions needed to achieve the results. Each key factor list should support the achievement of the other two key factors. Otherwise your client has not successfully integrated the Three Key Factors.

- **Leader interpersonal behaviors: "Increase your stamina to meet the relationship challenges you face in order to work more effectively with others."** You know your client has identified a good leader key factor list when a relationship challenge he has been avoiding is included on the list. He may feel some trepidation or resistance to face that challenge head-on, and it usually requires him to bring more backbone or more heart to his work relationships. For example, he might need to provide more clarity where in the past he maintained ambiguity in order to be less controversial and more comfortable. He might have to set aside his defensiveness in order to truly listen to others, even when they give him difficult feedback. You and he have left the world of logical puzzle solving and entered a landscape of emotional reactions and challenges. Your work with your client helps him increase his inner resilience to face these work relationship challenges that block achieving the business results.

- **Team interactions: "As the leader, identify and transform ineffective patterns co-created by you and your team."** Your client should discover the patterns at play between him and his team that sabotage his best intentions. Most often, neither your client nor his team consciously recognize these patterns. You can help him bring a thoughtful discovery process to something that is hidden yet so powerful that has negative effects on business results. If teams create effective interactional patterns, they can drive success far beyond what they previously achieved.

Simultaneous work in these three areas can drive a greater synergy compared to focusing your client on any one area. It requires equal doses of intellectual rigor and emotional intelligence on the part of both the coach and the client. Generic lists are comfortable but boring, useless for initiating change, and they keep the client at a safe distance from his challenge. The more specific and tailored each key factor list is, the more it can highlight the work relationship challenges that are most relevant to the business results. In addition, more specific lists are more likely to address the co-created patterns that need to be transformed. This is reason enough to keep asking your client to redefine, refine, and hone the items on each list.

Simultaneous work in these three areas . . . requires equal doses of intellectual rigor and emotional intelligence on the part of both the coach and the client.

Anne

I coached Anne when she was general manager of her division.[6] I was called because she faced several challenges: she had team members with long-standing interpersonal conflicts, corporate revenue goals were not likely to be met, and Anne's boss withdrew support because he was frustrated with her division's problems. Anne was considered a high-potential leader and was respected by many in the company for her demonstrated gifts and skills. At the time I met Anne, however, it was a stretch to get the kind of traction that would impress her boss. This had caused her to lose self-confidence.

Early in our conversations, Anne and I discussed the Three Key Factors and ways she could identify them. At first, she wanted to focus on "improved staff relations" as her business result because she spent so much of her energy dealing with conflict between team members. "Improved staff relations," however, is not a business result; it is a team behavior. I encouraged her to move it to the team interactions list.

After we explored many of the challenges she faced, Anne chose the business result of increasing revenue. Ultimately that was the results factor that the company and her boss cared most about. In order to boost revenues, Anne thought her own leader behaviors needed to revolve around resolving staff differences. As we talked, it became clearer to Anne that some of these differences might originate from her own lack of clarity regarding her expectations of her staff. So she put "define role clarity" on her leader behaviors list.

Anne perceived that the team members needed her to clarify her expectations so that they could prioritize their work better. The team lost energy to conflicts, both hidden and explicit, which slowed the implementation of all their plans. Clarifying expectations and collaborating to resolve differences mobilized Anne and her team to close in on their business goals.

A great challenge for the coach in working with a leader to identify the Three Key Factors is establishing the linkages among those factors. The factors may seem so self-evident that leaders do not pay much attention to them and consider the factors only on a vague, general level. This disempowers them and their teams. The real challenge comes in working to **customize and render measurable each of the Three Key Factors while demonstrating their interrelationships.** This is the first building block to establish a return-on-investment approach. "Link and make measurable, link and make measurable" is the mantra of Three Key Factors work.

Thus far, Anne's work in defining the Three Key Factors was a significant step, but was only the beginning. At that point she had determined business results (increase revenue), leader interpersonal behaviors (define clear roles), and team interactions behaviors (improve staff relations). Were they linked and customized to her situation? Her leader and team behaviors were indeed linked. We suspected that if she further clarified her team's roles, some of their conflicts with each other would evaporate. But how would that increase revenue?

As an executive coach, an important part of your job is to probe, and repeatedly emphasize, the interdependencies among the Three Key Factors. Rarely should you accept a leader's first answer. By repeated questions regarding the links among the factors, you can help the client focus on the crucial items under each factor. Your client should identify the ones that give her the most leverage and the greatest chance of success. Your collaborative skepticism, probing until you reach the specifics in each of the factors, builds a growing confidence in leaders that they have identified what is most critical to their situation. **You cannot convince them; they must convince themselves of the links by their own repeated refinements.**

Define the Measures: How Will You Know When You Get There?

Any item identified by the client must not only be linked to the other factors but must also be measurable. **Four basic categories to use in measuring business results are time, money, quality, and quantity. The measurable goals on the leader and team factor lists must be specific, observable, and repeatable.**

Exhibit 5.1 sets out a menu of categories that fit into each factor. Each client can choose the items that are most relevant to her situation and most interdependent with each other. This is not an exhaustive list. Nor are all of these menu items specific or measurable enough. They must be made more specific and customized to your client's situation.

**Exhibit 5.1 Menu for Identifying the Relevant Items
for All Three Key Factors**

BUSINESS RESULTS

Money	Time	Quality	Quantity
☐ Sales	☐ Project length	☐ Meet quality standards	☐ Production
☐ Revenue	☐ Production time	☐ Defects	☐ Number of services
☐ Profit	☐ Down time	☐ Prevention, relapse	☐ Service volume
☐ Discounts	☐ Task time	☐ Customer satisfaction	☐ Customers
☐ Employee absenteeism	☐ First-to-market innovation	☐ Meet environmental standards	☐ Inventories
☐ Employee retention	☐ Approval time	☐ Positive media visibility	☐ Market share

TEAM INTERACTIONS

☐ Paraphrase to clarify understanding.

☐ Give opinions, and raise concerns.

☐ Clarify readiness level to commit.

☐ Seek decision clarity.

☐ Give input outside their functions.

☐ Manage conflicts collaboratively.

☐ Hold peers accountable for mutual agreements.

☐ Own mistakes and initiate problem solving.

☐ Lead their own teams in alignment processes.

LEADER INTERPERSONAL BEHAVIORS

☐ Give goals and expectations.

☐ Ensure team paraphrases for understanding.

☐ Invite opinions, concerns, and reactions.

☐ Ensure commitment to goals.

☐ Clarify decision style.

☐ Give specific feedback.

☐ Encourage collaborative differences.

☐ Uphold expectations.

☐ Acknowledge achievements.

Anne, continued

Anne's assertion that the team needed to "improve staff relations" was not specific enough. They still would not know which behaviors served the goal of improved relations. However, "paraphrase each other's points of view" was a suitably specific way to improve team relations. Paraphrasing may seem an overly simplistic action, but when the right set of simple interdependent behaviors is chosen and applied simultaneously, they prove to be the key behaviors necessary to break through to a higher level of performance.

Another way to test the leader and team lists is to make sure they contain interactional verbs—actions that are directed toward someone. For example, my conversation with Anne was not done when she wrote "decision clarity" on her leader list. "Decision clarity" is a category, not an interactional verb moving toward anyone. When she wrote, "Identify decision-making style, and facilitate closure on decision discussions, summarizing both progress toward a decision and when a decision is made," *that* item includes specific interactions required for her team to achieve decision clarity—state her decision style and keep facilitating and summarizing the discussion with her team until a decision has been made.

Figure 5.2 lists the Three Key Factors that Anne chose to identify and manage. In terms of business results, Anne had specific numerical revenue goals for her business unit. She also believed that her team could best meet revenue goals by redesigning their sales process. The time line they had to achieve both the redesign and their revenue goal was one year.

Usually the leader and team behavior lists contain three to five items each. Individual behaviors can then build on one another and form a synergy of key interactions that will make the difference for the business. Anne's interpersonal behavior list

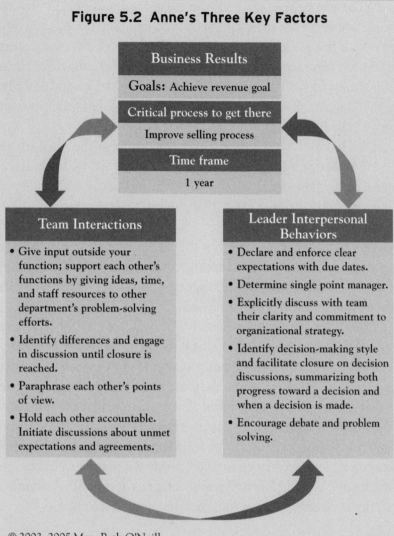

Figure 5.2 Anne's Three Key Factors

Business Results

Goals: Achieve revenue goal

Critical process to get there

Improve selling process

Time frame

1 year

Team Interactions

- Give input outside your function; support each other's functions by giving ideas, time, and staff resources to other department's problem-solving efforts.
- Identify differences and engage in discussion until closure is reached.
- Paraphrase each other's points of view.
- Hold each other accountable. Initiate discussions about unmet expectations and agreements.

Leader Interpersonal Behaviors

- Declare and enforce clear expectations with due dates.
- Determine single point manager.
- Explicitly discuss with team their clarity and commitment to organizational strategy.
- Identify decision-making style and facilitate closure on decision discussions, summarizing both progress toward a decision and when a decision is made.
- Encourage debate and problem solving.

© 2003–2005 Mary Beth O'Neill.

outlined specific ways in which she could continually clarify roles for her team. All team interaction items addressed the issue of improving staff relations. **The leader and team lists identified the critical actions they all needed to make *on a daily basis* in order to achieve business success.**

When you believe you and your client have successfully created a measurable list for each key factor, you can take the movie camera test. If the leader and the team pursue these behaviors during day-to-day interactions, could someone watching a movie of these interactions identify the desired behaviors and accurately describe them? Could an observer recognize the behavioral expectations set forth by the leader?

This level of specificity can aid the coach as she encourages the leader and team to use their plan on a continual basis. Both the executive and the coach should assess the frequency and quality of these interactions over time. How many times do they see these behaviors in meetings? Are they consistently and effectively used in every team meeting, whether the leader is present or not? Are expectations clear, and do team members seek the leader's clarification? Reinforcement of these specific and observable behaviors affects how the team does business.

These lists are not an exhaustive or complete list for any team that needs to increase revenue. Each situation is unique and therefore customized. **Although these may seem to be obvious behaviors for achieving business goals, they were built from the ground up so that the client was convinced that this particular combination would make a difference.** It does not matter that many of them also happen to appear on generic leader competency lists. For the same reason that leader competency lists rarely stir people to transform their leadership, leaders and teams tend not to mobilize around a generic list as effectively as they mobilize around *their* lists.

> *Leaders and teams tend not to mobilize around a generic list as effectively as they mobilize around their lists.*

Once the leader and her team incorporate these behaviors into their regular way of doing business, they can transfer these skills to other challenges and business results. These behaviors can be applied to other organizational goals. Once the leader and the team own the skills and have confidence in how they apply them, they can be brought to other contexts in ways they never thought of before. In a twist on the motto, "Think globally, act locally," this is an occasion where the client "learns locally" and then "applies globally."

When the list contains interactional verbs, the work relationship challenges of your client can become clear and mobilizing. The behaviors that she has until now avoided addressing often are the very ones needed to accomplish the business result. You know you have a high-quality leader key factor list when your client feels committed to a challenging new behavior but also daunted as to how to enact it. She has, in essence, created the agenda from which the two of you will work together to help her incorporate a new way of acting.

Truth in Advertising: Clients Will Balk

In many ways, working with a client to identify the Three Key Factors seems so straightforward as to be simplistic. However, dealing with a leader feeling pressure in the workplace is another matter entirely. **Executives are so compelled by forces internally and externally to act first and think later that they have a hard time settling down enough to be thoughtful, specific, and integrated.**

Often when you ask executives to identify the Three Key Factors regarding a business issue, they look at you blankly, or shrug the exercise off as a waste of time, or claim that they already have all of it in place. The problem, however, is an anxious leader rather than an irrelevant exercise. A coach needs to develop a thick skin to an executive's resistance to thoughtfully engaging with the Three Key Factors.

One way to begin a productive discussion of the Three Key Factors is to **start with the key factor that energizes the client the most.** The sequence is not important; you can start with leader interpersonal behaviors as easily as starting with either business results or team interactions. Although Anne was quite willing to take ownership for improving her and her team's performance, sometimes I work with executives who are fixated on laying blame on their teams. In those situations, I reflect and amplify that energy by asking for a list of all the ways in which the team does not function well. The executive typically has no problem creating a list, saying, for example, that they don't take initiative, they fight among themselves, and they are unprepared for meetings. The list can quite easily convert into categories for the team interactions factor by simply replacing the negative actions with positive ones: they take initiative, they collaborate with each other, and they prepare for meetings. This gives the coach and client a starting point to make specific, proactive, and measurable behavior goals for each item on the team interactions list.

Sometimes a client is much more open to looking at what she needs to do differently if you connect her leader interactions to the team list she just created. For example, you could ask, "Now that you know specifically what changes your team has to make, what are you going to have to do differently to lead them there?"

Defining the Three Key Factors requires discipline on the part of clients (and coaches) to face the complexity of executives' work situations. The process to finalize the Three Key Factors with a client is an iterative and creative exercise. The clients create their own criteria on which to build a successful enterprise and will know specifically whether they succeed or fail in each area.

Anne's first reaction to the Three Key Factors was that they were probably another canned coaching tool. It was not until she began using them that she saw their value and how they could help her with her team and business results. She said, "An important lesson for me was that although the Three Key Factors list was a generic learning tool, my Three Key Factors were completely customizable."

Having an outcome focus can make the difference between the client's continuing or giving up when she hits daunting obstacles. It keeps me from giving up as well. Sometimes new clients have told me they feel self-indulgent to be "merely" developing themselves with a coach. But it is not self-indulgent when that development is linked to results; their development is essential to the business. Insist that they describe how. In addition, linking the coaching effort to a business result will highlight and prioritize the business and leadership development areas that need attention.

It is important that your client keeps the ownership for deciding which goals and measures to pursue. You cannot have more investment in the goals than your client. It is your job to work hard to help her be specific about her goals, and it is her job to ensure that they are the right goals for the business. The connection builds among the Three Key Factors in the client's awareness so she knows what to attend to and where to look for gaps. Throughout the coaching process, you can inquire about all three: the business results, the team's interactions, and the leader's behaviors.

Building these links into your conversations increases the client's understanding of the connections, shows her how indispensable it is to keep the Three Key Factors interlinked, and eventually illustrates how valuable your contributions are to her efforts.

Let's go back to Barbara and see how her goals can be built from her presenting issue. This is another example of helping a client get specific about the Three Key Factors. She wanted excellence but was getting mediocrity from her team. The team was fragmented in their efforts because of an avoid-avoid pattern and a lack of strong sustaining sponsorship among her direct reports.

This conversation is long because it illustrates that a great deal of exploration is required to keep the Three Key Factors in play and interrelating.

Barbara

Coach: You'll get further and know when you have arrived if you set more explicit goals for the business, your team, and yourself.

Barbara: I've got goals. I want us to be the best game in town! Number one in the company.

Coach: But what does that mean? In what area and at what level? If you say, "Jump," how is your team going to know how high?

Barbara: Well, it's all about market share this year. We need to increase market share by four points [business results].

Coach: And as you have been learning about what works and what doesn't work on this team, what do your direct reports—the vice presidents—have to do to make this goal more achievable?

Barbara: Well, it's ridiculous that all the vice presidents don't have the same information on the key issues that have an impact on market share. They're still operating out of their silos and not thinking strategically about what information everyone should share [team interaction factor].

Coach: I see how critical that is, but how would you know if what they changed made a difference? If they just sent reports to each other, it doesn't mean they'll read them or use them strategically to increase market share.

Barbara: I see what you mean. We could dream up processes for information flow and still get nowhere. Wait a minute. Maybe the problem is what we cover in our meetings and how the whole meeting is run. I haven't thought to structure the meeting to match what I want them to be like. I'm going to charge them with restructuring our meetings to meet the information and design needs of the business.

Coach: Great. Now think about them working well. What would be happening if your VPs got out of their silos more and were better informed? And especially think of what they would be doing that would help increase the market share by four points.

Barbara: For one thing, we need to shorten our response time by a week between getting the latest sales figures and tweaking our sales tactics [team interaction goal].

Coach: Okay. That's a start. As you continue to work on this, you may discover other issues. You also need to define more specifically your expectations for team behaviors—how individuals need to act differently, to shorten their response time and to turn this whole thing around.

Barbara: Yeah, they need to step up more and deliver world-class performance.

Coach: And by "stepping up" you mean ... ?

Barbara: Do I have to spell everything out? These are vice presidents, for goodness sake! By now they should know what it means.

Coach: If that were the case, Barbara, you wouldn't be in the situation you're in and we wouldn't be having this conversation. You have really bright people reporting to you. But they've been pulled in so many directions lately that they have lost focus.

Barbara: So what are you saying? That I have to tell them how to be a team player? Isn't that insulting? I hate cheerleading senior people. It's demeaning.

Coach: I'm not talking about cheerleading or talking down to people. I'm talking about setting expectations that get everybody focused on key team behaviors that make a competitive difference. We're talking about soft skills, but it takes hard-nosed businesspeople to be explicit about them. When you think of your meetings, what about them would you say doesn't show world-class behavior?

> *We're talking about soft skills, but it takes hard-nosed businesspeople to be explicit about them.*

Barbara: Lackadaisical commitment. They say they're on board, but then they don't drive their managers to get the results.

Coach: You're talking about mobilizing team commitment. You're not going anywhere without higher commitment from them.

Barbara: How am I going to get that?

Coach: Exactly. How are you going to get it? Now you're talking about what you are going to have to do differently to have more committed VPs as sustaining sponsors. What more could you be doing [necessary change in leader interpersonal behavior factor]?

Barbara: Well, for one thing, I could talk more about the pressure I'm getting from my boss about market share. And I could be more active about talking to each one about their commitment too—especially their concerns. I know I'm not getting at the real stuff from them.

Coach: That would be great, because if you get the real stuff, you'll probably learn more about what they need to get more committed. By the way, what would be a measure of stronger commitment on their part?

Barbara: They would stop going around me to the HR director to find out what I want. And they would be commenting on the key issues, giving their best thinking, whether it directly affects their own area or not. Then I would know they were informed and up-to-date. They would be coming to me with ideas on how they're going to close the gap on market share that would include coordinating with other departments [team interaction measures].

Coach: If that's how you're going to measure it, you're going to have to track it, be aware of when it's happening and when it's not, and whether you're doing what you said you needed to do to get there as well.

Barbara: I think if we improved our decision making, we'd get there faster too.

Coach: Now you're on a roll. What's the problem?

Barbara: In meetings, the decision making is pathetic. It takes forever; then people don't remember what decisions were made, and so they have to get remade.

Coach: You run those meetings, Barbara. What do you need to do to improve that [necessary change in leader interpersonal behavior]?

Barbara: If I knew, I'd be doing it.

Coach: Often leaders don't tell people the kind of decision they are making, for example, if the decision is going to be consultative to the leader or consensual by everyone. Team members don't know how to be productive in the conversation. That's one thing you could do right away to make a change: be more explicit about which kind of decision you're making [leader interpersonal behavior measure].

Barbara: I could do that. I don't tell people the decision style I'm using. You're right about that; it could be confusing.

Coach: If you go in that direction, what do you want from them?

Barbara: I want them to give their input on decisions. I want to hear their reservations, and I want to hear alternative solutions. And I want everyone to remember what the decision was and follow through with their part of it [team interaction measures].

Coach: You've just named the measures for this one. What would be the easiest way to know that your team was on track?

Barbara: It would be easy enough for me to facilitate a summary coming from them at the end of each meeting about what decisions were made and the kind of decision each was. That way I could test against their understanding just how clear I was with announcing the style of decision up front and whether I stayed faithful to it. I could also scan to see whether I got sufficient participation and commitment from all the VPs.

Coach: To the extent that you tell them right away whether they got it, you will be concurrently measuring your progress on leader behaviors while giving them immediate feedback. Immediate feedback is a powerful tool toward improving bottom-line results.

These conversations are arduous but worth the investment the client and coach put into them. Barbara was able to identify goals and measures in each of the areas: bottom-line results, leader interpersonal behaviors, and team interactions. She made a connection between raising market share and increasing the quality of her business meetings. What is more, she knows her obligation to be clearer about the decision-making process in those meetings. Figure 5.3 shows the Three Key Factors that resulted from the conversation with Barbara.

Figure 5.3 Barbara's Three Key Factors

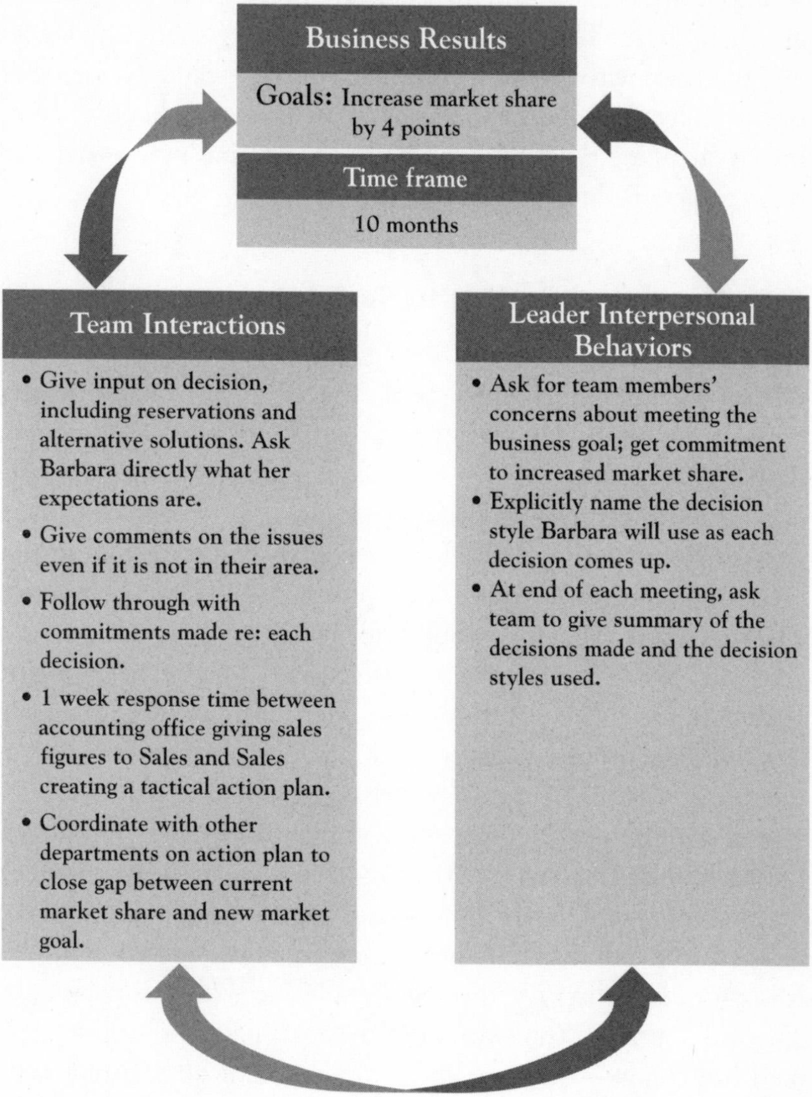

Business Results

Goals: Increase market share by 4 points

Time frame

10 months

Team Interactions

- Give input on decision, including reservations and alternative solutions. Ask Barbara directly what her expectations are.
- Give comments on the issues even if it is not in their area.
- Follow through with commitments made re: each decision.
- 1 week response time between accounting office giving sales figures to Sales and Sales creating a tactical action plan.
- Coordinate with other departments on action plan to close gap between current market share and new market goal.

Leader Interpersonal Behaviors

- Ask for team members' concerns about meeting the business goal; get commitment to increased market share.
- Explicitly name the decision style Barbara will use as each decision comes up.
- At end of each meeting, ask team to give summary of the decisions made and the decision styles used.

© 2003–2005, Mary Beth O'Neill.

The team interaction and leader interpersonal behavior goals are always the toughest to measure. The point of identifying measures for them is to provide a way for executives and their teams to know whether they are making progress toward those goals.

The ultimate measure is whether they make their bottom-line goal. But it is the team interactions and leader behaviors that will get them there. The measures for these goals provide the leader and the team with growing knowledge of the specific actions that directly affect business outcomes. They will be more likely to commit to changing their actions when they see that new leader and team behaviors directly affect results.

Slow Down Goal Setting to Speed Up the Action Later

Clients are often impatient to begin the coaching work during the contracting phase. Once they feel confident that they can work with a coach, they want action. However, without clear goals and measures for those goals, neither client nor coach is focused enough to know the most effective course of action. Clients are often impatient and irritated with protracted goal conversations. The time it takes is a real problem for them.

I used to think, "They're busy executives. Maybe they're right. I'm being too picky." Actually the client lashes out with impatience at the process because he draws a blank on getting more specific and more rigorous about his goals. It is too uncomfortable to experience the void in the conversation that stems from the leader's lack of clarity at the time. He would rather pop out of his discomfort and head for the action. He has been living, as have most people in modern organizations, in a fire-ready-aim mode. It is astonishing how often leaders ignore the goal-setting process. The task—finding the sweet spot between people processes and hard-line results—is easy to understand but difficult to attain with high quality.

A client's crankiness with you when you persist in a conversation that seeks specific goals and outcomes has little to do with you. It has more to do with his own reactions to doing the hard work of aligning himself and the organization and honing in on specifics. Stay with him, and keep inquiring about goals.

This is one of those opportunities to get a reputation for being a hard-nosed businessperson—not a bad rep to have!

This is one of those opportunities to get a reputation for being a hard-nosed businessperson—not a bad rep to have!

Although it may seem like swimming against the current, you need to slow the executive down long enough to establish clear goals so he can be productive during the implementation. With no clear guidelines, the action phase of a change effort slows down because of hurried, misdirected efforts. You need to keep the client from bullying you out of a clear goal-setting process. You must bring backbone and confidence to your conviction that there is efficiency in doing it. If you must, be a broken record about your conviction.

Now, there is no reason to be a perfectionist about this. Sometimes a business situation is too ambiguous to know confidently what team interactions goals would achieve the bottom-line results. A way to proceed is to encourage the client to establish, as best as he can, team interaction goals and measures that he believes will affect the bottom-line results. Then he can establish midpoint checks of the measures to calibrate them and see whether they take him and his team in the right direction. The specifics set at the beginning can be adjusted later if needed, but spend the energy up front to set them, and monitor them as the client proceeds with the action.

When the client connects improvements in his leadership to specific business goals, he builds in his own biofeedback system. He realizes how his own efforts have helped or hindered goal attainment and how he can sustain success. **With success in the experience of setting Three Key Factor goals, clients can get motivated to become more specific with other projects besides those discussed with their coach.**

Involve the Boss

So far I have been talking about setting up a coaching contract with a client as though the client and I will be working in a vacuum. While it is tempting to develop a strong one-to-one working relationship with a client and believe that his motivation to learn is enough to carry him through, the client works within a system, and that system has to be acknowledged, honored, and mined for invaluable data and direction for the coaching contract.

The coach is an adjunct resource in the client's system, not a replacement for any other role in his system, and certainly not a replacement for the boss–direct report relationship. And although many bosses wish otherwise, executive coaching cannot substitute for in-house performance management. All this requires that the boss stay involved with the client in the role of boss and evaluator and that the executive coach meet with the client's boss as part of setting up the coaching contract.

This is tricky terrain to travel. If I had a dollar for every time a boss met with me with the intention of delegating his responsibility to me, I would be a multimillionaire (okay, that's a bit of an exaggeration, but you get my point). Often they come to the meeting with an executive coach and say, "I'm glad to tell you what's needed and the background situation. My employee has a lot of challenges to face if she is going to perform at a higher level. Once you get into the work with her, let me know how she's doing. I really appreciate the work you'll be doing with her."

What the boss really means is, "Thank goodness you're here! I've avoided being straight and direct with my employee, and she hasn't gotten any of my hints or tips or advice [neither have I delivered any consequences]. Maybe *you* can light a fire under her. I'd also like you to evaluate whether you think she's truly executive material and tell me what you think."

Your first job meeting with your client's boss is to let him know that he will remain in the boss seat while you coach his direct report. Once that is clarified, the real reason to meet with the boss is twofold: **(1) find out what he cares about the most regarding his employee's development and performance, and (2) provide some "guerrilla coaching" of the boss to improve his supervision of his employee.** By "guerrilla coaching," I mean that the boss certainly does not see himself as the coachee or recipient of your coaching services. But he will probably learn more about how to be a better boss through his meetings with you than he ever imagined. And you can often turn these guerrilla coaching moments into a mini-contract to coach the boss to improve his supervisory skills.

Usually my engagement with the client's boss involves three types of meetings.

First are the preparation meetings, which have the benefit of a well-thought-out approach to the employee. This is the main agenda:

- Identify how the boss views the essential elements of the client's Three Key Factors: the client's business results, his leadership behaviors, and the team interactions that need to change on the client's team of direct reports.

- Discover how the client's Three Key Factors, if delivered well, allow the boss to obtain success with *his own* Three Key Factors: the boss's business results, leader behaviors, and the boss's team interactions. Get the boss to be specific about how these two sets of Three Key Factors, his direct report's and his own key factors, reinforce each other.

- Help the boss identify new leader interpersonal behaviors that *he* needs to change in supervising his direct report to increase the chances of success in the coaching contract.

- Discover the boss's time frame for when he wants his direct report to achieve the measures of the Three Key Factors and how he will monitor this progress.

- Prepare the boss for a three-way meeting with the boss, his direct report, and the coach. Offer to coach the boss during that meeting (see Chapter Seven for live-action coaching).

In three-way meetings, both the client and the coach experience the boss at the same time and the same information is shared with both, neither having to hear it second hand. In these meetings:

- The boss communicates his expectations to his direct report, sharing the Three Key Factors expectations, working on gaining clarity and commitment from his direct report regarding these issues.
- Client, boss, and coach cover when and how the boss will monitor progress.
- The boss offers the services of the coach to the direct report. He makes a distinction between the goals for the client (required) and how he gets there (optional use of a coach).
- The coach helps to keep the boss on track with his goals in the meeting.

Three-way meetings should be held over the course of the coaching contract so the boss can stay involved in his direct report's development.

Finally, **periodic follow-up coach-boss meetings heighten the boss's level of responsibility to supervise.** These meetings:

- Help the boss clarify his satisfaction with the client's progress and what areas need ongoing work.
- Identify an action plan the boss will carry out for any of the following: getting the information he needs to assess his direct report's progress, giving feedback to his direct report, and coaching the boss on his own progress on his new leadership interpersonal behaviors with his direct report.

All of these meetings provide rich material to work the systemic patterns that have been created between your client and her boss. If you work just with your client, you cannot easily change your client's behavior because she is constantly being reinforced in her current behavior by her boss even as the boss says he wants change in his direct report.

There are two important systemic principles embedded in the previous set of meetings. **The first is to help the boss identify new leader interpersonal behaviors that *he* needs to change in supervising his direct report to increase the chances of success in the coaching contract.** Most bosses have no idea how they perpetuate the undesirable behaviors in their direct reports. They do not see their contribution to a pattern that has been established between them. One of the best contributions you can make is to help the boss see this. But insight is not enough. You must challenge the boss to change his behavior with his direct report. The boss needs to see his new behavior as a significantly new leadership tool that he adds to his repertoire. This focus will help the boss to be more effective not only with your client but also with his other direct reports. The guerrilla coaching that the boss never asked for but now receives will have a longer-term effect beyond the results he originally imagined you would help achieve.

> *Help the boss identify new leader interpersonal behaviors that he needs to change in supervising his direct report to increase the chances of success in the coaching contract.*

The second principle is to **identify how and when the boss will monitor progress.** Every boss I have ever worked with asks, "How is he doing?" Or, "Does she have what it takes to get to the next executive level?" Or, "Does he have the capacity I need in that area, or is it just beyond his ability and always will be?" Or, "Is she truly motivated?" And it is sorely tempting to answer the boss's questions. But that will place you squarely in the Rescue Model of Coaching. If you answer these questions, you accomplish two things: (1) you feed your need to be seen as valuable to the boss without challenging the effects of feeding that need, and (2) you let the boss off the hook of his own responsibility to his direct report. You risk two things by *not* answering these questions: (1) the boss could get angry that you won't answer "a simple question—you're the one who's spending time with her and sees the real stuff," and (2) there is valuable information that may get lost if you do not share your assessment of your client's progress with the boss. What to do?

My policy is not to answer any question the boss asks that requires me to tell him my evaluation of his employee. This is beyond the issue of confidentiality. It's not that the boss is asking what is said in the meetings. This has more to do with the boss wanting my sense of my client as a whole.

Politically, it would be career limiting to give the boss your evaluations. When your clients find out that you shared an evaluation of their performance with the boss, they will lose all trust in you as their coach. They will lose the motivation to do anything more than try to look as good as possible. In addition, it will get around the company that you are in the back pocket of management and cannot be trusted.

There are also systemic reasons for not answering the boss's question that go beyond politics. Going back to the systemic principles of the triangled coach, how do you work in the midst of the boss–direct report relationship? It is the executive coach's job to keep the relationship between the boss and direct report the primary relationship. The relationship you have with each of them is secondary to their relationship to each other.

From the Client Responsibility Model's perspective, evaluating your client to the boss degrades the boss's responsibility to evaluate his direct report himself through direct experience. He is depending on your judgment rather than his own judgment. He is not standing on his own two feet to discern his employee's performance. If I am not the conduit of information between the two players, the boss must get that information from his direct report and the direct report's team by observing the real action himself. The real action is not happening inside my wise understanding of the client, no matter how insightful I think I am or the boss thinks I am. Therefore, **resist the boss's attempts to either flatter you or threaten you into an evaluation of his direct report. It is more disabling than empowering to the performance management relationship.**

What you *can* do is offer to coach the boss on ways he can get the information he needs to make an evaluation himself. He may even need help identifying what criteria he wants to define to evaluate progress, development, or performance. He may need help in thoughtfully weighing a direct report's strengths and challenges and how to communicate the results. This approach leads to much more useful and capacity-building coaching conversations that you can have with your client's boss.

Greg and Dan

An internal HR consultant had suggested that Greg call me to coach his direct report, Dan. Greg was VP of quality, and Dan was director of the customer service department. The department's job was to ensure not only a high level of responsiveness in its call center, but also that the customer service records and processing of issues were coordinated well with the information technology department, which handled the information storage and reporting.

When we first met, Greg impressed me as both friendly and decisive. He talked about Dan's strengths and weaknesses and why he wanted to get Dan some coaching:

Greg: Dan was promoted to director a year ago. He did quite well in his old job, and the company believes he could go far. He's great at making presentations to upper management and customer groups because he really understands his stuff and knows how to convey the most relevant information. He cared about quality work and delivered on his results. But he has stumbled since his promotion.

Coach: In what ways?

Greg: He intimidates his staff. If something goes wrong, he stresses out and takes it out on them. And then he doesn't fix the problem; he acts more victimized by the IT department and accuses them of messing things up. He doesn't address the issue and doesn't involve his staff in problem solving. When I see him in cross-functional team meetings, he clams up and doesn't contribute anything to the agenda.

Coach: How do you account for his behavior?

Greg: I think he really cares, but his personality causes him to pull in and mull things over when he's under stress, and then the whole thing caves in on itself. He probably needs help knowing how to adjust to this new level of managing. I think with coaching from you, he could adjust to his new position and learn how to include others more. I really want to invest in a coaching resource for him to keep him on track.

Coach: How much time have you spent orienting him and coaching him in this new position?

Greg: (jovial tone) Wait a minute! This isn't going to be about *me* is it?

Coach: Well, you don't want to waste money on an outside coaching resource when there are things you can do better than anyone on the outside. Do those first. Save your money for when you've done all that you can do and he's still stumbling.

Greg: Okay, so I could be spending more time with him telling him what I want, but I still think he's going to need help getting over some of his habits. I just don't get why he turns inward all the time, broods about what's stressing him, and then lashes out at his staff.

Coach: Have you asked him about it?

Greg: I've told him that his staff has gone to HR complaining about him, and they've just finished a 360 process on him; I'm going to share that information with him next week. He's pretty nervous about it. I told him this isn't a discipline thing, I think he's capable, but he's got to turn this around if he wants to succeed.

Coach: That's a good start, but you'll need to be more specific, and you'll need to get his commitment to change.

I talked to Greg about having very explicit expectations for Dan in the Three Key Factor areas: business results, Dan's behaviors as a leader, and Dan's team's interactions. We spent a couple of sessions helping Greg get clear about his expectations of Dan and how he would deliver that message. Figure 5.4 is Greg's first draft of what he sees as Dan's Three Key Factors, which shows how these lists began to shape up through the course of the evolving conversations with Greg.

Coach: Now that you are beginning to clarify the Three Key Factors expectations for Dan, it's time to make sure they dovetail with *your* Three Key Factors: what you need to accomplish in your job so you will obtain the greatest leverage from the changes Dan will make.

Greg: I see how linking the Three Key Factors up and down the division helps power up everything more effectively in my organization. Then I've got everybody working on what feeds success for the next layer.

Coach: Now let's customize your leader behavior list to this specific situation with Dan. Which of your leader behaviors do you need to alter to support the change you want to see in Dan?

Greg: Here we go again, making this about me! I didn't hire you to coach me. I'm hiring you to coach Dan!

Figure 5.4 Dan's Three Key Factors: Draft 1

Business Results

Goals:
• Minimum customer service level at 75%
• Internal quality standards maintained at 90%

Time frame

8 months

Team Interactions

• Go to Dan first (not HR) with issues, concerns, and differences with Dan.
• Give ideas on planning to end the top 3 recurring customer service issues.
• Raise obstacles and problem-solve top 3 issues in order to commit to plan.
• Go directly to IT when breakdowns occur, do not wait for Dan's directive.

Leader Interpersonal Behaviors

• Give ideas in cross-functional meetings.
• Initiate problem-solving discussions with IT and direct reports to end the top 3 recurring customer service issues.
• Gain commitment from IT and direct reports to the plan.
• Give Greg a plan for problem-solving breakdowns before he asks for it.
• Give performance feedback to direct reports in private.
• Ask for feedback from direct reports on management of them.

© 2003–2007, Mary Beth O'Neill.

Coach: Look at it this way: so far, whatever you have or haven't done with Dan hasn't changed his behavior. It's worth looking at how the two of you interact. There could be something you are unaware of that's reinforcing

Dan to stay the same. If that's the case, it doesn't matter if I work with Dan to change his behavior. I'm an outsider, and I'll be leaving when my work is finished. Everyone pays much more attention to their boss than to an outsider in terms of making behavior changes. Let's make sure you're doing all you can to support his change.

Greg: I'm not going to get out of this, am I?

Coach: Not when you work with me. My work is to make sure that the system between you two is effective, as well as helping Dan change his behavior.

Greg learned through our conversations that he was doing something to enable Dan to maintain his current behavior. When Greg approached Dan about his passivity, Greg would turn on his promoter self and work to convince, advise, prod, and exhort Dan to change his behavior. It was as though he were trying to cheer lead Dan into a change. Dan learned to withstand this chronic state of affairs. His boss tried to convince and cajole him to change, and then he would leave Dan to do what he did before. There were no consequences other than a few uncomfortable moments in these periodic conversations. Dan had only to act thoughtful and cooperative until the end of the conversation. Then he reverted to his old behavior.

It turned out that Greg was uncomfortable insisting that Dan change, getting his commitment to change, and establishing consequences when Dan did not. I encouraged Greg to think of a continuum of consequences that he could put into place with Dan and suggested that it was up to Greg to ensure that *he* did not lapse back into his old behavior. Here is the consequence continuum that Greg developed for his work with Dan (lowest to highest consequence listed):

1. "This isn't up to standard." (Have a discussion with Dan about how it happened. Dan gives lots of reasons why it

didn't happen the way it should have. Previously, this is the only option Greg used with Dan.)

2. "This is unacceptable. I'm disappointed." (Greg had never let Dan experience Greg's disappointment in him and feel the uncomfortable emotional sting of letting his boss down.)

3. "This is unacceptable. Do it over, and get it right." (This consequence goes beyond their conversation about it.)

4. "This is unacceptable. Do it over, and go public with it. Tell other key players you messed up and what you're going to do to fix it." (Insists on initiative from Dan.)

5. "This is unacceptable. This will affect your performance pay." (This consequence goes beyond day-to-day problem solving and affects Dan financially.)

6. "I'm putting you on a performance improvement plan." (This consequence contradicts the assumption that Dan is secure in his job.)

This list of escalating consequences provided Greg with his own map that gave him more flexibility in supervising Dan. It also gave Greg and me a map to use in subsequent conversations, as well as a way to talk about how Greg was monitoring Dan's progress. It signals to Greg that he needs to pay at least as much attention to how *he* manages Dan as to how Dan improves his behavior because of coaching.

Involving the boss in this way supports three sets of partnerships: the boss/direct report partnership, the boss/coach partnership, and the direct report(client)/coach partnership. When these partnerships are set up well, each relationship is effective and productive and supports the other partnerships. At the end of your contract with your client, he and his boss will have a greater chance of sustaining the changes they hired you for.

The example I use in this section on involving the boss has to do with an employee who was faltering in his performance. This may lead you to believe that involving the boss is used only with clients who are in trouble. That is not the case. I learned that it is important to involve the boss even with high-performance clients who were motivated enough to call me on their own. It is amazing how the bosses of these high performers are not clear about their expectations and how the lack of expectations can cause even high performers to derail. They did not involve their boss enough in their development work and headed in the wrong direction. That is when I learned that involving the boss is for clients anywhere on the continuum of performance in their positions.

When the client is a high performer and initiates the call for executive coaching, the sequence of involving the boss happens somewhat differently. You can do the preparation work with your client first. After helping her identify her Three Key Factors, you can meet with the boss and have him identify his direct report's Three Key Factors from his perspective and then initiate the three-way conversation. When the boss initiates the call to the coach, the boss runs the first three-way meeting. When the client initiates the coaching, the client can lead the three-way meeting.

A Word About Assessment Tools

Many executive coaches use assessment tools in their work with clients, either 360-degree surveys or any variety of style or type inventories such as the Myers-Briggs Type Indicator. Most businesses, as well as nonprofits and government entities, use these same instruments.

I travel another path regarding assessment instruments. Too many times organizations rely on the information from inventories to replace important face-to-face conversations. That work should include performance management, direct feedback, coaching, and building relationships in the workplace. How many times has a boss avoided performance management of his direct report by relying on her to get the information through a 360-degree process? How many times have people not given feedback directly to a boss or a peer and unloaded it in a 360-degree survey? How many times has a leader been bewildered by the feedback from 360-degree tools because it was the first time she received such a message? How many times has an executive been given an assessment and then not been given a coaching resource to help her develop to the next level of their skill? Too many times.

Some would say that this indicates the need for coaching to be applied to an executive's growth initiative after being put through these assessments, and they would be right. "Assessment + Coaching = Development" is a good development formula. In fact, I often meet prospective clients when they have recently finished a 360-degree process. The client's motivation to take on developmental challenges they would characteristically avoid can be increased by taking these assessments.

But there is something inherent in assessment tools that helps individuals in the work environment avoid each other. They rely on a tool, whether it's a feedback instrument or a style inventory, to do the job to deliver feedback instead of expecting themselves to deliver it. People can hide behind their anonymous feedback and hope that someone else—such as the boss, the coach, another peer, or another direct report—will face the leader in question with the feedback. Everyone hopes that *anyone else* will deliver the feedback instead of themselves.

> *Everyone hopes that* anyone else *will deliver the feedback instead of themselves.*

This indirect feedback mechanism promotes hiding out in organizations, which subsequently creates an overly politicized and unproductive environment that impedes effectiveness. This is why I have taken the position that assessment and style instruments are not part of my coaching services. When a client already has such feedback, I am happy for her to bring the information into our conversations so she can make plans to address the feedback. My main work with clients, however, is to help them **promote giving and receiving feedback directly, not triangulating their work relationships through another person or an instrument.**

You may ask, *But what if the executive is so intimidating that she creates a costly environment for anyone who gives her feedback, particularly her direct reports?* If that is the case, then that issue becomes a cornerstone of the coaching contract. I then coach my client to:

- Develop open-ended rather than closed questions for her direct reports regarding her behaviors—for example, instead of asking, "Do you think I'm intimidating?" use, "What do I do that shuts you down in meetings?"
- Show she listens to the feedback nondefensively—for example, "I see how my interrupting you wears down your initiative."
- Create a collaborative action plan based on the feedback— for example, "Here's what I'm going to do differently, and here's where I could use your help to change my behavior."

I also create coaching contracts with each of the direct reports, which include:

- Identifying the kind of feedback they have to give their manager—for example, "My boss doesn't trust me."
- Making that feedback more useful by making it more behaviorally specific and actionable—for example, "When you interrupt me and problem-solve an issue I bring to you before I ask for help, it seems to me that you don't trust me."
- Deciding what they can offer collaboratively to help their boss change their behavior—for example, "When you do that, I will remind you that I already developed a plan that I want to share with you, and that I'd like you to listen to me first."

When we conclude this preparation work, the client has a series of one-on-one conversations with each of her direct reports at which I am present and have contracts for live-action coaching for both parties (see Chapter Seven on live-action coaching). **I help the client ask for and receive feedback productively and without reprisals. The direct report gets my help in giving behaviorally specific and actionable feedback.** The conversations are initially uncomfortable for both parties until they realize that the discussions are neither dump sessions nor opportunities for punishing retribution.

It is exactly this transformation in work relationships that organizations need and often avoid through an overuse of assessment tools and an underuse of follow-up resources for executives. My own position not to use assessment tools at all and go immediately to developing direct relationships is my contribution to course-correcting assessment tool overuse by organizations.

I do believe it is possible to use assessment and style inventories in coaching in a way that gets to the same goal of developing direct feedback in work relationships, and many coaches have a robust method to get there. The thing to be wary of is the way in which your client organization may need help in becoming more direct. For example, your client's boss may be too eager to have you work with his direct report on the issues in the 360-degree assessment or style inventory as a replacement for his own direct conversation with his staff member. If that is the case, he is not facing his own job as a boss by establishing clear expectations, gaining commitment to the growth plan, fostering development, and monitoring his direct report's interactions over time.

This is another opportunity to involve the boss and coach the boss of your client to help him be the one to mobilize the direct report's attention and energy for the development ahead. Mobilizing a direct report holds a different level of responsibility and commitment on the part of the boss. He has to involve himself and give direct feedback to his direct report. If he does not, then all you have is a hearty yet passive hand-off of his direct report to you with a pile of assessment data attached. **Your job is to ensure that the boss mobilizes his direct reports for growth, even if his first impulse is to pass that job off to you.** When you take on the challenge of helping the boss be direct with your client, you develop the capacity of two people to increase their level of directness (your client and your client's boss) and the larger organization benefits from it.

Chapter Five Highlights

Join with the Client

1. Begin building a foundation for the relationship.

2. Engage in mutual assessment of the fit for a working partnership.

Familiarize Yourself with Your Client's Challenge

1. Listen. Follow your natural curiosity.

2. Empathize. Show you understand the client's core concerns.

3. Confront discrepancies. Help the client notice inconsistency in thought and action.

4. Show respect by demonstrating your belief in the client's capabilities.

Test Your Client's Ability to Own His Part of the Issue

1. Keep the client's response to his challenge as the central issue.

2. Test the client's willingness to reflect on his part of the issue.

Give Immediate Feedback to the Client

1. Feed back your impressions based on the here-and-now experience of the client.

2. Make your feedback relevant to the client's business issue.

Take a Systems View of Your Client's Issue

1. Identify both sides of a pattern shared by the client and the team.

2. You will feel the same pulls the members of the system feel.

3. Find your way to positional neutrality.

4. Identify how your client is creating a problem by her response to the problem.

Establish a Contract

1. Make the coaching offer explicit.

2. Describe the options.
   - Behind-the-scenes planning and debriefing
   - Live-action intervening

Encourage the Client to Set Measurable Goals

1. Set specific goals the client will work on during the coaching contract.

2. Do not confuse work relationship goals with business outcomes.

Use the Three Key Factors Methodology

1. Coach the client to identify the business results, her own leadership interpersonal behaviors, and the team interactions she needs to be successful.

2. Business results: Ensure the results are linked to key behaviors you need from yourself and others.

3. Leader interpersonal behaviors: Develop the stamina to meet the relationship challenges you face in order to work more effectively with others.

4. Team interactions: Identify and transform ineffective patterns co-created between you and your team.

5. Customize, and make specific and measurable, the items for each key factor.

Define the Measures: How Will You Know When You Get There?

1. Use four categories for business results: time, money, quality, and quantity.

2. Help the client create team interaction and leader interpersonal behavior lists that can be described, replicated, and enacted on a continual basis to achieve the business results.

3. Work with the client to build his team and leader lists from the ground up for his unique situation.

Truth in Advertising: Clients Will Balk

1. Resist the client's impulse to act first and think later.

2. Start with the key factor that energizes the client the most.

3. Keep the ownership with the client—not you—in deciding which goals and measures to pursue.

Slow Down Goal Setting to Speed Up the Action Later

1. Do not take the client's resistance to goal setting personally.

2. Encourage the client to use the Three Key Factors in other projects to continue to connect improvements in her leadership with specific business goals.

Involve the Boss

1. Find out what the boss wants most out of his employee's performance. Help him identify his direct report's Three Key Factors.

2. Provide guerrilla coaching of the boss regarding his supervision of his employee. It may give you a platform for an explicit coaching contract with the boss.

3. Conduct three kinds of meetings with the boss: preparation sessions for the three-way meetings, the three-way meetings themselves, and periodic follow-up meetings.

Leverage Change in the Boss–Direct Report System

1. Help the boss identify new leader interpersonal behaviors she needs to adopt in supervising her direct report to increase the chance of success in the coaching contract.

2. Identify how and when the boss will monitor progress.

3. Decline the boss's request for your evaluation of her employee.

4. Offer to coach the boss on ways she can get information to evaluate performance.

A Word About Assessment Tools

1. Promote giving and receiving direct feedback among people in organizations rather than letting them triangulate their relationships through assessment tools.

2. Help both sides of a challenged system—the leader to receive feedback productively without reprisals and the direct reports to give behaviorally specific and actionable feedback.

3. Involve the boss of your client in giving assessment feedback directly rather than through you.

6

PHASE 2–PLANNING

Keep the Ownership with the Client

Coaching should be more than an opportunity for the client to vent. To help your client create real change, you can use these planning steps:

- Move the client from general venting to a specific plan.
- Address issues inherent in change management, particularly ensuring role clarity.
- Help the client identify her side of the pattern in the situation.
- Help the client plan for the resistance she will encounter from doing something new.

Although these steps seem to flow in a logical order, in practice they do not necessarily happen in this sequence. Sometimes a next action makes perfect sense until you and your client work through the implications of the roles of the key players. Then it becomes clear that some other action needs to happen first to help align everyone's roles before the planned next step can happen. Or the next step is clear until the client realizes that it would merely replay an old pattern, and some new action needs to be planned that will break through to a more effective pattern. Actually, **each decision made during this planning phase needs to be double-checked against the other steps to ensure that they are fulfilling an action plan that addresses all the issues embedded in these four steps of planning.**

Here is another thing to keep foremost in mind: the planning phase is essentially about helping the client get emotionally prepared to face her challenge. Remember the motto for this phase: "Keep the ownership with the client." The client needs to come out of this planning phase not only knowing what she plans to do, but how she needs to remain persistent and determined while she is acting in new ways. Ironically, if you are not careful, the planning steps themselves can distract you and your client from this essential goal, especially if they are done in a mechanistic or wholly rational way without the client facing her anxiety about how she needs to work differently in her job. **During every step of this phase, help your client prepare to face her challenge by mobilizing her stamina for the plan she decides to put into play.**

Move the Client to Specifics

Once the issues surface and your client chooses goals, you can help him identify an action plan and focus on his immediate next step. The path from dilemma to goal to action can be difficult for a client immersed in an issue. The client may bog down in a variety of ways, such as avoiding specific plans, experiencing conflicted loyalties, remaining entangled in his anger at a subordinate, or fearing a conflict. In addition, he may feel overwhelmed by all the tasks required of him.

Some clients feel so relieved to get their problems off their chest that they do not move to the next step. Their stress may be temporarily alleviated just through conversations about the situation. Since they feel better (if only temporarily), they act as though the situation has improved. It has not. A coach does the client no favors to ignore his lack of directed action. Without a plan, the client will revisit the situation and repeat the same responses.

For example, I was in coaching conversations with Rich, a CEO who had a tendency to "stay in the talk," meaning that he liked talking about his situation but not doing anything about it. As he spoke about his issue, it became clear that he had a handle on it. He knew the key issues, and he knew how he contributed to it. He grasped the root causes of the difficulty and even had good ideas for solutions. But he was unwilling to focus on the uphill climb it took to change the circumstances. He never created a plan, and the problem was never solved.

To avoid this lack of action, you need to **encourage the client to identify a specific next step.** Sometimes a client can do this immediately. Other times, a client's next step will emerge from first reviewing the other three tasks of the planning road map from the beginning of this chapter.

Any step the client chooses probably has an element of risk to it. Otherwise he would have taken that step already and would not have needed your help to figure out what to do. Often clients try to choose a path that is devoid of risk, a very human response. Wouldn't we all rather take the easier road? But executives seldom have risk-free choices. Usually all paths have risks embedded in them. Even when the outcome is highly prized, the risks associated with the desired result can be daunting. Schnarch (1997) aptly describes this dilemma by stating, "We rarely accept we're choosing the anxiety we'll have to deal with. We want choices without prices and solutions without anxiety.... Anxiety per se isn't the problem. Anxiety is inherent in growth.... The real problem is our *intolerance* and *fear* of anxiety" (p. 302).[1]

One way to help a client view risk productively is to help him use two complementary ways to view the anxiety-provoking consequences of his decisions. The first is to look at outcomes and whether the risks taken are going to be worth the results. The second is to see the actions as an expression of who the client is, and he accepts the accompanying risks. An example of this second perspective could be a client who decides, "I know it's risky, but I can no longer go along with the group on this one. I want to become the kind of person who can tell the boss all the pros and cons and not protect her from bad news. I may be the only one, but it's more of who I want to be to do it this way." **When clients make a decision based on both of these ways of weighing risks—by outcomes and by defining who they are becoming—they can more readily stand**

behind their actions, tolerate the sting of their own anxiety, and accept the consequences of those actions, whether the outcomes are in their favor or not. It is when clients try to avoid all negative consequences that they are left with indecisiveness and underoptimized results. A client's plan therefore needs to use the most challenging level of action that the system, and the client, can tolerate.

> *When clients make a decision based on both of these ways of weighing risks—by outcomes and by defining who they are becoming—they can more readily stand behind their actions, tolerate the sting of their own anxiety, and accept the consequences of those actions, whether the outcomes are in their favor or not.*

Address Issues in Change Management and Role Clarity

A client does not manage in a vacuum, and she will not succeed if she focuses only on her own personal challenges as a leader. The change management roles (sponsor, implementer, agent, and advocate) need her attention and planning. You can assist the client by ensuring that her plan is appropriately aligned with key organizational issues—for example, sponsorship and authority in the system, decision-making processes, and clarification of the sponsor–implementer–advocate–agent roles and responsibilities for a specific task or project.

You can help your client by asking basic questions: Is she dealing with the right issue? Is she going to talk to the right person? In order to get answers to these questions, **you can delve into areas that help organize the client's action plan with questions that get at some of the most typically ambiguous or misaligned variables in an organization.** A client needs to clarify these areas before she can act effectively:

- Within the client's issue, who is the sponsor? Who are the implementers? Who is the agent? What role is your client playing?

- Can the client initiate and sponsor her own action, or does she need sponsorship from someone else? Answering this question can completely shift the focus of the coaching, and therefore the plan, to a more relevant, and thus powerful, arena.
- Who has decision-making authority on this issue? Is the client the decision maker?
- If the client is the decision maker, has she decided which decisions she will make and which she will delegate?
- How does the client want to increase investment within the work group?
- Are the relevant groups clear about their roles? Do they know to whom they are accountable and for which items? What is the client's responsibility to these groups?
- Has the client communicated these issues to the people who need to know?

These questions bring rigor to the planning process. By inviting your client to address issues of change management and role clarity thoroughly, you can help her leverage her plan to greater success.

Here is how change management and role clarity issues played out in a situation with one of my clients, Miriam. (The major players in the story and their roles are set out in Figure 6.1.)

Figure 6.1 The People and Roles in Miriam's Story

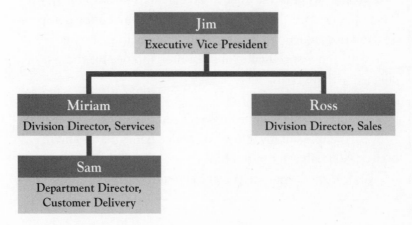

Miriam and Change Management Role Clarity

Miriam was the director of a division with ten departments under her. She had one manager, Sam, who was constantly underperforming by missing deadlines, not dealing with employee issues, and fighting fires rather than preventing them. Miriam was fed up with him, yet Sam had a real flair for the actual performance of the service that his department delivered. Customers loved him.

Miriam and I talked about the many issues she needed to address with Sam and which ones to tackle first. I asked the usual questions about her previous discussions with Sam. "How specific are you about the issues and your expectations? Do you ensure Sam understands what you require? Do you give deadlines?"

When Miriam and I discussed organizational issues, it became clear why Sam never changed his approach to his department. A peer of Miriam, Ross, constantly pulled Sam off his duties so Sam could resolve Ross's last-minute customer service issues (for example, overselling and therefore double-booking service delivery). Sam came out smelling like a rose. On top of that, Miriam's and Ross's boss, Jim, the executive vice president, congratulated Sam for these heroic efforts. Miriam wanted Sam to employ more advanced planning work so the heroic efforts would become unnecessary (they drove labor costs up, for which Jim gave Miriam a hard time). But no one puts on ticker-tape parades for "heroic planning."

Miriam would continue to be defeated in her efforts with Sam as long as this larger organizational issue involving her sponsor and peer remained unaddressed. She decided she needed to talk with Jim first to make sure her efforts to resolve these issues aligned with his goals.

Miriam: I can't believe I haven't addressed this before. Jim's undoing all my efforts to change Sam's management style. I've got to tell him.

Coach: And what are you going to tell Jim?

Miriam: That he's screwing up my development plans for my division! He says he supports me, and then he goes and does this!

Coach: Miriam, that and a dollar-fifty will get you a cup of coffee. Barging into Jim's office with your accusations will probably not change Jim, Ross, or the system.

Miriam: What do you mean?

Coach: This is going to be a huge change for everyone, including Jim. You've got to address this issue in a way that links it to something Jim holds near and dear to his heart. Otherwise there's not enough incentive for him to change. It's too much work for too little payoff. How could Jim benefit?

Miriam: Labor costs! He's always getting on me for my labor costs. And the biggest spikes in labor happen in Sam's department. That's what's in it for Jim.

Miriam had her conversation with Jim and linked what she wanted to accomplish with Sam to Jim's goals around labor. Rather than merely selling him on the connection, however, she genuinely asked Jim whether he saw a significant connection between what she wanted to accomplish and Jim's goals of lower labor costs. When Jim agreed that he did, she told him of the dilemma that his support of Sam's (and ultimately Ross's) firefighting had on her and his goals. It was not until Jim was willing to support Miriam's standards for Sam that this issue had any chance of resolution.

This led Jim to talk to Ross about his overselling. As much as Jim loved the revenue stream, he insisted that Ross find a way to sell at his pace while at the same time satisfying Miriam's parameters by providing enough advance notice for the delivery department to manage its labor needs effectively. Jim told Ross that unless he had Miriam's buy-in, he couldn't proceed. Jim said that if Ross was not able to get a workable agreement with Miriam, then he was to come to Jim, with Miriam, to settle the issue.

As you can see, while Miriam prepared for the next step in her planning stage, she discovered that her first action could not be with Sam. She needed to talk with Jim first. And Jim had to talk with Ross. Assessing change management role alignment issues has the potential of leveraging a client's plan to greater effectiveness. **This is why you encourage your client to study the context surrounding her action plan for role and change management variables; they could have an impact on the plan itself.**

> *This is why you encourage your client to study the context surrounding her action plan for role and change management variables; they could have an impact on the plan itself.*

Once the right action plan is identified, it is critical that coach and client discover which behaviors reinforce the patterns that have kept her plans from working. Here are some approaches to working with a client around the patterns she co-creates with others at work.

Help the Client Identify Her Side of the Pattern

Clients often think that planning strategies means figuring out what to tell others to do, and therefore they focus on how others need to change. Although attention to external variables is necessary, **the client must not ignore the ways she has been a critical variable in and contributor to the situation that now needs changing.** The client's own automatic reactive responses needs special attention. Does she plead, insist, and cajole; stonewall, deflect, and defend; or become philosophical and continuously entertain ideas while not committing to action? The plan should focus on the typical actions of the client and methods for changing her behavior.

The following example shows Miriam's discovery of her pattern of interaction.

Miriam and the Pattern

Miriam had already successfully broken one pattern by talking with Jim about his accolades to Sam and his tacit support of Ross that stressed the system. She had never before told Jim how his actions with others made her division more difficult to lead. That was a huge change in the right direction for Miriam. Now she needed to determine what she would do differently with Sam.

Miriam talked about how frustrated she became when she talked with Sam. We explored how these conversations usually went and Miriam's part in them. She first talked about Sam's unresponsiveness: "His passivity when I talk to him drives me crazy! He's a professional. Why doesn't he think for himself? He never anticipates beyond this week's demands. Do I have to do all his thinking for him?"

"Miriam," I said, "that's not exactly focusing on what you do. That's all about Sam. I know it's hard to get him off center stage, but don't let him take over your thinking! What's your part in this dance?"

When Miriam was able to talk about her side of their discussions, it became apparent that she had fallen into her dominant pattern. She often engaged in "selling" to Sam by telling him what was good for his career, how a different management style was going to benefit him, how great the department would be if he held a vision of excellence for his employees, and so on.

The pattern between them was one of overenthusiastic salesperson (Miriam) and indifferent prospective buyer (Sam). A two-verb description of the co-created pattern would be "sell/decline." His indifference was intolerable to Miriam, which led her to escalate her sales style, which caused Sam to dig his heels in even more.

Because she had not talked with Jim, the executive vice president, beforehand, Miriam's selling style was doomed from the start. Her style was actually a tacit plea with Sam to ignore Jim's kudos, which of course he would not do. Every time she went into her selling mode, Sam became more reluctant and more likely just to give lip-service to her ideas. Now that Miriam had Jim's commitment to support her efforts with both Sam and Ross, she was more likely to succeed with her interactions with Sam.

We focused on Miriam's contribution to the pattern between her and Sam as part of action planning and discussed how to alter the conversation by changing her side of the sell/decline pattern. At this point, the critical ingredient of our planning conversation was her response in the situation, more than the content of the conversation or Sam's response.

Here was a classic cycle of a two-sided, self-reinforcing pattern. Miriam's reaction fostered Sam's under functioning response, and her behavior undermined the very thing she wanted. Sam's action seemed to jump-start not him to action but Miriam to over action—and more of the same in an unending, subconscious cycle.

Miriam was so locked into this style that she lost sight of her goals in the discussions. Since she often sold ideas to others successfully, this lost sale knocked her off balance. Their conversations usually ended with Sam minimally promising compliance and Miriam feeling uneasy about any real prospect for change.

It can be very useful to the client to help her identify these patterns for herself. **Invite the client to notice her internal reaction when she gets into a repetitive pattern. If she is open to reflect on her experience and take responsibility for it, she may then discover the pattern and what triggers it.**

Any number of internal states can signal an automatic pattern:

- Indecisiveness or lack of direction
- Frustration that has no apparent resolution
- Self-blaming
- Feeling closed-minded toward another's input
- Wanting to blame someone else
- Feeling frantic and the need to speed up the pace of activities

In Miriam's case, the internal signal was her high level of frustration and her negative judgments about Sam's "passivity" and "unprofessionalism."

When a client is so frustrated that she can focus only on what the other person is doing wrong, it is a sign that she is truly stymied in her own side of the pattern. This is an example of internal homeostasis that will keep the client from doing anything different. She needs to develop the ability to step back and gain enough distance to see both sides in a more neutral way, including her own contribution to a pattern that no longer works. Only then will she gain some freedom to think creatively about how she might change her side.

One way to get used to thinking of patterns as truly co-created by both contributors is to start charting it out in a simple picture. Once you become adept at seeing patterns and charting them in this way, you can transfer this skill to your clients and help them visualize the patterns they co-create at work.

To begin, draw two arrows like those in Figure 6.2. This is a picture of a self-reinforcing dance that two people, or a leader with her team, create together. Whatever the person (represented by the top arrow) does elicits the reciprocating "dance steps" of the other person (represented by the bottom arrow). And those steps reinforce and draw out your client's response. By the time you meet your client, he and his team have probably been within the same pattern for so long that it has become invisible to them—both what the pattern is and who contributes to it. At best, clients can sometimes see the other person's contribution, but often not how they feed into it.

Figure 6.2 A Co-Created Pattern

Now label each side to represent the key players. I will use the people from the story, Miriam and Sam, for the example in Figure 6.3.

Labeling the two sides of the pattern is a process of generating hypotheses from both you and your client. The titles are less important than getting at the essence of the pattern. I have found it most useful to think of a single verb that would describe your client's contribution and a single verb to describe the other party's contribution. Thus, **you have a two-verb description of the self-reinforcing pattern.** Remember Miriam and Sam's pattern: Miriam was the overenthusiastic seller and Sam the indifferent prospective buyer. Their two-verb pattern is charted in Figure 6.4.

Figure 6.3 Key Players in the Co-Created Pattern

Figure 6.4 Co-Created Pattern with Titles

Sell

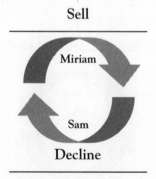

Decline

Here is an example of how to structure the conversation to identify both sides of the pattern when the client does not see it at first:

Miriam and the Process of Pattern Identification

Coach: **What do you do?**

Miriam: I talk until I'm blue in the face.

Coach: **And what does Sam do?**

Miriam: He just sits there!

Coach: **And then what do you do?**

Miriam: I usually think of another creative way to say what I've
said before, hoping it will light a fire under him this time.

Coach: **And then what does Sam do?**

Miriam: The most I can get out of him is a mumbled excuse.

Coach: **Then what do you do?**

Miriam: I either explode, or I say we'll talk about it later.

Coach: **Then what does Sam do, to either reaction?**

Miriam: He usually skulks out the door.

Coach: So you both are reinforcing each other to do the
same thing over and over again. Your last response *seems*
different, but it doesn't get different results. **What name
would you give to each side of this circle [draws self-
reinforcing arrows]? If you could say it in as few words
as possible, even one verb per side, what would it be?**

Miriam: I'm talking until I'm blue in the face; he's sitting
back nice and relaxed.

Coach: Good: "talking until blue" [writes that above the
top arrow]; "sitting back" [writes that under the bottom
arrow]. Does that say it? Does that give the tone?

Miriam: That's about it!

Coach: Give yourself a little credit here. The way you've
described it before, you're actually sincerely wanting
to show Sam how a change in his behavior could help
him, right?

Miriam: Yeah, that's what I don't get—that he doesn't understand that a change would be good for him.

Coach: That's because patterns aren't rational. But I'm thinking that you're not just talking until you're blue in the face for no reason; you're actually trying to sell him on these ideas.

Miriam: Yeah, I'm a lousy salesperson when it comes to Sam!

Coach: That's because he's so good at his part in the sales process. If he saw you as a used car salesperson, what would his "sitting back" style be saying to you?

Miriam: "Thanks, but no thanks, ma'am."

Coach: I'm thinking that too. He's declining your sales pitch. Would it be accurate to say that your one-word side is *sell* and his one-verb side is *decline*? [The coach draws another circle of arrows and writes *sell* above the top arrow and *decline* under the bottom arrow.]

Miriam: It's embarrassing to put it so bluntly, but yeah, that says it.

Eventually Miriam could see some humor in the knee-jerk, fits-like-a-glove nature of her side of the pattern, her impulse to oversell to reluctant buyers. She wondered why she had not seen it beforehand.

Notice the coach's questions to Miriam that are in bold type. They are repetitive questions. The coach keeps up the same litany: "What do you do? Then what does he do? Then what do you do?" These repetitive questions help you and the client see the circularity of the pattern and how each side reinforces the other. The client begins to see that she is part of it and what she does that keeps the pattern going. What is important is the client's ownership of the pattern and seeing that she contributes as much to the pattern as the other person does. It is up to her to change her side, rather than expecting the other person to be the only one who changes.

There are many typical co-created patterns that frustrate people at work. They also decrease effectiveness and productivity. Figure 6.5 lists some of the ones I have encountered with clients. One way of thinking of pattern work is that each side of the pattern is lacking either backbone or heart. Clients usually have to develop the side of them that is weak on either delivering

Figure 6.5 Typical Co-Created Patterns Between Leaders and Teams

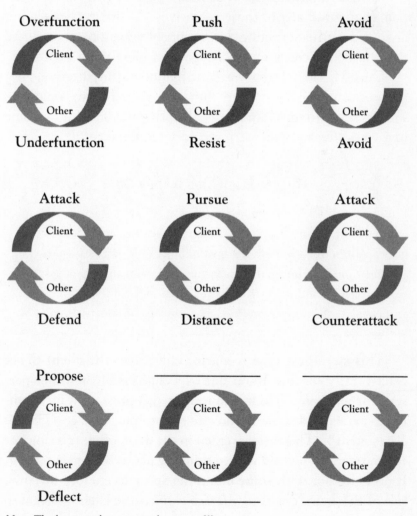

Overfunction	Push	Avoid
Client / Other	Client / Other	Client / Other
Underfunction	Resist	Avoid

Attack	Pursue	Attack
Client / Other	Client / Other	Client / Other
Defend	Distance	Counterattack

Propose	_____	_____
Client / Other	Client / Other	Client / Other
Deflect	_____	_____

Note: The last two elements are for you to fill in.

backbone or weak on showing heart. The same is true for these typical nonproductive patterns: each side is missing at least one element of backbone and heart.

> *The same is true for these typical nonproductive patterns: each side is missing at least one element of backbone and heart.*

Miriam finally realized that she knew very little about what Sam thought of any of these initiatives. At first that made her angry. On further reflection during our conversations, she realized that she did not create much of a space for him to air his opinions.

Once Miriam saw that her contribution to the pattern did not allow Sam to give her the very thing she wanted (Sam's opinion), she was ready to set a different goal, both for a different outcome in the meeting and a different way to act in the meeting.

Miriam Identifies a New Goal

When I first asked Miriam what different behavior she wanted from Sam, her response was, "I am so frustrated by his lack of vision that I can't describe what having it would be like." After struggling for some time with her irritation at Sam, she came up with a description: "He would initiate meetings with me, coming to me with ideas about how to streamline labor costs in the department."

This step (best-case scenario) challenges the client to get behaviorally specific about her expectations of the other person (for example, "He would initiate meetings with me, coming to me with ideas about how to streamline labor costs in the department"). This opens a crack in the door, often relaxing her commitment to her old way of thinking about the other person. It provides her with some breathing space to explore her own side of the dance creatively. It also requires the client to begin to focus on the next step of planning: considering what resistance she can expect to her new way of acting in meetings.

Remember that resistance means there are forces in place that operate to keep things the same. In earlier chapters, I covered how strong the interactional field is and therefore how homeostasis will pull all players back into their habitual ways of doing things within the system. Since it is a natural response, you and your client can count on it. It is the savvy coach who focuses the client on the resistance to her plans. It is the prepared client who girds herself for the inevitable push-back.

Help the Client Plan for Resistance

Some good old-fashioned skepticism can sometimes be useful with executives. What's to say that the client's plan will work? There is a reason the client wants coaching on the issue. If it were as simple as fitting alignment pieces of a puzzle together, the client probably would have moved beyond his dilemma on his own by now. Your contribution is to discuss with the client the powerful forces in place that will push back on him, even as the client makes good plans toward ensuring a more functional alignment of the issues. The move in the system toward homeostasis—keeping the current balance of forces stable—is powerful, irrational, and often unconscious or unacknowledged (see Part One). Even when Miriam receives Jim's sponsorship for her plan with Sam, that does not guarantee success when she turns her plan into action with Sam.

Clients need to plan for the inevitable resistance they will experience in executing their plan. Sometimes clients enter into a coaching process enthusiastic about their plan but unprepared for the resistance. Afterward they might say, "Well, that was a lousy idea; it didn't work out." Instead of allowing them unrealistic illusions, you can invite them to think about what they are going to do when their plan does not work. After all, the real challenge is to bring clients fully to the moment in a different way than they ever experienced before.

Planning for resistance can help clients develop a realistic persistence rather than pursuing a plan based on ungrounded optimism. It can build their capacity to remain in sticky situations that activate anxiety. They may not be so easily thrown off course when they experience the inevitable static in the system.

There is power in imagining a successful situation beforehand and rehearsing for its outcome. There is also power in imagining what to do about the resistance that might derail an action step. Both preparations pave the way for success. **It can be highly productive to encourage your clients to imagine the resistance that could sink their initiatives. This includes their internal resistance as well.** Sometimes it is not a pleasant experience, but by pinpointing their individual vulnerabilities to the forces that keep things in place, you can improve a client's chance for pushing through the resistance.

For example, a client may know that he never fails to back off from his plan when three specific people in the department come up with objections to it. He can then choose to keep moving ahead even if those three people predictably play their part in the dance. It also helps to identify the judgments he thinks people will have when he persists: "Well, they'll think I'm being unreasonable or unreliable. They may even complain to my boss."

You can encourage the client to imagine beyond the impasse. Ask him what he will do to stay on course. You may go through many repetitions of, "Then what will you do?" In that way, you are helping him build tolerance for his own discomfort at facing the resistance to his new pattern. When he fully explores these scenarios, it can be liberating, sometimes even funny. He can see how transparent everyone's resistance can be when he has pictured himself withstanding it, making it possible to last long enough to get to the other side. In Miriam's case, planning for resistance helped her prepare for the change she wanted.

Miriam Plans for Resistance

We had discussed what Miriam could do differently in her pattern with Sam. She decided that she could do less of the talking and Sam could do more and thus decrease her selling and create a space for him to be more proactive.

Coach: Miriam, this is not going to be easy street. You and Sam have been operating like this for years. In fact, you could repeat the old pattern in your sleep. You and he are going to do and say things in the conversation that will keep the "strong selling–no buying" dance locked into place. What will he do to keep it going?

Miriam: Get a blank look on his face and slouch in his chair. That drives me crazy.

Coach: Actually it drives you to stronger selling. And what will you do to keep the old pattern going?

Miriam: I can't stand his sullen silences. Five seconds of pause in the conversation is all I can take. Then I'm off again.

Coach: So what are you going to do differently?

Miriam: We'll have a give-and-take discussion, and I won't take it over.

Coach: Sounds great. Then what are you going to do when you're on your second round of selling because you've just blown past the pauses in the conversation?

Miriam (with a blank look on her face): What do you mean?

Coach: Well, you know it's going to happen. This conversation isn't going to be perfect the first time. You have to give yourself a break. Rely on getting stuck in the old pattern and be willing to do something different when you notice it. Here's an example. No matter where you are in the conversation when you notice you've gone on automatic, you can stop and ask Sam a question. And don't say a word until after he answers it, even if that's longer than five seconds, even way longer than five seconds.

Miriam (reflecting on how the conversations usually go): Yeah, that would be different.

Coach: It's also good to plan for more than one course of action. Another way to get Sam to be more active while you are less active would be to ask him to paraphrase what it is you said. That requires him to do active listening rather than just wait you out.

As you can see in this conversation, the coach offers a couple of different actions the client could take, anticipating the push-back response from the other person. The client imagines both falling back into her old pattern and then moving beyond it to a distinctly different response that keeps her on track with her plan.

You can use another tool to help your client plan her actions to counter push-back resistance by drawing on a worksheet the contrast between the old and new patterns like those illustrated in Figure 6.6.

Figure 6.6 Pattern Shift Worksheet

Business Issue: _____

From: _____

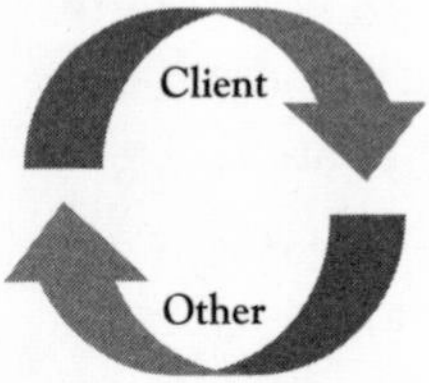

Client

Other

_____

To: _____

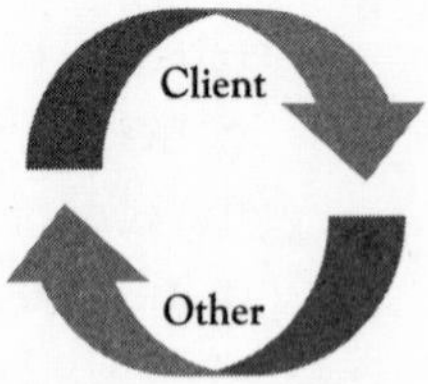

Client

Other

_____

Likely "Push-Back" to Client's New Behavior:

_____

Client's Response Options to the "Push-Back":

_____

_____

Once that is clear, the client lists the likely push-back and new responses she could use. Figure 6.7 shows how Miriam and her coach used the worksheet.

Because patterns are so ingrained and often unconsciously reinforced, your client may not shift the pattern on her own without help *while* she is implementing it. This is the main reason to do live-action coaching with your client. It is an art in and of itself. The next chapter explores this particular kind of coaching. It also continues Miriam's story so you can see what happened with her plan with Sam.

Figure 6.7 Pattern Shift Worksheet: Miriam's Case

Business Issue: ———————————— Decrease Labor Costs

From: Sell

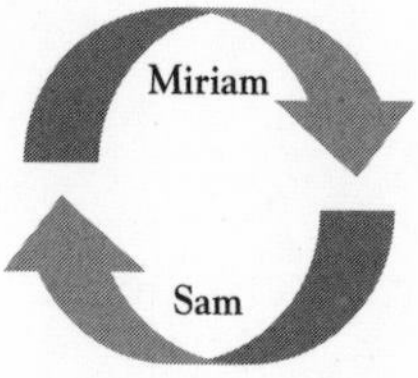

Miriam

Sam

Decline

To: Ask Question and Pause

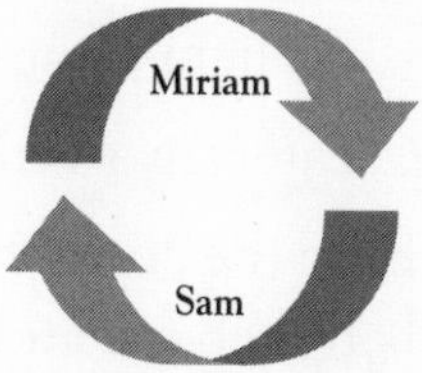

Miriam

Sam

Respond and Initiate

Likely "Push-Back" to Miriam's New Behavior:

• Sam will continue to not respond, wait out Miriam until Miriam starts to sell again so he can remain passive.

Client's Response Options to the "Push-Back":

• Ask question and pause. Do not say anything until Sam responds.
• Have him paraphrase what Miriam said.

Chapter Six Highlights

Move the Executive to Specifics

1. Move from general venting to a particular plan.

2. Identify a next step now, and check to see how it may change after looking at all five steps in the planning phase.

Address Issues in Change Management and Role Clarity

1. Ask the client questions that uncover change management issues.

2. Ensure the client's strategy takes into account the alignment of roles.

Help the Client Identify Her Side of the Pattern

1. Focus the client on *her* pattern changes.

2. Help the client connect her internal experience with her characteristic pattern.

A Tool for Naming Patterns

1. Chart out the pattern with the client using a very simple picture.

2. Label the two sides of the pattern as hypotheses from you and your client using repetitive questioning.

3. Create a two-verb description of the self-reinforcing pattern.

4. Help the client create a new specific behavior that breaks both her side and the other side of the pattern.

Help the Client Plan for Resistance

1. Help the client anticipate the push-back response.

2. Invite the client to plan for internal resistance as well.

3. Use a pattern shift worksheet so the client has a full picture of the change she will make and the challenges she faces.

7

PHASE 3–LIVE-ACTION COACHING

Strike While the Iron Is Hot

Live-action coaching is more like improvised jazz than a choreographed dance. You intervene in unexpected yet useful ways to help your client achieve his goal in the session.

Live-action coaching is more like improvised jazz than a choreographed dance

---

Since live-action coaching means you are present when your client conducts business activities and interactions, you face a built-in awkwardness. Few people feel at ease when someone observes them doing their work. Nevertheless, they begin to see the benefit when it provides feedback that can increase their effectiveness. One new client recently told me, "I want a coach so I can see myself in action—someone who can observe what I can't."

Before embarking on an in-depth exploration of live-action coaching, I provide a brief overview of **a coaching developmental sequence** that I often use when working with clients over time. These stages represent the usual flow of activities and events when the client has chosen the complete process that includes live-action coaching. You can use this evolutionary sequence to assess your approach to your clients. The sequence is as follows (see Figure 7.1):

Stage 1: Behind-the-scenes coaching of the client.

Stage 2: Observation of the client in a business meeting with her directs and in one-on-one meetings with staff members.

Figure 7.1 Developmental Sequence for Coaching Contexts

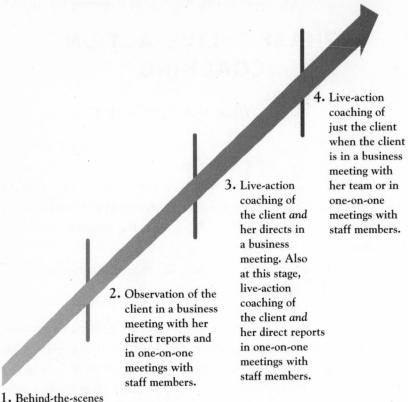

4. Live-action coaching of just the client when the client is in a business meeting with her team or in one-on-one meetings with staff members.

3. Live-action coaching of the client *and* her directs in a business meeting. Also at this stage, live-action coaching of the client *and* her direct reports in one-on-one meetings with staff members.

2. Observation of the client in a business meeting with her direct reports and in one-on-one meetings with staff members.

1. Behind-the-scenes coaching of the client.

Stage 3: Live-action coaching of the client *and* her direct reports in a business meeting. Also at this stage, live-action coaching of the client *and* her directs in one-on-one meetings with staff members.

Stage 4: Live-action coaching of just the client when the client is in a business meeting with her team or in one-on-one meetings with staff members.

All of these coaching stages demand a range of experience and skill levels from the coach, but the most demanding is stage 3. You can use this survey of the coaching sequence to assess your skills and ascertain which currently represent your skill level when you coach executives. This sequence provides a blueprint for increasing your repertoire of coaching. The more of this sequence you can master, the greater value you bring to your clients.

Stage 1: Behind-the-Scenes Coaching of the Client

On one end of the coaching continuum is behind-the-scenes coaching, which includes contracting, planning, and debriefing with the client. This type of coaching was the focus of the previous two chapters (contracting and planning), and we will revisit it in Chapter Eight (debriefing). Many clients may want this kind of coaching exclusively and choose to implement their plans on their own without your presence. It is a bit misleading to think of behind-the-scenes coaching as the simple end of the coaching spectrum. As I have already discussed, coaching requires a tremendous amount of personal presence and organizational savvy. It is on the far end of the continuum, however, for two reasons: (1) it does not have the added complexity inherent in live-action coaching, and (2) it encompasses a necessary set of coaching tasks that accompanies live-action coaching. Live-action coaching depends on effective contracting and planning beforehand, and debriefing afterward.

Skills required: We explored most of the skills for behind-the-scenes coaching in the previous chapters: maintaining a strong signature presence, having the ability to see systems, working from the Client Responsibility Model, and helping the client set goals and plans for action.

Stage 2: Observation of the Client with Her Direct Reports

It is one thing to hear a client's own account of her leadership challenges, but it is quite another to actually see her implementing her leadership goals. I suggest that you set time aside during all of your coaching contracts to observe your clients. At some point, I want to see my clients in action rather than merely hear their accounts of their decisions and actions. I also get a fuller sense of the reinforcing patterns that my client and others contribute to the co-created dance between the client and her team.

My goal for observation is to see clients at least every other month during the length of our coaching contract. This keeps us both honest about how much progress has been made during the coaching work and how much further the client has to go to make her leadership goals a reality.

For live-action coaching clients, the goal of this stage is to observe the client with her team of direct reports when they conduct their business and factor this observation in when it comes to intervening with clients. The purpose of the observation is two-fold: (1) to see how the leader and the team interact with each other on their own, without intervention from a coach (the observation operates as a bit of a pretest to see how they do without help) and (2) to see how much capacity and resilience the leader and the team have with each other—for example, are they brittle, defensive, open, curious, engaged, disconnected? It is useful to recognize the skill set and emotional tones that emanate from this leader and team. It helps prepare for the live-action stage of the coaching.

Skills required: The coach must notice themes in the client's strengths and challenges and describe them back to the client in specific and observable ways that will help develop a targeted action plan for next steps.

Stage 3: Live-Action Coaching of the Client and His Direct Reports

Live-action coaching can be helpful to clients who are stuck within ineffective patterns with their teams. This intervention helps the client experience kinesthetically the opportune times for changing a pattern because the coach can stop a client midstream and suggest an alternative action. The in-the-moment self-correction can help the client recognize and eventually anticipate those times when he responds automatically. Live-action intervention combined with behind-the-scenes coaching can speed up the change process.

Many times consultants do not use the live-action coaching option (stage 3 or 4) even though it could empower their client to a new level of effectiveness. Sometimes change agents gravitate toward one of the extremes of intervention: they either take over the full facilitation of the group's process or coach the leader in isolation from her team. Both of these methods are viable tools in and of themselves. Depending on them solely, however, can leave a blind spot for both the leader and the coach. This kind of live-action work combined with behind-the-scenes coaching is powerful and effective.

Live-action coaching is just-in-time, on-the-job training and reinforcement of the executive when it counts the most. The greatest level of complexity is live-action coaching in which you intervene with your primary client and his team of direct reports simultaneously. This differs from the classic group process consultation model for which organizational development specialists are best known because the coach does not facilitate the meeting. Instead, while the client leads and facilitates his own meeting with his team, a coach intervenes as the process unfolds. By acting in the moment while events and patterns are in play, the live-action coach can help accelerate the leader's and the team's performance and focus on their strengths. It can also help a leader and team get back on track if they have become ineffective as a group. The live-action coach can offer suggestions along the way or stop the meeting at critical times to provide on-the-spot debriefings and opportunities for the leader and team to give each other feedback. Incidentally, the transition from observation to live-action intervention is an easier one to make rather than diving right into live-action coaching the first time the team encounters the coach.

Skills required: In addition to all the skills of behind-the-scenes coaching and observing the client, stage 3 requires the ability to track and intervene on four levels in the midst of the meeting by (1) maintaining the leader's effectiveness as the meeting facilitator, (2) keeping track of and helping members advance the business agenda, (3) coaching each team member and the leader regarding their individual goals for effective work relationship behaviors, and (4) helping the leader and the team shift out of ineffective patterns and into more productive patterns at the very moment they are unfolding. The Client Responsibility Model has to be foremost in mind so that you do not overstep the boundaries of the coaching role and start to manage the group in place of the leader. Because of the complex elements that the coach needs to track and consider in choosing a course of intervention, I work with a colleague to ensure that there are two coaches working with all of the clients in the room.

One example of stage 3 live-action team coaching is the work a colleague and I did with Len, the vice president of marketing, and his team while he led his team meetings.

Len and His Team

Len wanted to improve two aspects of how he led meetings: (1) getting more input from team members that increased the quality of the discussions and (2) better defining of and making decisions. We contracted for live team coaching at his meetings to help him and his team improve in these areas.

At the beginning of each meeting, Len let everyone know not only the agenda of the meeting, but also what it was that he wanted to work on and why we were there to help him.

I had coached Len to add one more thing: if anyone on the team noticed that he was straying from his two goals, they should speak up and mention it rather than wait for me or the other coach to intervene. This places some of the responsibility on the team for making sure the meeting is run well. After all, the team is always there; we are not. Building more self-sufficiency in the team around effective interactions reduces reliance on outside coaches.

We had a coaching contract with each team member to help them initiate the behaviors that Len desired from them and attain the goals each had identified to improve their individual effectiveness at meetings.

As we witnessed the team meetings, under Len's leadership this group continually lost track of the discussion and was not clear about the decisions being made. A few minutes into the first agenda item, the discussion became disjointed, tangential, and unproductive. Len did not notice this or attempt to get the meeting back on track. Instead, he further contributed to a discussion that was going nowhere. At that point I intervened directly with him in front of the group so that the team members could also hear what I had to say: "Len, the discussion is covering several topics. What do you want to focus on right now?"

We used a variety of live-action interventions throughout the meeting directed to either Len or his team as a whole, or to specific team members when the conversation got off track. The following are some more examples:

> *To Len:* "A decision was just made, and I don't think there is clarity among the team members about what exactly it was. Can you ensure that all team members are aware of what they are committing to?"
>
> *To the whole team:* "The goal that was stated earlier is to hear from everyone. You can help Len make sure that happens either by inviting comments from those who haven't spoken or speaking up if you haven't weighed in yet."
>
> *To Len:* "Are you ready to move on, or do you want to hear from more people?"

> *To a specific team member:* "In keeping with your goal of
>   tying your comments to others' ideas, now would be
>   the time to show Lisa you understand what she just said
>   before giving your opinion."
> *To Len:* "You have exceeded the time you said you were
>   going to take for this topic. Do you want to take more
>   time on this or close it off?"

Saying all comments and suggestions aloud so that everyone can hear them helps the most people break the trance of the leader and team's old pattern. Then anyone can take the initiative to make the meeting more productive and thus contribute to the pattern change. We did not take over facilitating the meeting or change direction of the discussion, which left Len in control of the meeting. We made sure not to overstep Len's authority to facilitate and make decisions.

> *Saying all comments and suggestions aloud so that
> everyone can hear them helps the most people break
> the trance of the leader and team's old pattern.*

What is absolutely critical in live-action interventions, in either stage 3 or 4, is not to give evaluative feedback to your client. Evaluative feedback, such as, "You aren't listening to your team members," "That statement was too harsh," or "I see why team members ignore you," can easily contribute to a defensive response from the person you are delivering the feedback to in such a public forum. I tell my clients in advance to expect to hear short statements of observation or suggestions—for example, "You are over the time you allotted for this topic." It is important that they are suggestions, not mandates. The point of the statements, suggestions, and questions is to break the trance of the old pattern, not to demand blind obedience from the client. When the trance is broken, the client may actually generate better alternatives than those a coach would suggest.

Len, continued

Each time we intervened directly with Len, he considered the input and then decided what he wanted to do next. At the end of each meeting, he solicited feedback from his team on both his effectiveness in leading the meeting and his level of success at meeting his two goals. Team members also reported on which specific team members helped move the meeting forward and what could improve effectiveness at the next meeting. Over time, Len became more adept at running the meetings. Team members also learned to intervene and shift the team to a more effective pattern. As Len and his team became more self-sufficient, their dependence on coaching diminished.

When a client needs to make a dramatic shift in his business results, leader behaviors, and team interactions, stage 3 live-action team coaching, combined with behind-the-scenes-coaching of the client leader, can help shift patterns and achieve breakthrough results in all of the Three Key Factors of the client's landscape.

Stage 4: Live-Action Coaching of Just the Client When the Client Is with Her Direct Reports

The fourth level of the developmental sequence is live-action coaching of the client when she is either in a team meeting or in one-on-one meetings with her staff members. As you help the client articulate her thinking and as she puts her plan into action, you may detect room for improvement in her leadership and management in both team and one-on-one meetings.

At first, this may seem to be the same as stage 3 leader and team coaching. However, there is a subtle but significant difference between the two. In stage 3, your client is everyone in the group—both the leader and each team member. You work with everyone live during the meeting, and everyone is a candidate for receiving on-the-spot coaching. In stage 4, the executive is your sole client. Unlike stage 3, you do not directly address or coach the group as a whole or as individual members. Nor do you facilitate the meeting since this would deprive the leader of developmental opportunities. Stage 4 live-action coaching focuses solely on how the leader functions.

You are working specifically to improve the executive's leading skills so she can accomplish her goals in the ensuing meetings. It is a bit like driver's education instruction in that the leader, not you, has her hands on the steering wheel of the car.

You may wonder why coaching your primary client individually comes developmentally after coaching the full team (stage 3). After everyone has been coached in stage 3, they are much more amenable to live-action coaching solely of their leader. They no longer find it strange that the leader is being coached in stage 4. By contrast, team members are more guarded and less likely to learn if I initiate stage 4 live-action coaching of the leader when the team members have not been clients of coaching themselves. Having been coached, they are less likely to view the coach as a foreign element and their boss as deficient.

Developmentally, I use stage 4 to start weaning the client away from my live-action interventions. Self-reliance has more of a chance to emerge at this point if the coach addresses only the leader rather than the full team. The leader feels more responsibility to make the meeting effective. Since the coach no longer intervenes with team members, the leader has to work to increase team members' productive interactions.

Skills required: In stage 4, the coach takes a "bifocal view" by watching and diagnosing the quality of the group process while directly intervening with the leader. It takes discipline to have an opinion on how the group is doing and yet not speak directly to the team members. It is not that you are impeding their development, but rather building capacity in the leader to develop the team.

Individual live-action coaching requires the ability to notice the precise moment when the leader strays into her old pattern.

You can then take advantage of that moment and help the executive shift her pattern in real time.

Sometimes coaching the client in a one-on-one session with a staff member can be especially uncomfortable for your client since there are just the three of you in the room. This kind of live-action coaching requires that the client have a high degree of trust in the coach and a great deal of comfort with herself. She has to be willing to put herself under a powerful microscope in this close setting. Although it would seem to be a less vulnerable forum than in front of the whole team, I have found that executives sometimes feel more vulnerable with a coach as witness and intervener in one-on-one sessions.

Stage 4 coaching in one-on-one meetings depends on your track record with the client. This type of session enables a client to get coaching in real time while she attempts to manage her reactivity in a potentially hot situation. It is usually when the client has reached an impasse with one other person that she will consider a one-on-one live coaching session. You must be able to balance respect for her authority (if she is in a manager-employee conversation) along with challenging her in real time to communicate more effectively with her staff.

The coach engages in some hefty self-management in these one-on-one sessions. This is the Client Responsibility Model at its most fundamental and challenging level. A hot triangle can form when only three people are in the room and two of them have some entrenched pattern. The client's temptation to subconsciously draw you in as interference or a distraction will be great. It can be as simple as the uneasiness between the two inducing you to step in and rescue.

You need to maintain the bifocal view of stage 4 by keeping your focus on your client. You will feel impelled to be a third-party intervener or a human resource policy expert addressing performance management issues. These roles have their place at other times, but they involve a different contract. It takes skill to discern the difference and advise your client as to which role would best suit her development needs at the time.

Setting the Stage for and Using the Live-Action Coaching Method

Now that the developmental stages have been laid out, let's look more closely at stages 3 and 4, where the live-action coaching options are used. Four activities are crucial to the success of live-action coaching. Two of them happen behind the scenes as you contract with clients specifically for live-action coaching: (1) clearly defining what your role will be in the session and (2) ensuring that the client can sponsor you well in the session. The other two activities happen during the live-action coaching itself: (3) interventions aimed at the specific goals the client sets for that session and (4) promotion of effective pattern change between the client and her team. Before embarking on these four activities, you must determine whether it is appropriate, necessary, and useful to use live-action coaching with a particular client.

Determine Whether You Have a Live-Action Coaching Role

Since live-action coaching means that you are with your client while he is on the job, you can directly observe how he executes his plan and what strengths and challenges he has in implementing it. As I mentioned before, the coach can intervene in the moment to help keep the client on track. Under what circumstances should a coach suggest live-action coaching to a client? **There are two criteria to keep in mind when considering live-action coaching:**

- **The level of trust built up between the coach and the client.** The higher the trust is, the more likely it is that live-action coaching will be successful.

- **The degree to which the client fails to see and self-correct his pattern when he is in the middle of it.** Live-action coaching is a tool to create a shift in the client's pattern that he continually plays out with his staff.

Level of Trust. The client has to trust the coach enough to bring the coach directly into his live work setting. **Trust entails two key elements: (1) the belief that the coach will not overstep his boundaries in the client's work life, and (2) the coach will not confront the client with a disrespectful challenge in front of her employees.** This is tricky business because the purpose of live-action coaching is to effectively challenge the client in front of others in a way that the client welcomes as highly useful. The client needs to know that you act respectfully when you challenge her and also needs to trust that you will not overstep your bounds and act as a replacement for the client with the client's employees.

Because of these fine lines, live-action coaching usually follows an established client-coach relationship that is already working effectively. I use this coaching either when executives have been long-term clients or they have shown their capacity to receive feedback from me and learn from it during the extensive contracting and planning phases for live team coaching. Both the coach and the client have already walked down the path of immediacy and feedback to the extent that they are ready for live-action coaching.

Client's Failure to Self-Correct His Pattern. People cannot change what they cannot see. Even with the best of intentions and new plans for action, clients will enter familiar situations and go on automatic, completely forgetting their intention to change their behavior. There was nothing wrong with their plan. It is just that the old behavior and the forces to stay the same are overpowering your client.

When you experience your client not being able to see or change his behavior, then live-action coaching may be the best way for him to change. You provide an immediate biofeedback loop that helps him see his behavior and gives him something that he can respond to right in that moment. Opportunities to change are pointed out for him to take advantage of. He can familiarize himself with a new habit of interaction with his staff, which is reinforced as it is happening.

Define the Live-Action Role

Rigor is required for live-action coaching. **The role of the coach needs to be clearly defined beforehand, with the full range of available options discussed and agreed on** (see Figure 7.2). Otherwise the client may feel blindsided or abandoned during the session due to a mismatch of expectations.

At one extreme end of the spectrum, the least active option, is observation (stage 2 of the developmental sequence of coaching interventions). As the coach, you benefit from seeing the client in action. You receive information beyond the client's account of the experience. Also, the client is more aware of her goals for the meeting because of your presence. However, if I am in the room, I prefer to offer as much feedback as possible, and observation gives the coach less influence than the live-action coaching options.

The other end of the spectrum is the "stop action" option. You contract with the client that you may call a time-out at any time and debrief with her right on the spot about what she is doing. This highest-impact option requires the greatest trust between client and coach. The client has to be comfortable with the possibility that she could be in a debriefing conversation regarding her weaker skills in front of others. Clients who have confidence in themselves as learners and have a sense of humor about their own foibles are the best candidates for this option.

Figure 7.2 Live-Action Coaching Interventions

Observe	Offer suggestions	Stop action, debrief
	Make statements	Give feedback
	Ask questions	Restart action

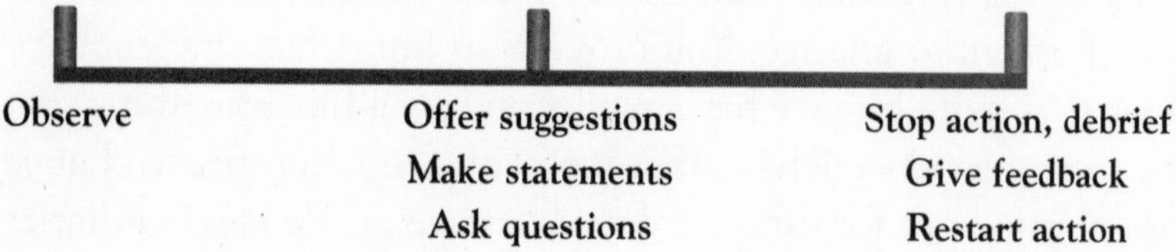

A middle-ground option that is used most frequently is to offer the client suggestions or questions during the action that do not interrupt the flow of the meeting. When this is done well, the client continues with her train of thought, either using or ignoring the coach's suggestions, depending on whether the client can incorporate the suggestion in the moment.

The following example shows planning for live-action coaching with Miriam to determine the coach's role:

Miriam Plans for Live Action

I offered to Miriam that I could sit in on her next session with Sam:

Coach: It's one sure way to notice when you get into your selling pattern.

Miriam: How would it work?

Coach: You would have your conversation with Sam, and I can coach you right in the moment. I won't do your work for you or take over the conversation.

Miriam: I'm game for it—at least to try it once. Given my track record with Sam, there's nowhere to go but up. What will it be like? What will you do?

Coach: It will be more like an occasional suggestion to remind you of what you've been preparing for, to keep you moving toward the goals you have for your discussion with Sam. It will still be your meeting. I'm there to help you stay on track.

Miriam: Won't that be weird to have you there with Sam? What if he clams up?

Coach: He already clams up. If anything, that could give us both an opportunity to see what you do when he clams up.

Miriam: So I still don't know what it will look like.

Coach: It could look like this. You get lost in your selling pattern, and I say something like, "Miriam, remember that you wanted to ask Sam a question," or I could say, "Miriam, try something besides selling," or I could say, "Do you know whether you've been clear? Why don't you ask Sam to paraphrase what you said."

Miriam: Oh, I get it: you give me suggestions I use right then when I've lost it.

Coach: Yes. I help remind you of your action plan and the new pattern you want to create.

Prepare Your Client to Define and Sponsor the Live-Action Coaching Role

At the beginning of the live-action session, **the client needs to sponsor your presence as her coach in the session. This means she will define your coaching role to others who are present during the coaching session.** Some time spent before the live-action session discussing how the client will explain your role goes a long way to preventing others from misunderstanding it when the client describes it at the session. For instance, team members should be aware that you are not there to facilitate everyone at the meeting or evaluate your client's staff members.

An example of a client giving a well-sponsored explanation of the live-action role in stage 4 (only the client receives coaching) would go something like this: "I've asked John [the coach] to be here during our conversation so he can coach me to be more effective. He has been working with me on some of my leadership goals. Improving how I conduct one-on-one conversations is one of them. Although John's sitting in on the discussion, he's focusing only on how I'm doing, not on you. He's raising the heat on me here. John might give me some suggestions in the middle of the conversation so I stay on track. Do you have any questions about his role?"

Live-Action Coaching Tasks

Many of the tasks for live-action coaching are used both when coaching only the client in one-on-one sessions with a staff member and during live-action coaching when the whole team is involved. As I describe these tasks, I will use one consistent example from stage 4, live-action coaching of just the leader in a one-on-one session. **Here are the essential live-action coaching tasks:**

- **Ensure proper sponsorship and structuring of the session.**
- **Follow the client's goal.**
- **Foster pattern breaking.**
- **Maintain alignment in the system.**

Ensure Proper Sponsorship and Structuring of the Session

Stage 4 live-action coaching when the client is having a one-on-one session with a staff member can get tricky for both the client and the other person in the session. It can seem like a dynamic of two against one (client and coach versus staff member). Very little can be said that guarantees that this third person will feel comfortable at the beginning and not intimidated by the coach's presence. Several elements of structuring a live-action session can be particularly helpful in this situation. They show the other person that the coach is not there to be an enforcer for the client, or an arbitrator, or an evaluator, or even a third-party facilitator.

In the first task, the client sponsors the coach by explaining to the other person the purpose of the session and the purpose of the coach's presence. Although you may have prepped your client to give such a sponsoring statement, there is no guarantee she will say it effectively. I learned this lesson the hard way when I did not prepare clients around their introductions of me.

In their nervousness, they would give a completely misleading interpretation of my role.

> *Although you may have prepped your client to give such a sponsoring statement, there is no guarantee she will say it effectively.*

Do not allow yourself to be a victim of your client's definition of your role. Although it is important that she sponsors your presence by defining the reason you are there, feel free to fill in gaps and fine-tune her definition. I tell the client beforehand that I will augment her introduction of me if I need to. It is a way I can add my voice early in the conversation as a joining activity, a way to become known a little bit to the other staff member if he has not met me previously. It is better for him to hear me speak first during this early structuring time in the session rather than first hearing from me during a more intense time, when a higher-impact intervention becomes necessary.

Someone in the staff member's position is often skeptical about the coach's "real reason" for being there. **You truly need to live up to the stated purpose in the session and maintain your independence from your client's content agenda.** This also means not focusing on the staff member midway through, no matter how tempting it is. It is important that you show in some way that you are not in your client's "back pocket" or so fused to her view of the situation that you do not have your own perspective. I often let my client know the importance of attending to this emotional landscape and tell her beforehand that at some point in the session, I will probably challenge her as a way of communicating a viewpoint that is independent from her own.

A way to lessen the two-against-one perspective without shining a spotlight on the other person is to sit next to him rather than next to the client during the session. This allows you to share the literal point of view that the staff member has as he experiences his boss.

These small actions can help you **position yourself as emotionally neutral to the content outcome of the conversations** because you show that you do not side with either the client or the employee in the session, even as you focus solely on your client's skill development.

Follow the Client's Goals

It seems obvious that you will be guided by the goals the client established in the contracting and planning phases. Nevertheless, all kinds of distractions can divert you along the way. One big snag is the need to be useful and have something to do. You can easily think, "Here I am, invited by the client to sit in on this session and contribute to his effectiveness. I better not just sit here. I better contribute and do something!"

The challenge you face in live-action sessions is to be prepared to be very active at any time, while also being prepared to do nothing if no intervention is needed. This is the ultimate challenge of the Client Responsibility Model of coaching. "Doing nothing" while staying attentive and engaged takes a lot of energy. You are observing the extent to which your client is accomplishing what he set out to do.

Turning your observations and your considered judgments into action can be difficult. I said earlier that I have a bias for action in these live-action settings. However, the motto from the Client Responsibility Model is, **"Stay active *and* stay out of the way."** You want to act in the moment to increase the client's learning, but you can err in a number of ways that can block the client's full learning potential. One way is to pseudo manage, that is, fill in during all the pauses, missteps, and hesitations of the client in such a way that you take away his leadership. You need to let him manage the session.

You are also not a third-party intervener, particularly when your contract is for stage 4 live-action coaching with one party of the conversation. It is not your job to ensure that the communication or relationship of both parties is mutual or successful or resolved. Your job is to ensure that your client is attending to that, not that you make it happen—a subtle but powerful difference. The more you facilitate as a third-party mediator when that is not what you are contracted to do, the more you increase your client's dependence on you to make it happen the next time.

So, you may be wondering, *what do I do, and what does it look like?*

You already have a map that you can bring into the session to help you stay on track: your client's plan that he developed with you in the planning phase of your coaching work together. It was there that he decided what he wanted to accomplish (the specific next step to advance his business goal) and how he needed to accomplish it in a new way with others (his work relationship challenge).

These two goals—your client's next specific step and your client's work relationship challenge—are quite enough to keep track of and intervene around. There is so much going on between people in a meeting that it is easy to get lost or overwhelmed by everything that needs to be worked. You can also become mesmerized by their established patterns.

Sometimes it is tempting to address something you think your client needs to work on when you have no contract to live-action-coach him on that issue. You will feel pulled to take action addressing these new behaviors. Most of the time, that impulse is a distraction from the contracted goals that your client has set forth. Those goals should be the center of your attention when you help him in the session. Do not let the complexity or novelty of other growth opportunities keep you from helping your client in the very ways he thinks you will be helping him. Live-action coaching is nerve-wracking enough without challenging your client with uncontracted learning goals. It will seem to him as if it is coming out of nowhere.

Foster Pattern Breaking

The coach's role is to look for opportunities to change patterns precisely when they are operating in the conversation.

Let's revisit the situation of the overselling director, Miriam, and the reluctant manager, Sam. She and I spent some planning time looking at her side of the unsuccessful pattern of their interaction. By attending to the gaps in sponsorship that were undermining her effort, she was able to get sponsorship from Jim (the vice president) to pull Sam out of firefighting situations with Ross (Miriam's peer).

Miriam was now ready to address her own part in the ineffective transactional pattern with Sam. She set out to eliminate her side of the co-created pattern as a major step, and she wanted me to be present at the session to help her do it differently. As you will recall when last we left Miriam (Figure 6.7), she had a plan to stop the "sell" (Miriam)/"decline" (Sam) pattern between them and work to shift it to "ask something, then pause" (Miriam)/ "Respond and initiate" (Sam). Sam was likely to work to keep the old pattern in place by waiting Miriam out and continuing to neither respond nor initiate. Miriam's job was to outwait Sam's waiting until he responded or ask him to paraphrase what she had said.

Miriam in Live-Action Coaching

Once we were in the live-action session, after the initial joining and structuring of the session, including defining my role as her live-action coach, Miriam outlined the goal for the meeting: settle on a course of action to turn Sam's department from one based on crisis management to one that performed well through proactive measures, saving on labor costs.

Then, leaving no room for Sam to respond to her agenda, Miriam went on automatic. She completely forgot about her goal to shift her side of the pattern. She started to sell the idea of how great the new era of the department would be, how Sam would benefit, and how employee morale would increase. The more animated she was, the quieter and more sullen Sam became. He started to slouch back in his chair with his feet straight out in front of him. The more she talked and gestured, the more horizontal he became in his chair.

I interrupted at that moment (my action was between a midstream suggestion and a directive, stop-action intervention). I had enough history and trust with Miriam that I was able to say simply, "Miriam! Try something besides selling." It was as though she woke from a trance (which is what a stuck pattern becomes). She stopped, and a moment of recognition flashed across her face. Then she laughed and muttered something to herself about losing it. Then she folded her hands and said, "So Sam—this is where I am going, with Jim's support, in the division. I expect you to be a proactive manager rather than a crisis manager. What are your ideas on how to head your department in this new direction?"

Sam was silent at first, then gave a one-sentence answer: "I could talk to my supervisors and get their ideas." He stopped, still comfortably slouched in his chair. In the past, a one-sentence, half-hearted reply would be enough to spur Miriam back into a protracted sales pitch, and Sam could relax through another one of Miriam's monologues. This time Miriam asked, "And what good will that do?" Sam was silent again. Miriam was silent. Could she outlast Sam's silence?

After some time passed, which seemed excruciatingly long to Miriam, Sam sat up in his chair and haltingly began listing some initiatives he and his supervisors could take. Miriam asked, "What are you willing to commit to now?" Sam paused and then gave two priorities for action. "Fine," said Miriam. "It's a start. This is the kind of thinking I like hearing from you."

Although this result was less than stellar, it began to break up the old dance and build something new on which Miriam and Sam could create a new pattern of interaction.

Miriam spent the rest of the session both trying on a new pattern (making short statements or asking questions followed by a pause to elicit Sam's initiative) and falling back into the old selling pattern. When she fell into the old pattern, I reminded her to either just pause or to get Sam to paraphrase what she had just said. It was useful to her to become aware of the different ways she experienced herself in these two patterns. She felt clumsy, but she could see how Sam interacted differently with her when they were not dancing in the old pattern. She often had difficulty finding words to fit the new pattern, but when she did, she could see the difference in the conversation.

The coach has to stay within the contract that is established between the coach and the client. What I did not do during the awkward silences was turn to Sam and interact with him, for example, "Sam, are you buying this?" or "What do you think?" or "Could you paraphrase what Miriam is telling you?" These statements are more along the lines of stage 3 live-action coaching of all parties involved, which I was not contracted for in this situation. It is the difference between asking Miriam if she thought Sam got what she said rather than asking Sam to paraphrase Miriam. The more she can stop what is not working, the more she can eventually manage herself in this relationship without the presence of her coach.

Maintain Alignment in the System

Because it is so elemental, pattern breaking can be a powerful intervention that a client can use to shift a situation. For increased effectiveness, however, the coach needs to keep an eye on the process of organizational alignment before and during live-action coaching. It made no sense to address the pattern between Miriam and Sam before Miriam worked out with her boss that he would support the direction in which she wanted to proceed with Sam. Once that was in place, helping Miriam use her authority to align her direct reports to the business goals was the right issue to address. Miriam's pattern with Sam then became the right one to focus on in live-action sessions between them. Miriam was, after all, the sponsor of her division and needed all of the departments within her division, including Sam's department, to be run proactively, not in a crisis mode. Such a change would boost productivity and employee morale. She needed to communicate to Sam her expectations of him as a department manager, as well as laying out time frames and other parameters.

Therefore, what you as a coach need to look for is an opportunity to **help your client change a pattern that can also support the best use of her authority to align the organization to attain its business goals.** This is why so much time is spent up front on establishing the bottom-line, leader interpersonal behaviors, and team interaction goals. **When the client stays focused on the Three Key Factors goals, the interactional pattern that needs to be changed becomes clearer. Otherwise there is no compass to discern whether a particular pattern is on or off the mark.**

> *When the client stays focused on the Three Key Factors goals, the interactional pattern that needs to be changed becomes clearer. Otherwise there is no compass to discern whether a particular pattern is on or off the mark.*

Supporting alignment in the system also honors the hierarchy as it already exists in an organization. No matter how badly the client stumbles during the session, it is critical that you do not take over her job as the manager by speaking for her, establishing your own priorities for the employee, or deciding on the ensuing steps between the two of them. Maintaining alignment means staying out of the boss-employee relationship while coaching the client to attend to that relationship, and helping her see how she can try a new way of interacting with her staff.

In some ways, Miriam's selling pattern is a substitute for old-fashioned performance management. She undercuts her own goals through selling, which telegraphs to Sam, "You can either buy or not buy what I want you to accomplish. It's up to you." I helped Miriam manage the dilemma of how to take a firm stand (backbone) while maintaining a strong connection (heart) with those who work for her. **Coaching along this backbone and heart intersection is what a live-action coaching session is all about.** Actions you take can be in the form of directives, questions, suggestions, and debriefing on the spot, all to support the client in creating new patterns and better alignment to achieve her goals.

I have found this combination of stage 3, live-action client leader *and* team coaching, with stage 4, live-action client leader coaching, to accelerate the leader's learning while developing the leadership of all the team members. This is a three-for-one deal for organizations: the leader client is developed, the business results are accomplished, and the team members (often leaders of their own teams) are developed too. That is a return on investment of executive coaching about which everyone can be happy (see Chapter Nine for more on the return on investment of executive coaching).

Chapter Seven Highlights

Assess Your Skill Regarding the Developmental Sequence of Coaching Contexts

Stage 1: Behind-the-scenes coaching of the client.

Stage 2: Observation of the client in a business meeting with her direct reports and in one-on-one meetings with staff members.

Stage 3: Live-action coaching of the client *and* his direct reports in a business meeting. Also at this stage, live-action coaching of the client *and* his direct reports in one-on-one meetings with staff members.

Stage 4: Live-action coaching of just the client when the client is in a business meeting with her team or in one-to-on meetings with staff members.

Determine Whether You Have a Live-Action Coaching Role
1. Weigh the two criteria of live-action coaching for each client.
   - The level of trust built between the coach and the client
   - The degree to which the client fails to see and self-correct her pattern
2. Clearly define the role of the coach in live-action.
3. Define the range of available intervention options.
4. Assist the client in preparing a sponsorship statement for your role in the live-action session.

Define the Live-Action Coaching Role
1. Clearly define the role of the coach beforehand.
2. Help the client choose what kind of interventions the coach can make.

Prepare Your Client to Sponsor the Live-Action Coaching Role
1. Help the client prepare a definition of your role that she will explain to others in the live-action session.
2. Encourage the client to distinguish the live-action role from other roles her staff members may have observed, for example, people who play facilitator roles.

Live-Action Coaching Tasks
1. Ensure proper sponsorship and structuring of the session.
   - The client defines and sponsors your role.
   - Establish your independence from the client's content agenda.

2. Focus on the client's goals.

- Stay active, *and* stay out of the way.
- Keep the client's goals foremost when guiding your interventions.

3. Foster pattern breaking.

- Look for opportunities to change patterns.
- Stay within the contract you established about how actively you will intervene.

4. Maintain alignment in the system.

- Help your client change the pattern that is most related to getting alignment into his organization.
- Honor your client's authority in the system.

8

PHASE 4–DEBRIEFING

Define a Learning Focus

Executives usually spend their work lives racing from activity to activity. They long to have time for reflection but rarely take it due to the demands of the job. Consequently executive coaches need to insist early on that the sequence of coaching activities include time for evaluation.

For best results, the coach should build debriefing time right into the coaching contract. Agree on times that the two of you will sit down and debrief the client's experience. Particularly following a live-action coaching event, it can be challenging to get the time with the client to debrief. She is already charging off to her next commitment. To make it easier for her and me, I explain up front that the debriefing event is a seamless part of the time commitment to live-action coaching. For example, a client's team coaching time commitment is not over when the team leaves the room. The client and I have already scheduled a session immediately afterward that lasts between twenty and sixty minutes. We evaluate her effectiveness during that session and make plans for any next steps. The method outlined here shows how to use debriefing time effectively.

This chapter covers the following debriefing tasks:

1. Evaluation of the client's effectiveness:
   - Assess the client's strengths and challenges.
   - Review the client's skill in management competencies.
   - Customize your debriefing to each client.

- Debrief tough clients.
- Debrief at the end of a coaching engagement.

2. Evaluation of the coach's effectiveness, including building a mutual feedback loop into the coaching relationship

A thorough evaluation of the client's effectiveness provides him with a kind of biofeedback mechanism. He can compare his own experience to the feedback he gets from his coach. During the debriefing phase, the client can be open to learning and thus improve how he manages.

Sometimes you may encounter a client who resists developing his leadership ability. In the debriefing stage, you need to plot a course for working with the client or in some cases, determine whether to continue to work with him at all. A section in the chapter addresses this challenge.

The last phase of debriefing, evaluating the coach's effectiveness, builds mutuality into the coaching contract. It is an opportunity to get feedback from your client and share your own assessment of your coaching in a way that serves as a model of self-assessment for the client.

Evaluate the Client's Effectiveness

The process of debriefing is fairly straightforward. **You start by asking your client to self-assess her effectiveness before you give her your feedback.** If you give your feedback first, she is more likely either to swallow it whole or become defensive without thinking through her own evaluation of herself.

Assess the Client's Strengths and Challenges

Usually clients focus on what they did wrong and what needs improvement. You can insist that they speak to both areas: to what they did well, **identifying their strengths, and to the challenges they experienced in their performance.** Keep your client's business goal front and center. Ask her if she achieved her business goal and to what extent, and ask her to reflect on what, if anything, was missing. One resource that provides useful questions for generating greater awareness in clients is Whitmore (1996). Whitmore helps clients see their actual behaviors in a more objective light, thus encouraging them to self-correct.

After the client gives her self-assessment, you can follow with your own feedback. To what extent do you believe she attained her goal? What are the challenges she continues to face? How effective was her leadership, and what blind spots might she be missing? The debriefing session most often falls into four categories:

- Celebrate achievements.
- Identify recurring patterns that were either successfully broken or that remain ingrained.
- Assess the alignment of roles.
- Develop a plan for the client's next step.

Celebrate Achievements. It is important to emphasize the client's successes. Clients spend very little time concentrating on their strengths and instead tend to look at the gaps. While that can be a strength in itself, they need to remain mindful of the assets that help them succeed. For example, when I debriefed with Miriam, she noted these positive aspects: there were two ways she clearly defined her expectations of Sam, and she also induced Sam to commit to two specific action steps.

Debriefing the successes with a client also cements that successful behavior into her repertoire, and she is more likely to apply those skills when the situation calls for it the next time. Her brain is literally building a new neural pathway that recognizes the opportunities to replicate the sequence that worked before (not unlike the building of neural highways in the toddler's brain). The more the client succeeds and enjoys the emerging competence t comes from this new set of behaviors, the more these behavior become habitual and increase the client's effectiveness. Debriefing captures the moment of success and the taste of satisfaction that the client experiences and helps her transfer that moment into long-term memory. Your job as a coach is to ensure that these transferring and reinforcing opportunities happen so that the client benefits from the full arc of her learning.

> *Your job as a coach is to ensure that these transferring and reinforcing opportunities happen so that the client benefits from the full arc of her learning.*

Identify a Key Pattern. Pattern recognition develops the client's ability to take a more objective look at himself in order to see the big picture and how he fits into it. Again, this activity is business focused. Rather than identifying all patterns that were played out in the situation, **you encourage the client to identify the one pattern that most affected his results.** He may notice it right away and recognize where he repeated the same old pattern. Or he may not see it at all and resist your description of it. The more he invests energy in ignoring his reactive patterns, the longer he will remain in them. A little "there I go again" view of his own defensiveness can help him move beyond it. Your ability to specifically describe his behavior and its subsequent consequences can help him to view himself more objectively.

It helps if the client can develop a healthy dose of humor about his foibles. You can convey that all is not lost because he tripped and fell into the same hole. Your debriefing conversation can con-
 these questions: How can he put a neon sign around this pat-
 notices it earlier the next time? How can he detect his
 lues more quickly? This develops a more neutral
 ally ingrained positions.
 rsation, Miriam was able to see, feel,
 nce in herself and in Sam's actions when
 ual pattern with him. She was able to stop

midstream, notice an opportunity to do something different, and self-correct. This is a powerful skill for a leader to acquire.

Assess the Alignment of Roles. During the planning phase, you spent a lot of time talking to your client about how her plan can support the best alignment of roles in her work world. During the debriefing phase, you return to this important topic and **help the client assess how effective she was in aligning her role and her colleagues' roles relative to their specific issues.** Here are some questions you can ask your client when you debrief alignment issues: Did she follow the mandate in her role as a sponsor, implementer, advocate, or agent? Did she ensure that the other party, whether it was the team or boss or a subordinate, successfully worked within his own role in the conversation? What loose ends, if any, such as authority, decision making, the goal itself, and participation, still need to be clarified? In a debriefing session, Miriam realized the importance of her sponsor's agreement and alignment regarding switching Sam from firefighting to prevention. Thus, she was able to enjoy a much more successful session with Sam.

Develop a Plan for the Next Step. Now is the time to identify a learning focus. Sometimes increasing awareness of her challenges can cause the client to get bogged down and feel immobilized. **Planning for the next action step prioritizes and breaks down these global challenges into manageable steps, all the while keeping coach and client focused on the goal.** For example, after her session with Sam, Miriam and I talked about her next step, which was to set a date to follow up with Sam around his action plan.

Review the Client's Skill in Management Competencies

During debriefing sessions, you may discover the client's stren and weaknesses in a number of typical management arena might find that he concentrates on only a few and neglects the rest. For example, he may excel in the areas that require global thinking but fall short in facilitating discussions that uncover important information.

The following list of management competencies can help you scan for the areas in which the client needs to become more effective in order to produce organizational results. Look over these skills, and assess your client's ability and confidence to perform these leader activities. You can **examine the list with the client and set a developmental agenda as you continue to coach him.**

Management Competencies

Strategic thinking

- Understands the whole picture. Sees complex functions from the perspective of the whole.
- Can weigh external and internal variables that affect the organization's productivity and results.
- Comprehends business issues, how an organization works, and can develop ideas to maximize the organization's effectiveness.

Vision

- Develops a clear vision for the organization and self.
- Identifies specific and measurable goals (which are challenging) to achieve the vision, and effectively communicates the vision and goals.
- Engages constituents in conversations to further the vision, gain greater clarity, and increase collective commitment.
- Perceives the customer, vendor, internal customer (employee), and larger community (civic context) relationships as mutually reinforcing.

	• Works to streamline processes to aid these relationships.
Cultivating external relations	• Promotes a significant presence in the larger community of shareholders, customers, vendors, civic leaders, and others to increase partnership and influence in these areas.
	• External to one's division, influences all cross-functional groups to coordinate their efforts for maximum productivity.
Meeting facilitation	• Develops an agenda and prioritizes items for the optimal use of time.
	• Facilitates discussion to gain maximum participation.
	• Helps group members identify key needs, ideas, and plans for action.
	• Uses a variety of group process methods to achieve effective engagement, leading to synergistic results and productive outcomes.
Promoting conversations	• Clarifies the parameters of discussions to maximize their effectiveness.
	• Helps all constituents to be heard and to speak to each other directly.
	• Seeks to unearth new information and break habitual thinking.
	• Addresses underlying issues. Talks about the tough issues.
	• Takes a learning stance in conversations, that is, can expand one's position based on others' input.
Decision making	• Takes responsibility for clarity around who makes decisions.
	• Uses several decision styles effectively; for example, consultation, delegation, majority vote.
	• Can firmly say yes or no and remain connected with constituents.

Gaining commitment	• Articulates behavioral expectations as specifically as possible.
	• Ensures that the employee understands expectations.
	• Discerns the differences in employee resistance, everything from the legitimate raising of obstacles to an unproductive pattern between the leader and the employee. Deals with the resistance effectively.
	• Ensures commitment to the expectations.
	• Encourages employee initiatives toward the goals and expectations.
Sponsoring project teams	• Gives direction effectively. Specifically, identifies key roles, responsibilities, and time frames of projects. Allocates the people to provide expertise and support for the projects and identifies decision makers. Clarifies the single point agent for each project. Sponsors the kickoff.
	• Ensures monitoring processes are in place and works to strengthen cross-functional sponsorship.
	• Uses staff in change agent roles.
	• Directs staff agents to high-priority business issues.
	• Ensures sustaining sponsors are using their agents well.
	• Insists that agents remain in agent role without overstepping bounds.
Team coherence	• Looks for signs of group cohesiveness or breakdown.
	• Takes action to build group identity, values, and synergistic work relationships.
	• Promotes the team's presence and contributions to the larger organization.

	• Ensures the team has the necessary resources to fulfill their mandates. Helps the team keep a whole-system view of their work.
Performance management	• Sets clear expectations and standards of performance for others. • Gains commitment to those expectations. • Gives behaviorally specific feedback. • Actively holds people accountable to those standards: asks for updates, solves problems with participants, and links consequences (praise or discipline) to people's performance in a direct way.
Coaching	• Coaches only after performance expectations are clear and committed to. • Promotes leadership and initiative in people in all organizational roles. • Gives specific feedback of others' strengths and challenges, thus building competence and commitment in others. • Is able to train others in discrete tasks and skills relevant to their performance, or delegates training resources for their development.
Systems functioning	• Expands awareness of the presenting issues to include (1) the effectiveness of the organization's infrastructure, (2) the systems patterns at play, (3) the emotional tugs and pulls lying underneath organizational issues, and (4) the larger communities that support the organization. • Includes oneself as an important player in co-creating the patterns at work in the system.

	• Works to increase the resilience of leaders and subordinates within the system.
Advocacy	• Effectively advocates for ideas and for one's role in the organization in order to achieve the goals.
	• Communicates understanding and commitment to the larger goals when advocating.

This management competencies list is by no means comprehensive. Its purpose is to stimulate your thinking regarding your client's breadth of competence. There may be whole arenas that he and you overlook because of the intense scrutiny you are giving other areas. I advocate that you take an occasional pause to scan for other ways your client can develop to become a more comprehensive leader of his organization. You can also spend time with him and his boss looking at the areas that your client needs to ascend to the next layer of management.

For other resources, another way to sort leadership competencies is to use the framework of Lencioni (2002, 2005), which requires both backbone and heart skills from the executive while he is creating a strong "first team" of direct reports. Kouzes and Posner (2002, 2003) identify five practices and ten commitments of exemplary leadership that you can use with your client to assess his strength and challenge areas.

Customize the Debriefing of Each Client

As you and the client assess her skill and confidence levels in the management competencies, you will profit from using a situational leadership approach. Blanchard, Zigarmi, and Zigarmi (1985) present variables (competence and/or confidence; required direction and/or support) applicable to clients' capacities and motivations around management competencies. (For a fuller explanation of this approach, see Chapter Eleven.) Blanchard developed this approach for managers working with direct reports, but I find his methods useful for coaching clients as well.

Your clients face the same fluctuating set of variables as their employees regarding skills or motivation in leading and managing tasks. **Your clients have unique developmental needs that require customized attention.** Depending on the level of attainment and commitment that clients have for the preceding leadership competencies, you can become more or less directive and supportive regarding their next steps. One example is the client from the previous chapter, Len, who needed a lot of direction but not much moral support from me regarding his ability to facilitate his team meetings. He had no idea what he could do to improve and wanted all the direction I could offer in the coaching session and during the debriefing times. He needed very little coaching support in terms of motivation because he was so committed to improving his facilitation leadership.

Len had this profile in three management areas:

- Facilitating team meetings: low competence with high motivation
- Creating budgets: high competence and high motivation
- Managing performance: low competence and fluctuating motivation

As Len's coach, I needed to approach my work with him very differently for each of these management tasks. My coaching style had to shift as his ability and motivation shifted with each management task:

- I gave him high direction with little support in conversations regarding leading his team meetings.
- I spent very little time directing or supporting regarding creating budgets other than ensuring that he understood the parameters he had to work within for his budget.

- I offered both high direction and high support on the topic of managing employee performance.

You cannot expect to use the habitual style of coaching that falls within your own comfort zone with every client you work with or even consistently with any one client. Leaders are as individualistic and quirky in their development needs as their employees are. **You have to match your coaching style of direction and support to your clients' needs at the time.**

> *You have to match your coaching style of direction and support to your clients' needs at the time.*

Debrief Tough Clients

The majority of clients progress well on the path to greater skill development during coaching in both their work relationships and their pursuit of business goals. There are occasions, however, when a client does not put her plans into action. When this happens, it is typically discovered in the debriefing phase unless you discover it during live-action coaching. When the coach and client reconvene, the coach realizes that the client is not following through and has resistance to implementing her action plan.

It is important to probe the client's lack of action to discover whether you have a tough client or whether the real issue is that she lacks confidence or feels threatened by change. Many times seemingly tough clients are really clients who are fearful, skeptical, awkward, or anxious or possess any number of attitudes that may accompany the learning process. Only if these issues have been surfaced, worked on, and therefore ruled out should you determine whether you have a tough client.

Another definition of *tough* might describe clients who are cantankerous, argumentative, or dominating, but these traits can be dealt with as long as the client is working along the learning curve and knows that she is the key to necessary changes. It is important not to confuse the personal style of a client with her deeper intentions and aspirations for learning about herself.

I define a tough client as someone who does not learn from her experiences. For any number of reasons, she does not take input well, cannot actively listen to alternatives, never takes action on action plans, or does not take ownership for her part in work dilemmas.

The truly tough clients say they want change but do not make it happen. They never get around to it or never get beyond resistance to taking action in the first place. A case in point is Rich, the CEO in Chapter Six, who never took action but just liked to talk about his situation.

The really difficult cases are the clients who say they are committed to changes they need to make in their management, but their automatic knee-jerk responses to stressful situations prevent them from forging a new, more effective pattern. They stay in their reactive mode all the time and remain defensive about their reactions. Then the coaching sessions cease to be productive.

Okay, you may be thinking. *You've named my coaching nightmare. But what do I do if I discover my client isn't committed? What if I have a client who persistently does not follow through on her plan and is not in a learning mode?* The first thing you must do is realize that you are living your worst nightmare. Sometimes when you get reactive to this kind of client, you can get into a loop of either placating or blaming her. To realize you are entering an unproductive pattern with your client is the first step out of a dance that is not working. This was the realization I made when I worked with Chris.

Chris

Chris was a can-do kind of person: smart, decisive, opinionated, and impulsive. As executive vice president in a service industry company, he juggled a lot of stores, executives, and headaches. He needed a turnaround in one of his underperforming stores and was quite critical of Jason, the general manager who ran it. When I asked him what Jason was doing that slowed the store's progress, Chris gave me a blank stare. After some thought, he said, "I suppose I've been too tolerant." That led to a conversation of what he needed to do differently, including being clearer about his expectations and staying connected and tuned into his relationship to Jason. We outlined a process that Chris could use to engage with Jason and Jason's executive team to increase productivity.

It became clear in the process that the relationship between Chris and Jason was cool and distant. Jason and his team had no consistent understanding of Chris's expectations of them. A month went by, and Chris continued to avoid Jason. Apparently this behavior was typical of Chris. When he became disappointed with someone, he distanced himself from that person. We continued to meet and talk about his plan to address Jason and his reticence to do so. Another month went by, and nothing had changed between Jason and Chris. But Chris's complaints about Jason were just as strong and critical.

Before my next meeting with Chris, I found myself making all kinds of judgments about him. I was irritated that he hadn't followed through. How did he expect things to change? My anxiety was unusually high because it seemed that this was an entrenched pattern, and things were not likely to change. So what leverage did I have? Chris was impulsive too. If I confronted him with this, he might write me off as well. "Oh great," I thought. "And I've got a meeting with him tomorrow morning."

Then the light bulb went on. "Wait a minute. I'm getting sucked into the system," I thought. I was on the brink of distancing myself from Chris just as he distanced himself from others. And my anxiety was keeping me from more calmly sifting through the information I had in order to provide constructive feedback to him.

Although such a realization can be deflating, it is actually the beginning point to taking more decisive action. That is the beauty of systemic realizations: when you know a system's pattern has caught you, that change in perspective can lead to a way out.

One way out is to ask yourself, "What would I do if I weren't triggered by all this and my client was one of my most motivated clients?" In other words, if you were at your best and this client was ascending the learning curve, what would you be doing? These questions help to clear your thinking from your knee-jerk, fight-or-flight reactions. A challenging situation like this needs you at your best because your client is responding automatically and is currently unable to create a new outcome.

This is not Pollyanna thinking. It is challenging yourself to meet the demands of being an executive coach, which in this moment requires giving straightforward feedback to this client rather than blaming or avoiding him.

What has often been helpful to me in these situations is to think of the central pattern at play and call it to the client's attention. I then present my position relative to that theme. In other words, I give the client my best thinking on what is happening and what is required in this situation.

In the case of someone like Chris, I avoid distancing myself from him, even as we are going through some rough water. I continue to partner with him by offering him creative approaches to the issue. I also need to identify my bottom line and ask myself what I am willing or not willing to do with this client, including perhaps terminating the contract if he does not show enough movement toward change. Ending the contract should not be regarded as a punishment or an emotional cutoff. It is a regretful but respectful termination rather than a harsh one. It comes from a realization that we cannot do any further fruitful work without a significant change in the client's behavior.

In summary, when dealing with a tough client who is not ready to change, a coach should:

- Identify the central pattern and share it with your client.
- Give the client your best thinking on the situation.
- Identify and communicate your personal bottom line regarding involvement with the client.

Here is how these tasks played out with Chris:

Chris, continued

In my next meeting with Chris, I asked him for an update—whether he had anything different or more to report. He had no additions and was not forthcoming in committing to do anything differently. He seemed to be waiting for me to come up with interesting thoughts about Jason's deficiencies and discuss what Jason would have to do to change.

"Chris," I said, "you are continuing to keep a safe distance from Jason [name the pattern]. And you are setting him up to fail. It's like you're at a gunslingers' standoff. You're facing him from a careful distance, and neither of you is making a move. What usually happens in these situations [give best thinking] is that it continues until one of you can't stand it any longer, and then you blow each other's head off. No communication, then blasto! Obviously that doesn't lead to increased productivity. One or both of you will be casualties for not engaging with each other. Ultimately Jason's productivity is affecting your productivity. Do you really want to go down with him over this? Unless you decide to take action, I don't see a reason for us to keep working together. If you are not going to work on changing your work relationship with Jason, I can no longer be useful to you" [personal bottom line].

> Chris hadn't considered his own vulnerability in the situation. That perspective actually motivated him to address the issue with Jason. His new awareness of his self-interest raised his energy to push against his own resistance to change.

This tough client turned around enough to enter a learning mode and change his behavior, but the story does not always end this way. Even when you do what I suggest with tough clients, some clients do not take the action they need to take. Then you need to activate your bottom line and respectfully end the contract.

Evaluate the Coach's Effectiveness

At some point in the client-coach relationship, you should solicit feedback from your client regarding your effectiveness as a coach. A natural time for that to happen is during the debriefing phase. This builds **a feedback loop in the working relationship** and ensures that you are serving the client well. A side benefit is that you serve as a powerful model of someone who initiates and receives feedback. You can show that someone can maintain a professional presence while in learning mode.

When you receive feedback on your effectiveness, **it is important for the client to give feedback to you first.** This ensures that she gives you her unedited list, and you see what it is that she pays attention to in your sessions. You have the opportunity to ask questions to clarify what she says about your work with her. You can show what a nondefensive stance looks like when someone receives feedback.

Listening to your client's assessment of your sessions places you on the receiving end of the client's feedback, an experience you now share with others in the client's workplace. You learn how skilled your client is at giving feedback. You can then give her feedback on her feedback. Kind of clever, no? Actually, clients *could* use help giving better feedback. Generally clients need to be more specific in their feedback and more balanced both in noting strengths and giving suggestions.

Next, you evaluate your own performance and thus tutor your client on the fine art of self-assessment.

The degree of your candor with your client about your strengths and weaknesses depends on the strength of your working relationship. Not surprisingly, with new clients, it is important to establish credibility about your effectiveness before launching into a litany of your weaknesses. Clients turn skittish if you self-assess too thoroughly before they know you well. The session is, after all, supposed to be about them, not you.

What is essential is your tone in evaluating your work with your client. You must be an equal partner with your client. When you mention anything that you did not do well, it is important that you stay on that equal footing and not demote yourself with self-flagellation, guilt, or diminishing your position with your client. **When you can maintain your emotional equality, you are doing your client a great favor. She can see what it looks like to take responsibility for imperfections while maintaining confidence in her ability to move on and improve, all without getting defensive or placating.** Clients need to develop the ability to self-assess with this same emotional tone. Often they have never seen how it is done. If more leaders had this ability, organizations would be less politically charged places.

> *Clients need to develop the ability to self-assess with this same emotional tone. Often they have never seen how it is done.*

During your self-assessment of your own coaching, you **identify your strengths and weaknesses** in this particular coaching partnership. This includes **reviewing the ways you may have become stuck in patterns that were not useful to the client.** You could have fallen into the same dance patterns of the system or contributed to an ineffective pattern between the client and yourself. Some examples of a self-assessment review may include the following:

Strengths

"I helped you get crisper in articulating your goals."

"I stayed on top of your dominant pattern with you and your team and thus helped you catch yourself in two critical moments."

Weaknesses

"I backed off from pushing you on the issue of measures, which left you vulnerable in the meeting with your boss."

"I underestimated the degree of challenge you experienced in managing yourself with Steve during the meeting. We could have created a specific strategy for that."

Besides serving as a good model, your self-assessment also helps the client sift through and prioritize what she may want to further improve. For example, after listening to your self-report about how you did or did not help her manage herself, she may decide to put more effort into managing herself the next time she faces her coworker.

The last part of debriefing therefore is **recontracting**. Since this is a continuing relationship, it is useful to recycle through the four phases. This can mean shifting the contract to fit the client's new or continuing goals rather than assuming that what she needs now is the same as before. It is the time to **revisit the measures for the goals of the initial contract, see to what extent the outcomes have been attained, and course-correct if necessary.**

Debrief at the End of a Coaching Engagement

Debriefing with the coach can help the client build a capacity to continue these planning and debriefing phases on her own once the contract is completed. When you approach the end of your coaching work with the client, it is time to enter into a more formal debriefing session. Essentially you accomplish two items: **(1) give and receive feedback regarding the whole arc of the coaching contract, and (2) calculate the return on investment (ROI) on the coaching work** (see Chapter Nine). In terms of a final feedback session, **you can use the same debriefing framework outlined in this chapter: self-assessment by the client and then feedback to you as the coach.**

The client sees with new appreciation where he has grown, and you see the impact of your work. Giving your client a summary of his growth, with a litany of specific ways he has developed new strengths, can be very satisfying. I ask the client to give this summary first. The more he can see for himself, the better. Then **your summary becomes, at best, an expansion on his self-assessment.** For a detailed agenda for this kind of meeting, see Pomerantz (2007). Pomerantz outlines a "lessons-learned meeting" that not only covers this kind of feedback but incorporates a natural way to encourage the client to help market your services to others.

A concluding debriefing process with your client should also include the calculation of the ROI for the organization for the coaching contract. Chapter Nine outlines such a process. When the client tells you what impact you have had on his leadership development, it becomes part of the inquiry into the ROI. As you will see in Chapter Nine, all the specifics you worked on during the initial contracting phase, the Three Key Factors and identifying the internal and external variables that influence the outcomes, now help you to determine the ROI of your work with the client.

Chapter Eight Highlights

Evaluate the Client's Effectiveness

1. Encourage the client to self-assess first.

2. Discuss the client's strengths and challenges.

3. Identify a key recurring pattern.

4. Assess the alignment of roles.

5. Plan the client's next step.

Review the Client's Skill in Management Competencies

1. Scan for management skills that the client needs to strengthen.

2. Build a development plan for the client that addresses these areas.

Customize Your Debriefing of Each Client

1. Recognize the unique development needs of the executive you coach.

2. Match your coaching style to the client's level of competence and motivation.

Debrief Tough Clients

1. Identify the central pattern at play, and share it with your client.

2. Give the client your best thinking on the situation.

3. Communicate your personal bottom line regarding involvement with the client.

Evaluate Coach Effectiveness

1. Ask for feedback from the client first, and follow with your own self-assessment.

2. Identify your strengths and challenges when you coached the client.

3. Identify patterns you participated in.

4. Recontract for further coaching.

Debrief at the End of a Coaching Engagement

1. Give and receive feedback regarding the whole arc of the coaching contract.

2. Calculate the return on investment of the coaching work.

9

AN ROI METHOD FOR EXECUTIVE COACHING

Have the Client Convince the Coach of the Return on Investment

Although executive coaching is a well-established practice in the corporate environment, its benefits are more obvious to clients than to the accounting department.[1] This chapter presents practitioners with a method for demonstrating a quantifiable return on investment (ROI) for their work with clients and addresses the needs of executive coaches working in the field rather than those of researchers and academics regarding research methodology.

The main focus of this chapter is a how-to method for an executive coach or consultant. It not only addresses the issue of ROI but also directly involves the client in evaluating the bottom-line benefits of coaching. An experienced practitioner who understands how organizations work can successfully implement this ROI strategy.

> *An experienced practitioner who understands how organizations work can successfully implement this ROI strategy.*

I use *ROI* here as it is colloquially applied in our culture, generally to refer to the financial gains that business executives want to see compared to the costs they pay. There is an ongoing conversation

© 2005, Mary Beth O'Neill. Chapter Nine is excerpted and revised from an article by the same name that first appeared in the *International Journal of Coaching in Organizations*, 2005, 3, 39–52.

in the training, organizational development, and executive coaching fields about what formula is more useful for clients: ROI percentages or benefit-cost ratios. Each of these terms has a specific meaning and formula. I prefer the benefit-cost ratio because I think it is more accessible to coaches and clients, particularly those who are just beginning to apply fiscal thinking to coaching interventions.[2] However, when referring to the general discussion of measuring coaching's effects on bottom-line results, I use the term *ROI* because that is the language most frequently used in conversations and the media.

The Dilemmas

Most practitioners I talk to are stymied by three dilemmas in identifying the ROI of their work. **The first dilemma** goes like this: "I work on the soft side of business: the development of people skills in a client. How could I ever define and measure that? Besides, I'm completely intimidated by research and statistics. It's not my thing."

The second dilemma for those who have some confidence in their quantitative skills is uncertainty about how to link a client's development to measurable business results: "I can measure the shifts in a leader's attitudes and the team's perspective on the leader's effectiveness, but how do I link those to the bottom line?" Some practitioners may say, "I've even been able to measure shifts in organizational goals among those I have coached, such as retention and promotions, but I don't know what elements of the coaching and consulting effort, if any, created the change."

The third dilemma comes from a values conflict best expressed as, "If I take on the responsibility of measurement, then I'm doing the client's job for them. I've stepped over the line. I've become responsible for bottom-line results rather than for methods that lead to executive development. Anything I do that weakens the client's sense of responsibility for results erodes my effectiveness."

If you have experienced any of these dilemmas yourself, take heart. There is a way to determine what effect the client's changed behaviors have on bottom-line results. Over the past ten years,

I developed a coaching strategy, beginning with the contracting phase, that not only links client development to the bottom-line results but also allows the client to retain full responsibility for her business results, linking her developmental challenges and improvements to those results.

The Three Key Factors Methodology

You are already familiar with the first step in setting up executive coaching efforts to calculate ROI: identifying a client's Three Key Factors (see Chapter Five). Besides giving the client targeted goals to work toward, the Three Key Factors have two other advantages: (1) they identify the bottom-line results and the leader and team variables that could most affect those results, and (2) all Three Key Factors lists are measurable.

The business results are measured in time, money, quantity, or quality metrics. The leader interpersonal behaviors and the team interactions are specific and observable actions that are verifiable in quantity (Did it happen? How often did it happen?) and quality (How well did it happen? To what extent did the behavior include all the components necessary?). This is another critical reason to drive to observable behavior rather than using global terms when your client first creates the lists.

For example, "Be more decisive" will never be measurable with any satisfaction. But "Identify when a decision is going to be made," "Declare which decision-making style I am using," and "Summarize at the end of each meeting what decisions were made" give you and your client measuring sticks for decisiveness that can be tracked.

During your early work with your client in defining the Three Key Factors, you can tell her that you and she will return to those lists at the end of the contract to calculate ROI. It is another reason to be thorough in setting up the Three Key Factors on the front end. In addition, it gives you and your client a checklist or biofeedback mechanism to use during your coaching engagement to check progress toward each of the Three Key Factors.

Assessing Other Variables

In order to identify a return on investment for the coaching engagement with the client, **it is essential to explore with your client the other variables besides coaching that will affect the likelihood of success of all Three Key Factors.** I do it early, right after identifying the Three Key Factors with the client. This will be important when a formula that isolates the coaching variable is calculated at the end of the coaching contract.

I have learned to ask the client to create a list of four kinds of variables:

- **Variables internal to the organization that improve the chance for success,** including the current strengths and assets of the leadership team and the larger organization
- **Internal organization variables that detract from success**
- **Variables external to the organization that help lead to successful results**
- **External variables that may jeopardize success**

Executives need to be reminded to consider positive internal variables. They are used to assessing negative threats. They forget what they have in their favor.

There should be a list of many items for each variable. Remember Anne from Chapter Five and her Three Key Factors (for a quick review, see Figure 5.2)? Clients can usually identify three to ten items for each variable. Here is one example from each of Anne's four lists of variables:

- *Internal strength:* She had a team of skilled people who understood the business challenges they faced.
- *Internal challenge:* Executives higher in the organization made decisions that diminished the ability of Anne and her team to control outcomes.

- *External opportunity*: There was untapped revenue in the marketplace.
- *External challenge*: Other formerly reliable customers were cutting back business because of a dip in the economy.

Truth in Advertising: What It Takes to Get There

The focus of this chapter is on a benefit-cost ratio calculation. The rest of this book details the specific executive coaching implementation methodology that helps clients like Anne and her team achieve results in all Three Key Factors. However, here is a broad sketch of the work I did with Anne and her team that helped her to achieve the results she needed.

We worked with the Three Key Factors constantly throughout the coaching process. After setting them up in the beginning, they remained as a standing agenda item for nearly every meeting afterward.

With a colleague, I did live-action team coaching with Anne and her team members while they were all present and working on business issues at their meetings. We helped her sequence a series of concentrated efforts, from communicating the Three Key Factors to her team and getting feedback from team members on whether the factors were on target, to gaining commitment to them, to helping them communicate more directly with each other.

The executives with whom I work have team members who are leaders themselves. This offers the added benefit of teaching team members leadership skills that they can then apply to their own staffs. **We focused on three ongoing learning challenges: (1) the leadership behaviors and work relationship challenges that Anne found most daunting, (2) her ability to "learn live" with her team so team members were willing to take on more of their own learning challenges, and (3) a shift by Anne and her team to more effective co-created patterns of interacting with each other.**

Typically the leader interpersonal behaviors factor list is incomplete until coach and leader identify behaviors that are a stretch for the leader and thus often avoided. Executives are more willing to face their own leadership challenges when they see how necessary these behaviors are to achieving specific business results. Anne showed courage in several areas, including entering uncharted territory for her and her team, staying the course, and learning about herself with an open mind. Thus, the coaching engagement was satisfying for all involved: the leader, her team, and her coaches.

Midway through the process, we discussed progress on each factor and whether Anne and her team were likely to achieve them. At the end we had a formal conversation assessing results for each of the Three Key Factors.

The Benefit-Cost Ratio: Clarify the Connection

At the end of the contract with your client (or for ongoing projects at the ten- to twelve-month time frame), you can review the results for each of the Three Key Factors and begin to see the financial benefit from the coaching endeavor. **First, ask your client for specific measures he did or did not accomplish regarding the business results. Then return to the team behaviors list. To what extent did the team enact them? How does the leader know that? How often and where do they show up? Coaches can use this same line of inquiry for the leader behaviors.**

A question you can ask repeatedly during this discovery conversation is, **"What connection do these behaviors have with reaching your business results?" Your job is to be a collaborative skeptic.** You ask questions like a good anthropologist who may have an inkling but still asks the naive questions—for example, "How did improved decision making increase your market share?" If there truly is a connection, they can tell you, but you may have to continue to ask them to show you the connection from the leader or team behaviors factors to the results factor to identify the link. As a coach, you should keep pursuing the connections until your client has convinced you that there is a link. In the meantime, they have deepened their own confidence in the links among all Three Key Factors. Let's review Anne's situation to see what results she achieved (Figure 9.1).

> *You can ask, "What connection do these behaviors have with reaching your business results?" Your job is to be a collaborative skeptic.*

Anne's Results

Anne achieved $244.8 million revenue for the year, 3 percent over the budgeted goal and 10 percent better than revenues of the year before. This is very impressive, given that her peers in the region were 6 to 14 percent lower than their revenue targets in achieving the year's revenue goals. Also, the selling process that Anne's team designed was incorporated into the corporate planning department for the whole company.

Anne accomplished all her goals in her own leadership behaviors and those of her team. They had an impact on nearly every meeting they had. In fact, the leader and team factors show unanticipated improvements beyond her expectations (see the "plus" lists in Figure 9.1). In addition to meeting the stated goals for team behaviors, they redesigned the staff meeting to improve problem solving. The team continued to hold these meetings when Anne could not be there, and they asked for deadlines. Anne learned how to aid the team in resolving their issues by referring them back to each other when they avoided interaction by approaching Anne. Because of her team's improved effectiveness and her financial results, she received increased support from her boss.

As further evidence that Anne and her team exceeded their behavioral goals, the team received the regional Team of the Year

Figure 9.1 Anne's Results

Business Results

Goals: Achieve revenue goal.

Actual Results:
3% over revenue goal
(when other divisions missed their revenue targets by 6–14%)

(Selling process approved and used by corporate planning department.)

Team Interactions

- Give input outside your function; support each other's functions by giving ideas, time, and staff resources to other departments' problem-solving efforts.
- Identify differences, and engage in discussion until closure is reached.
- Paraphrase each other's points of view.
- Hold each other accountable. Initiate discussions on unmet expectations and agreements with each other before going to Anne.

Plus:
- Ask for deadlines.
- Redesigned staff meeting allows time to resolve issues. Can continue even in the absence of the leader.
- Team of the Year Award.

Leader Interpersonal Behaviors

- Declare and enforce clear expectations with due dates.
- Determine single point manager.
- Explicitly discuss with the team their clarity and commitment to organizational strategy.
- Identify decision-making style and facilitate closure on decision discussions, summarizing both progress toward a decision and when a decision is made.
- Encourage debate and problem solving by insisting on varying points of view.

Plus:
- Effectively work with triangles—redirect staff to talk directly to each other.
- Increased support from boss.
- Promotion to next level of management position.

Award, and Anne was promoted to another leadership position within the company. Her new division was rife with challenges, and she brought me in to begin work with the Three Key Factors and the live-action team coaching process with her new team. Using the Three Key Factors in a new area, Anne said, "My second time around is a different story in terms of owning the customization process to create the Three Key Factors methodology for this team, as I have personal experience with how it all works. With every coaching session, the Three Key Factors felt more real and actionable. Time and practice are absolute key ingredients for making the Three Key Factors come alive, spurring a leader and team into action."

Solidify the Connections Among the Three Key Factors

It was through my questions such as, "How do you know that you and your team's behaviors made a difference in the bottom line?" that many of the behaviors over and above the set goals came to light. Because Anne and the team focused so persistently on their behavioral factors, they created new synergies that allowed them to achieve their revenue results.

By remaining conscious of the decisions they were making and the specific commitments necessary within each phase of their work, Anne and her team were able to create efficiencies that affected their bottom line. Anne is convinced that without managing specific behavioral leader and team factors, she would not have achieved her results. She named specific decisions that executed the Three Key Factors well and directly led to her business results. Her ability to focus on these customized behaviors sowed the seeds for success. She knew what her team was like before the Three Key Factors focus. Now she had evidence in their daily interactions that underscored the success of incorporating the Three Key Factors into their work routines. It is also possible to use pre- and post-surveys of the leader and team behaviors which track their frequency before and after the contract.

The Benefit-Cost Ratio: Quantify the Impact

Once Anne identified the behavioral key factors and showed that they led to bottom-line improvement, it was necessary to assess how much the coaching contract affected her results. **What percentage of the change can be attributed to the executive coaching variable as opposed to the other variables that Anne named earlier?**

Often leaders are so pleased with their results that they enthusiastically exclaim, "One hundred percent! The coaching is 100 percent of what got us there!" This comment is reminiscent of happy participants immediately after a training class giving a high rating because they had a good experience. It is not necessarily tied to the training's effectiveness. Therefore, **it is our job to be skeptical about the "grade inflation" our clients give because they are satisfied with the coaching work.**

You must ask clients not only to connect one key factor to another, but also to assess to what extent the internal and external variables they had named earlier were important to their results. I see it as my duty not only to remind them of all the variables that could have affected their results but to paint them with bold strokes. I once told a client who claimed the coaching variable was 100 percent of the impact, "You can't give me 100 percent of the credit. Your leadership alone was a huge variable. You made it happen. What are you, chopped liver?"

Through deeper questioning, healthy skepticism, and light-hearted humor, I help clients knock down the percentage they give to coaching as they more seriously consider the host of variables at play. This adds to my credibility as a hard-nosed business partner. **I am not looking for an unearned compliment but rather a realistic picture of the business variables and the impact of the coaching variable.**[3]

Anne was able to weigh all the variables in her situation and acknowledge the competent team she started out with, the opportunities in the marketplace, and her own business market instincts. After some careful consideration, she assigned the coaching effort a 25 percent contribution to their success. She underscored that although the other variables weighed in at 75 percent, she and her team would not have managed them to success without coaching. They absolutely needed the 25 percent coaching variable to get them the rest of the way. As one client said, "We would have gone 60 percent of the way ourselves, some expert consultants helped us achieve another 20 percent, and you delivered 20 percent. But without that 20 percent, we wouldn't have made it. There was no in-between: we had to either reach the goal completely or fail. Given what we were dealing with, without the coaching, we would have completely failed." By now the client is confident that the percentage of the impact attributed to coaching is realistic. Based on my experience of clients' evaluations regarding the impact among all variables, the impact executive coaching has had on bottom-line results averages between 15 and 33 percent.

Now let's look at the numbers. The formula I use to calculate benefit-cost ratio that accounts for the coaching impact's effect on the outcome is:

$$\frac{\text{Business results} \times \% \text{ impact of executive coaching}}{\text{Cost of executive coaching}}$$

This is a generic formula that needs to be customized to your client, the client's system, and what the client values and measures when deciding if something is worth the investment. The business results metric that you and your client use has to have credibility in the client's system.

The most rigorous approach is to insert net contribution in the business results portion of the formula. *Net contribution* means taking the increased revenue they obtained and subtracting it by other customary costs associated with earning more revenue, such as increased labor cost or increased materials. Companies routinely calculate net contribution not just for the whole enterprise but also for separate divisions and departments. Your clients may already have net contribution calculated for the areas they oversee.

Many clients do not focus on net contribution when they are thinking about what they got out of the coaching effort. They are focused on the one economic indicator that they and their boss care most about for that year. It is not as comprehensive a calculation as net contribution. It could be, for example, revenue or market share or increased productivity. Because of a big push during a fiscal year to focus on one category over another, clients may even have incentive packages that are tied not to net contribution but to a specific economic indicator that the company is pushing their staff to achieve for that year.

Clients should be the ones to decide which economic results to put in the business results portion of the formula. The real test is whether the formula is useful and credible to your clients and if the formula they choose stands up to the internal scrutiny of their organizations.

For clients who are not in the top two levels of their organization, it may be wise to give them some "truth in advertising." Although they may care more about a specific indicator such as market share, the officers of the company may care more about net contribution. If you relay this bias of the top to your clients and your clients still choose a business result other than net contribution to calculate ROI, they are doing so after having been educated by you.

My client Anne tracked revenue. That is what she and her boss cared most about for the year that Anne did her work with me. Because of the enormous emphasis on increased revenue generation, it was by far the most compelling indicator for which Anne was accountable, and that priority was set by those who were two layers above her. Any increased rigor to focus on net contribution actually demotivated the client system. So revenue is the business result that we used.

Once the business result category is chosen, I calculate an intentionally conservative benefit-cost ratio to offset any doubts clients harbor regarding the lack of a strict one-to-one statistical correlation between the behavioral key factors and the business

results factor. Therefore, rather than using the coaching impact as 25 percent of total revenue ($244.8 million), we took just the portion of Anne's revenue that was the difference between her performance and the next best department's revenue, which was 6 percent of revenue target (again, taking the most conservative number, 6 percent, from the 6 to 14 percent missed targets of her peers' performance). This is even more conservative because you could say it was a 9 percent difference (Anne was 3 percent above target; her peer was 6 percent below target). Six percent of $244.8 million is $14.69 million. Since many of Anne's internal and external variables are shared by all departments in Anne's division, you can think of other departments as a kind of control group that did not have the variable of executive coaching applied to their efforts for the year.[4]

Now we can plug Anne's numbers into the formula (the coaching costs of the contract were $76,025):

$$\frac{\$14,690,000 \times .25}{\$76,025} = 48.3$$

Benefit-cost ratio = 48:1

The benefit-cost ratio is forty-eight to one: Anne received forty-eight times the financial benefit of what she paid out for the coaching effort.

I recommend asking clients how they normally calculate ROI for the projects they evaluate. This will indicate how extensive the research needs to be to calculate costs. The more fully loaded the costs are, the more extensive the research needs to be.[5]

I would not, however, engage the client early in the coaching contract in a lengthy conversation of calculation options. Most clients have not calculated ROI benefits for skill development in their own divisions. The discussion would tend to be too abstract and frustrating. I wait until the end of the contract to discuss a specific formula. By then you have the highest chance of engaging them in a relevant conversation. You can give your thoughts and your perspective, but they decide on the actual formula. It is their discernment of which formula is most useful to them that is the deciding factor. (For those interested in a variety of perspectives regarding formulas, see notes 2 to 5. Readers who are math phobic may want to take three deep breaths first.)

The client is aware that we are not calculating all the benefits they actually receive. Although the leadership, team, and process skills gained through coaching are transferred to other business issues, they are not counted in the analysis. Anne and her team approached subsequent business challenges much more productively because of the development they underwent through coaching. This further reinforces the worth of the coaching investment. Additional benefits not calculated include the contributions that Anne and members of her team make to groups elsewhere in the company as they left this team to join other teams. I personally enjoy knowing that the beneficial waves of the coaching effort will continue to break on the beach after my work with the client is done.

Step-by-Step Process

As an experienced practitioner, you can use this practical analysis with your clients so they convince themselves of the value of their executive coaching investments. Exhibit 9.1 outlines the entire process. It requires a subset of the analogous skills that you use as an executive coach to develop your clients: deep listening to uncover crucial facts, striving for concrete behaviors rather than accepting generalities, and understanding how organizational components interact with the external environment in order to recognize critical areas of impact and development.

Exhibit 9.1 Overview of the ROI Process for Executive Coaching

Step 1:	Coach the client to **identify the Three Key Factors** she wants to improve that relate to a business need in the organization and a change in leader

and team behaviors. The Three Key Factors are business results, leader interactional behaviors, and team interactions.

Step 2:   Customize and **hone the Three Key Factors** until they are specific, measurable, and interrelated.

Step 3:   Ask the client to **identify other variables** that affect results, the internal and external advantages and obstacles.

Step 4:   Check in and **assess progress** toward achieving the results and enacting the behaviors of the Three Key Factors throughout the process.

Step 5:   **Evaluate ROI.** Your client:

(a) Identifies the **final business results in dollar amounts** and other bottom-line metrics regularly used in the organization.*

(b) Assesses any interconnections or synergies created between the improved leader and team behaviors and the business results.

(c) Recalls the significant **internal and external variables** that affected the business results.

(d) Names the **percentage of impact** that the executive coaching variable had on the results, relative to other variables.

(e) **Calculates the benefit-cost ratio** of the executive coaching variable:

$$\frac{\text{Business results} \times \% \text{ impact of executive coaching}}{\text{Cost of executive coaching}}$$

You then have the benefit-cost ratio.

---

*When I say "final results" I realize that the client may continue to work on these goals or the results are intended to be ongoing. At some point, however, it's time to evaluate progress. For significant changes to occur in all Three Key Factors, I find that ten to twelve months is the time frame most frequently used with my clients for evaluation.

The rewards of using this approach are many. Leaders are more likely to remember to use the behaviors they know give them results. They will tend to expect their teams to interact in specific ways that create results. Executives are more likely to invest in using you as a coach in the future when they have a new team or more challenging set of results to achieve. Clients are happy to be strong references for your executive coaching practice if it specializes in linking leader development to business results. This set of rewards for using the benefit-cost ratio strategy can build a healthy portfolio for executive coaches who consider themselves business partners with their clients.

Chapter Nine Highlights

The Dilemmas
1. Some coaches are intimidated by research and statistics.

2. Others are uncertain how to link a client's development to measurable business results.

3. Still other coaches fear that coach involvement with calculating ROI lessens the client's responsibility for business results.

Use the Three Key Factors Methodology
1. Business results are measured in time, money, quantity, or quality metrics.

2. The leader and team behaviors are specific and observable actions verifiable by quantity and quality.

Assess Other Variables
1. Explore the other variables besides coaching that affected the success of accomplishing the Three Key Factors.

2. Ask the client about internal success, internal detractor, external success, and external detractor variables.

Truth in Advertising: What It Takes to Get There

1. Work with the Three Key Factors continually throughout the coaching contract.

2. Use live-action coaching with the leader and the team.

3. Focus on three learning challenges:

   - The leader's most daunting work relationship challenges
   - The leader's ability to "learn live"
   - A shift in co-created patterns between the leader and the team

The Benefit-Cost Ratio: Solidify the Connection

1. Ask for data on specific business measures.

2. Ask the client to outline any connection between changes in team functioning with the business results.

3. Ask the same question regarding changes in leader behaviors and the business results.

4. Be a collaborative skeptic.

The Benefit-Cost Ratio: Quantify the Impact

1. Ask what percentage of the change is attributable to the variable of executive coaching.

2. Be skeptical of the "grade inflation" of satisfied clients, and help them name a conservative percentage of impact.

3. Use the formula to calculate the benefit-cost ratio.

4. Customize the formula to what business results metric has credibility in the client's system.

5. When there is a judgment call on which of a range of business metrics to use, calculate an intentionally conservative benefit-cost ratio by choosing the lower number in the business metrics.

6. Use the overview of the ROI process as a guide to the steps in the process.

Part Three

SPECIAL APPLICATIONS

10

MAKING A STRATEGIC TRANSITION TO THE ROLE OF EXECUTIVE COACH

This chapter is for organizational consultants, human resource leaders, or organizational trainers who want to move more into the role of executive coach. This assumes that you have the necessary **traits of an executive coach,** including those that have been explored in this book, such as the following:

- You know how business functions operate and interrelate.
- You are business and results focused.
- You can make connections between bottom-line results and work relationship behaviors.
- You are an excellent listener and are well versed in basic coaching skills.
- You can steer conversations from the global to the specific.
- You hold a systems perspective.
- You have a strong sense of self. You are not intimidated by people in positions of authority.
- You can work in the middle of others' anxiety.
- You can give immediate feedback.
- You are equally able to support and to challenge.
- You have a sense of humor about human foibles—your own and those of others.
- You can let others create their own successes and mistakes.

That's an impressive and enviable list of characteristics and skills! Who *wouldn't* want to use you as a coach?

You may be working in companies with dozens of leaders throughout the organization, yet none are asking you for coaching, even though you possess the necessary skills to be an executive coach. This was my situation when I was director of training for a corporation that had a team of seven executives and twenty-five next-level leaders who directed the efforts of the organization. However, I was not hired to coach them. Initially I was expected to carry out training duties for the organization. Offering to coach anyone, let alone the top executive, would have seemed absurd to them. Yet later I found myself in the enviable position of being sought after as a coach by those very executives when leadership dilemmas intersected with their strategic and tactical issues. You too can bridge the gaps between your current situation and the more developed coaching relationships you want in your practice.

Concerns About Making the Transition

Typical questions and dilemmas people have in making this transition include the following:

- What do I do when I have an executive who doesn't know how to use me as a coach?
- How do I start from where I am now? How do I create an opportunity?
- What if the leader has a completely different map for change and my role within that change?
- How do I deal with the executive's resistance to spending time on coaching?
- How do I get the leader to view me differently?
- How can I ensure that an executive's initial experience with me as a coach will be a positive one?
- What do I do when I have a good idea before the leader does?

- How do I deal with an inadequate or weak executive?
- How can I help the leader see my coaching role as leverage toward the leader's greater effectiveness?

These concerns about role expectations boil down to three areas:

- Anxiety that you do not see eye-to-eye with your sponsor about what your **role** should be
- The need to get the right **contract** for coaching, so you can be successful with the executive and help her succeed
- The skill and presence needed to get into the **right conversation with the leader** in order to address the first two concerns

Concerns over Your Role

There are clues that indicate your sponsor does not see your role in the same way that you do. Here's one clue: when you offer to coach him on his leadership dilemmas, he gives you a quizzical, somewhat impatient look, which leaves you squirming. Or he approaches any work with you from the Rescue Model. He wants you to take things into your own hands rather than help him address them. You might hear him make comments such as these:

"So what can you do to get this implementation off the ground?"

"Just go tell them that the deadline is unacceptable."

"Why are you coming to me when you need to be spending your time getting the team going?"

These reactions and others like them indicate a mismatch in understanding about your role. They come from an executive who will not consider his own responsibilities to provide strong leadership for the organization. He will often assume you should engage in activities that, from a Client Responsibility perspective, are really his responsibility as a sponsor and not yours as a change agent. He may be unable or unwilling to view you as a resource able to help him think through and maintain those sponsor activities, the most important ones being communicating the direction and goals of the organization, ensuring commitment to the goals, clarifying decision-making authority with key players, managing performance expectations and consequences, and providing resources.

The Contract

This situation demands that you negotiate **the right contract** as a change agent (remember, coaches are change agents) in the project, including offering to initiate conversations that would lead to executive coaching. You know you have the right contract when the leader and you are both working from the same page, that is, from the Client Responsibility Model. The executive understands her responsibilities as the sponsor and sees you as a resource to keep her honest about them. You may also be assigned other duties as a change agent to help get a project under way. You can better leverage that agent role when it is pursued in tandem with the sponsor responsibilities that the executive maintains herself.

Here are a couple of common questions and complaints about leaders in these situations:

> "I have an inadequate sponsor who doesn't accept his responsibilities but thinks of plenty of activities to dump off on me."
>
> "What if my sponsor does not know the Client Responsibility Model? Do I have to teach it to her?"

Very few people are born great sponsors; most have to develop into the role. Some sponsors are lucky enough to connect with a great coach who can develop them. The coach does this by acting as an effective change agent who evokes stronger sponsorship from the executive. Rather than looking at the inadequacy of your sponsor, perhaps the question is, "Are you being a great change agent?" And, if not, "What can you do to be a stronger one?"

The Conversation

You do not have to teach your sponsor the Client Responsibility Model. Rather, you must embody it without using fancy jargon. This requires getting into **the right conversation** with the executive. It means shifting with your sponsor into the Client Responsibility perspective, not jumping there yourself and then blaming her for staying unknowingly in the Rescue Model. To manage yourself in your relationship with the leader, you should focus on acting differently with the leader rather than waiting for her to act differently with you.

> *You should focus on acting differently with the leader rather than waiting for her to act differently with you.*

Guidelines for the Conversation

We will explore several guidelines for the coach-client partnership that you may recognize from other chapters. These guidelines will help you initiate and sustain conversations that promote your coaching skills:

- Act *as though* you and the sponsor are both already in the Client Responsibility Model.
- Focus on the executive's goals.
- Provide a sample of what you can offer; demonstrate it right in the conversation.
- Find a way to say yes to the leader's goals.
- Have goals for managing yourself in the conversation.
- Offer loyal resistance, a form of advocacy, if necessary.

In acting as though you are in the Client Responsibility Model, always maintain focus on the executive's responsibility for keeping a strong connection with his people and establishing clear expectations. Define explicitly how you will help him build greater clarity and stronger relationships. Act as though your sponsor is capable of joining you in this perspective, even if he has never demonstrated this ability before.

What should you actually discuss? **Build credibility as a business partner** by talking about business goals and results. Then **link business challenges to the leader's challenges,** which provides a natural **segue into executive coaching.** Therefore, you need to **discuss the executive's goals, not your aspirations to coach.** What you wish to accomplish professionally is not what executives stay up at nights fretting about. **Concentrating on anything besides what preoccupies executives is fundamentally counterproductive to your own interests.** Therefore, engage them in what they care about. You need to define your role within the context of what they are motivated to achieve. This is a realistic approach to leaders: they sponsor best when they have vested self-interests. Expand their horizons by linking new ideas, insights, and your capabilities to their passions, concerns, and interests.

Once you find yourself talking with an executive about his goals, here are some typical questions to ask in order to get more deeply into the conversation (Schachter, 1997, p. 1):

- What do you want to accomplish in this effort?
- What is your best thinking about this issue?
- Have you met this type of challenge successfully before?
- What are the barriers to surmounting the same kind of challenge this time?
- How urgent do you feel this issue to be?
- How do you account for not being able to accomplish this?
- Do you have any sense of your part in not meeting the challenge this time?

- In your position as leader, what challenges do you personally face regarding this effort?
- What outcomes do you want?
- What would be achievable results in what specific time frame?
- To what extent do the people who report to you hold the same perspective or urgency that you do?
- Does your team know as much about what you're thinking as I now know?

You probably recognize these questions as conversation starters for the contracting phase of coaching. The contracting phase is the perfect opportunity for focusing on the leader's goals and strategies for attaining them.

These questions are potent tools for developing the executive's thinking about his relationship with his team and the expectations he has of them. **Congratulations! Just by asking these goal and team relationship questions, you open the door to coaching conversations and help the leader reflect on issues that may conceal ingrained challenges to the leader.**

However, it is not wise to define the discussion beforehand as a coaching conversation, which can scare off many leaders. Instead, you can give your potential coaching customer a sample of what you can do. The experience, plus a debriefing of the conversation afterward (what was helpful about it, what further clarity he now has, and so forth), establishes a track record for your coaching skills. After a number of these conversations, you can point to the experiences and offer to facilitate further coaching conversations about the projects the executive finds particularly challenging. To the extent that you have managed your relationship well with the executive, he is more likely to take you up on your offer.

Find a way to say yes to the leader's goals. Most organization consultants who also provide executive coaching take on other change agent responsibilities: facilitating, training, data gathering, mediation, or project management. The sponsor may draw you both back into the rescue perspective. This is the critical moment in the sponsor-agent relationship. Find a way to say yes to his goal by redefining for him which change agent tasks will better help him achieve his goal. Articulate your role and responsibilities in the light of the sponsor's goals and responsibilities and discuss the interplay between the roles.

You may be asking yourself, *What kind of dialogue can I have that would attend to both of our roles and work to align them?* An example of this kind of conversation follows (it also gives your sponsor a heads-up on chances for success of his goals):

Agent: You say you want the managers to enact the new performance standards.

Leader: You got it.

Agent: And you want me to train them on the new approach.

Leader: I can't think of a better person for the job.

Agent: And you said you are unable to take the time before the training to talk to the managers about their reservations about the new system.

Leader: You've seen my schedule! We've barely had time for this conversation.

Agent: Don't get me wrong. I'm happy to do the training. But let me be frank about the chances of this training "sticking" with the managers. They will know how to do it, but if you neglect their concerns, you have less than a 40 percent chance of putting an organizationwide system in place. If you deal with their concerns beforehand, even if that means having some tough discussions, you dramatically increase your chances of successfully initiating and introducing the new standards.

Leader: Increase it by how much?

Agent: You call the shots on that one. You decide what percentage you're satisfied with. You work their commitment until you get the percentage you want.

Leader: Why don't you just explain the need for it at the start of the training?

Agent: Even if I said it eloquently, they would continue to
   covertly resist you by not doing it. Hearing me talk about it
   is no substitute for airing their concerns directly to you. And
   you know what? They deserve that from you.

Leader: You sure know how to increase my workload.

Agent: It's a pay-now or pay-later scenario. You either deal with
   their commitment on the front end, or try to get it from
   them later while the project unravels. The second option
   takes up more of your time, as you and I have both painfully
   learned from experience.

This kind of conversation requires your signature presence in
managing yourself in the whitewater rapids of the leader's urgency,
anxiety, and impatience. This conversation will succeed if you
avoid blaming the sponsor for his shortcomings, or giving up on
him for being stubbornly resistant to strongly sponsoring the very
changes he wants. **Replace the impulse to blame or criticize with
offering neutral information that is related to the sponsor's
interests.** You are painting pictures of outcomes that the sponsor most cares about, for example, an organizationwide change in
implementing standards. You describe your role relative to his and
link both to the results that he wants.

---

*Replace the impulse to blame or criticize with
offering neutral information that is related to the
sponsor's interests.*

**It is also important to solicit the executive's reaction to your
position.** What is his best thinking about what you just said? What
are its merits, and what are his nagging concerns?

Agent: So what do you think about what I just said?

Leader: Okay, okay, I see your point. I can't wiggle out of this
   one. But I still don't see how I'm going to pull this off.
   I haven't got the time for it!

Here is a critical juncture in the conversation: Do you rescue the leader from his responsibility or continue to let him struggle with it?

Agent: You're in a tough spot. And you know what strikes me as ironic? Lack of time to implement is exactly one of the managers' reservations about this new system. You are struggling with the same issues they are. By dealing openly with your own challenges as you assign priority to the project, you serve as a model and a resource to the managers on how they can make it a priority in their work. Positioning the challenge as a common dilemma among all of you allows you to build your credibility and connect with them regarding this issue.

Leader: That's a tall order.

Agent: That's what you and I can talk about: how you're going to fill that tall order [the coaching opportunity].

The critical juncture in this conversation is when the change agent avoids becoming distracted by the leader's frustration. Instead, the agent stays on course by keeping the challenge front and center with the leader and **bringing immediacy to the conversation** (his time constraint is the same issue that the managers face).

The more often you find these moments of immediacy, the more powerful your coaching will be, and the more likely the leader is to see you as a coaching resource. In this case, using immediacy segues to the real issue of how daunted the leader feels in dealing with time pressures and managing his leadership team.

As this example demonstrates, you can have a jargon-free conversation while operating within the perspective of the Client Responsibility Model. One of the model's requirements is to stay on the task of building the sponsor's responsibility, even if you feel obliged to rescue him from that responsibility. You do not have to be eloquent or graceful, just effective.

The kinds of conversations I have been promoting in this chapter are what I call *coaching moments.* They happen outside the context of a formal coaching contract but within the context of the executive's work world and high-priority concerns. Opportunities to have these conversations are plentiful. They happen as the leader is focused on something else. You can build your credibility as a resource for the leader in ways he may not have imagined at first. Coaching moments can cover some of the same territory as the coaching phases, though in smaller increments. You can still:

- Listen carefully to the executive.
- Help him get more clarity about what the issue is, the goal he wants to accomplish, and a next step.
- Give feedback on his dilemma that can shed light on how he is leading this particular effort.

These moments over time build your portfolio of coaching skills that can later develop into more formal coaching relationships. When you enter conversations with the leader that highlight the need for him to exercise stronger sponsorship, you get closer to his personal leadership challenges. **When you show that you are calm enough, sturdy enough, and direct enough to have these leadership challenge conversations with him, he is more likely to invite you into more of those conversations.** And leadership challenge conversations are coaching conversations.

Having goals for managing yourself within this kind of conversation is essential for staying on course (these are the same as the process goals from Chapter Two). Goals keep you from getting sidetracked by your own anxiety in the face of the leader's impatience or irritation. Here are some examples of goals that I have had for myself, taken from several of these kinds of meetings in the past:

- When the executive gets impatient, focus on results.
- Don't jump into awkward silences. Let the leader take the initiative with pauses in the conversation.

- Stick with only one personal bottom line. Don't complicate the picture with too many requirements from your side.

- Find a moment to be immediate; the pattern "out there" is going on "in here" between the two of you.

- He doesn't need to hear how this project complicates your life. You must tell him whether you think it will work.

- Don't speak for other people. Speak for yourself, and invite the leader to seek out the opinions of others.

I do not pursue all these goals in each meeting. They are tailored to the executive, the situation, and my particular anxieties at the moment. It is best to have only one or two of them in a specific conversation.

Loyal Resistance

You may notice a tone that comes through in the example conversation and these sample goals for the coach. It is what I call loyal resistance. When an executive chooses methods or approaches that I judge to be counterproductive to the very direction she wants to take, I initiate my loyal resistance.

Loyal resistance is a form of advocacy. Actually many of the activities I suggest in this chapter, **such as focusing on the leader's goal, tying your role and aspirations to what the leader wants to achieve, and finding a way to say yes, are forms of effective advocacy.** As you recall from Conner's definition (Chapter Four), **advocacy** means promoting an idea, solution, or role that you espouse in a way that induces the leader to sponsor it as something she wants and owns as well. Loyal resistance occurs when an executive wants something from me that I cannot support because I do not believe that it will work. Notice that the emphasis is not on whether I want to do it, but rather on whether I think it will *work*.

Loyal resistance is a form of advocacy.

With loyal resistance, you are positioning yourself in a different, sometimes oppositional, place from the executive. However, since your intent is not to polarize your position with the leader, you show your willingness to support the deeper interests that she holds. In loyal resistance you do three things simultaneously:

1. **Get on board the leader's train. Show that you understand her goal and support it.**
2. **Articulate clearly how you differ with her approach.**
3. **Offer alternatives that can satisfy both her interests and your concerns.**

When you use this triple focus, you are invaluable to the sponsor.

Getting on board the leader's train shows her that you deeply understand what she is trying to accomplish. You do so by showing that you understand and support her goal and are finding a way to say yes to her interest behind that goal.

The tricky part is most often **articulating your differences** with her approach—*how* she wants to get there. You need to be thoughtful about your own perspective and have weighed its merits and obstacles carefully. If you can offer your viewpoint as useful information rather than a crusade or battle for the "right" position, the leader is more likely to listen to you. This is particularly true when you can tie your thinking to the executive's desired outcomes. You can save a leader from herself by highlighting what she may not be noticing in a situation. In these circumstances, if you do not share your knowledge and reservations, you are holding out on the leader and withholding your best thinking from her.

When you add the third ingredient in loyal resistance, you add power to your position. **Offer alternative solutions** that address your concerns while fulfilling what the executive wants to accomplish. After all, leaders are most interested in getting to a destination, not in the pathway to get there. Presenting ideas consistent with their goals can sometimes open leaders up. The ensuing brainstorm can generate options no one had yet mentioned, and the conversation gains renewed synergy. You show again how valuable you are as a business partner. Leaders are very attracted to people who can join them in commitment to their goals, respectfully and robustly bring differences to the table, and offer alternative ways to think about an issue.

Pace Yourself

Once you and your sponsor are in the right conversation, you build your experience base as an executive coach. Success is built on hundreds of these small conversations. You may start out with fifteen-minute discussions that veer in this direction. If you are just embarking on the adventure of coaching leaders, do not sabotage yourself by expecting to have full-blown, brilliant, lengthy executive coaching conversations the first time out. Neither should you call it "executive coaching" until you have a track record with the leader and the two of you begin explicitly to call the conversations "executive coaching." You need time to evolve your role, and the leader needs time to make changes in her expectations of you in your role.

Chapter Ten Highlights

Identify the Leader's Understanding of Your Role
1. Look for misalignment in expectations about your role between you and the leader.
2. Avoid taking on Rescue Model activities.

Get the Right Contract
1. Work for sponsor-agent alignment.
2. Ensure that all your change agent duties come from the Client Responsibility Model.

Get in the Right Conversation

1. Evoke stronger sponsorship in the leader.

2. Use the following guidelines for the conversation:

   - Act as though you are in the Client Responsibility Model.
   - Talk about the leader's goals.
   - Provide a sample of what you offer.
   - Find a way to say yes to the leader's goals.
   - Find moments of immediacy.
   - Have goals for managing yourself.

3. Offer loyal resistance, a form of advocacy, if necessary:

   - Partner with the leader's goals.
   - Articulate your differences.
   - Offer alternative ways of approaching the goals.

4. Pace yourself.

11

HELPING LEADERS EFFECTIVELY COACH EMPLOYEES

As an executive's coach, you often can help clients become better coaches to their employees. There seems to be not a little confusion in the minds of managers as to how to coach their employees. They know there is this hot new management tool called, "coaching employees." They may have been hounded by their own bosses or the HR department to do more of it. But it is still a mystery to them. Much of the perspective of this book can help leaders coach employees more effectively. *However, bosses are responsible for special and distinct performance management responsibilities they must do first before coaching their staffs.*

In this chapter, we explore areas you need to address when you help a boss become a better coach. **One is role clarity, for there are two roles the boss takes on when coaching employees. The other deals with an effective sequencing of those role responsibilities.**

Role Clarity

When leaders coach, they commonly make the mistake of downplaying their role as the employee's boss. This creates confusion in the employee and unproductive coaching on the part of the boss. An executive who wants to coach his employees must keep his roles clear. In terms of Conner's alignment roles, a boss is a sponsor, and

---

Note: I acknowledge the significant contribution that Rob Schachter has made to my perspective and practice. His influence in this book is most directly felt in the coaching models of Chapter Four and our codevelopment of the role 1, role 2 approach in this chapter.

a coach is an agent. As I mentioned in Chapter Four, it is possible to play multiple roles, that is, to be both a sponsor and an agent. However, an executive must be clear about which role he assumes at any given time as a way to **manage the complexity created by the dual roles.**

For example, bosses hold employees accountable for results, while a coach helps people improve the skills needed to achieve those results. Bosses who coach both mandate the goals and help people develop the ability to accomplish them. That is no small feat. When a boss coaches a staff member, he never stops being the boss. He cannot pretend not to have performance expectations of his employees while he is coaching them. His performance expectations are always there.

> *Bosses hold employees accountable for results, while a coach helps people improve the skills needed to achieve those results. Bosses who coach both mandate the goals and help people develop the ability to accomplish them.*

There are common pitfalls when people act as both a boss and a coach. One extreme is the boss who soft-pedals his bottom-line expectations because as a coach, he wants to develop his employees. A boss may try to coach an employee into compliance (replace the word *coach* with *nag, cajole,* or *plead*). This faulty thinking goes something like this, "Maybe if I coach them, they'll do what I want." Coaching is not a substitute for performance management. Yet another extreme is a boss who thinks coaching means being directive and giving an employee constant mandates on how to accomplish expectations. Nobody (neither the bosses nor the employees) truly enjoys being in either of these two extremes. True coaching of an employee is something altogether different.

There are separate and sequential roles a boss should use when coaching an employee:

Role 1: Articulate performance expectations, and ensure that the employee commits to them.

Role 2: Coach and develop the employee to accomplish those expectations.

Bosses should not confuse the two duties, and the first role must be completed before the second. Role 1 places the leader's coaching within a larger context of work expectations. Trying to coach without first addressing expectations is wasted coaching time and produces poor results. Your job as an executive's coach is to help a boss through this sequence so he can incorporate coaching effectively within his management responsibilities.

Role 1: Articulate Expectations and Ensure the Employee Commits to Them

Many managers live by the "read-my-mind school of management" philosophy—they are not explicit enough with their expectations. Then they wonder why they are not getting results when they "coach" employees. The leader's first job as a boss is to be clear about her expectations and to gain employee commitment to those expectations.

Clarity in expectations means being behaviorally specific. The employee needs to know:

- What the leader wants accomplished,
- by whom,
- by when, and
- how much decision-making authority the employee has to accomplish the goal.

Here is an example of clear and specific expectations:

I want you to head the task force on new employee orientation. Jovan, Bill, Priya, and Sue will work with you [who]. I want you to come back with a program, the length of time each new employee is needed for it, and a draft training manual [what]. You have two months to make a recommendation to me [when]. I want the task force team to have majority vote on the specifications of your recommendation [decision-making authority].

Here is another example:

> You have to handle the conflicts that come up in your department instead of allowing employees to come to me to resolve them. Beginning immediately [when], you [who] will ensure disagreements are resolved so that your staffers are coming to me only with issues that are outside your control [decision-making authority]. In fact, I want you to be the one who comes to me with those issues [who].

When the boss has clarified her expectations with an employee, she dramatically raises the employee's chance of success, as well as the boss's. (For more on giving explicit and specific expectations, see Fournies, 1998.)

Just because the boss has been clear, however, does not mean the employee gladly accepts the task and implements it. Sometimes an employee resists the boss's expectations, either explicitly through argument or covertly through lack of follow-through.

Role 1 also includes gaining commitment from the employee, an essential step before moving on to role 2. An employee's commitment is shown in three ways:

- **Understanding the goal**
- **Emotionally committing to the goal**
- **Taking initiative toward the goal**

Without all three in place, coaching an employee is premature.

Understanding

The employee needs to clearly communicate her understanding of the business goal. Even if the employee does not agree with it, she must understand what is required of her and the level of importance the boss places on it. To ensure understanding, it is important that the boss ask the employee to paraphrase her understanding of the boss's expectations. Then the boss is assured that the employee does in fact understand the expectations.

Commitment

Understanding is a necessary but insufficient criterion. An employee must also communicate her commitment to accomplish a business goal. As long as she sees the goal as the boss's issue and not hers, role 1 is incomplete. The boss needs the employee's commitment to the goal. Otherwise the boss resorts to berating, coaxing, or begging her to do it. The employee must assign the priority for her work that corresponds to the priority accorded it by her boss.

Part of the commitment process is allowing the employee to express her concerns, worries, and resistance to the boss's expectation. Although it may not sound like it, discussing obstacles and giving reactions is a way that the employee starts to imagine herself actually doing what it takes to accomplish the goal. The boss's job is to listen to the concerns and assure the employee that he understands what these reactions are.

At some point, the boss must determine the level of commitment that the employee has to the expectation. The boss needs to hear a clear answer, whether it is a no reservation commitment, a commitment with reservations, or no commitment at all, and must determine if he has secured an adequate commitment from the employee to move forward. A commitment with reservations can be a productive commitment if the reservations are solvable problems that the employee and the boss are committed to addressing, especially as these may indicate organizational obstacles.

Initiative

With commitment comes initiative. The boss knows the employee is ready and mobilized when she spends energy addressing the issues and obstacles inherent in the business goal. The following are signs of commitment and initiative: they begin to speak of the expectation as part of their work; they let the full weight of the expectation's implications sink into their awareness; they take on some of the anxiety of the responsibility for it and accept the management of the positive and negative consequences of the expectation. Another sign of initiative is when employees bring their own ideas and communicate them to the boss without him having to solicit them.

Sometimes a boss is eager or anxious to get on with a project, and will settle for one or two of the criteria for role 1 instead of all three. This is where you as the executive's coach can save the boss from himself. You can continue to challenge the boss to be thorough in role 1 so the rest of his work does not unravel later. You can be particularly useful when the process does not go smoothly, for example, when the boss runs into an employee's resistance to commit to the expectation.

Dealing with Resistance

When an employee balks at a boss's performance expectations, one of three things may be in play:

1. **A legitimate concern about organizational obstacles or priorities that interfere with attaining the goal**
2. **An unproductive boss-employee pattern that distracts the employee from the goal**
3. **A lack of the skill or confidence necessary to accomplish the business goal**

The first two must be addressed during role 1 before moving on to coaching in role 2. The third is a legitimate coaching issue and can be addressed in role 2: coaching for increased performance. We address the third kind of resistance when we explore role 2 later in this chapter. But let's look at the first two and how to handle them during role 1.

A Legitimate Concern About Organizational Obstacles. An employee may identify legitimate obstacles within the structure of the organization, contradictory priorities, or resource problems that must be addressed up front for it to be possible to accomplish the goal. If they are not addressed, the employee's efforts may fail, no matter how committed he is.

Many times the boss does not want to hear about these obstacles, but she must if the goal is to be successfully achieved. This is an example of the loyal resistance I mentioned in Chapter Ten. You can help leaders listen to this kind of "resistance" as a positive contribution. **The employee's objections are intended to improve the organization and can lead to an appropriate readjustment of the boss's expectations. This kind of loyal resistance is good feedback to the boss.** The boss needs to let the employee know that the boss will better structure the project so that the employee can accomplish his mandate. (For more on the conversation between a manager and employer on organizational obstacles, see the "improving performance" section of Kinlaw, 1993.)

> *This kind of loyal resistance is good feedback to the boss.*

An Unproductive Boss-Employee Pattern. A second reason an employee resists a boss's direction has more to do with an unproductive, well-established pattern between the two of them. There may be an unintentional but quite ingrained habit of relating to each other that increases the employee's resistance to the boss's direction. It happens more often than most executives think. If the executive tries to coach the employee before they break the pattern, the boss actually reinforces the problem and continues to thwart progress toward the business goal. **You can coach the boss to look for and identify her unproductive pattern with the employee.** Some possible patterns include the following:

- The boss raises concerns, and the employee questions the validity of those concerns.

- The boss invites, and the employee declines.
- The boss brings up issues that feed the fears of the employee, who then gets paralyzed rather than mobilized.
- The boss placates the employee, and the employee demands more from the boss.
- The boss threatens, and the employee threatens back.
- The boss avoids being clear about expectations, and the employee avoids asking for more clarity.
- The boss enthusiastically sells a great idea, and the employee becomes a passive buyer (this was Miriam and Sam's pattern).
- The boss complains to others about the employee, and the employee complains about the boss to others.

Missing from all these relational patterns are straightforward conversations about performance expectations. Expectations arise not in a vacuum but within a relationship, and the boss-employee relationship pattern can make it difficult to set straightforward expectations. As the boss's coach, you need to strongly advocate against coaching (role 2) until this pattern is shifted and allows for the communication of and commitment to expectations.

There is, of course, the issue of homeostasis, or the push-back against any pattern change. As the boss changes her side of the pattern—stops inviting, or stops raising concerns, or stops threatening, or stops feeding fears—and starts being clearer and more straightforward about expectations, the boss may get resistance to the very change she makes. The boss might say to you, "First, he won't do it, and now he's fighting my shift in the approach I'm taking with him!" This double dose of resistance is common before the boss and employee establish a more productive pattern. The boss must learn to expect this kind of resistance and increase her own tolerance level for it rather than returning to the old pattern just because the employee's resistance makes her uncomfortable.

That is why the boss has hired you. You can help the boss plan for this kind of resistance and explore options to increase her tolerance in the face of it. Besides the discussion on breaking patterns in Chapters Six and Seven, here are **guidelines you can give the boss.** This sequence of actions helps to gain an employee's commitment and initiative when there is an unproductive pattern between boss and employee:

- **The boss clearly states her business goal and measurable outcomes.** She is specific and thorough in her expectations. This starts the first step of the three-step process of role 1 and setting expectations.

- **The boss stays the course** in her position through the storm created by the employee's tendency to maintain the old pattern. The boss anticipates the employee's push-back, plans what her response will be, and stays on track anyway. This is the backbone part of managing.

- **The boss reinforces the change** in the employee's side of the pattern once he has joined the boss with a more productive response. The employee is manifesting his change through his (1) understanding of the goal, (2) committing to the goal, and (3) taking initiative toward the goal. That is something the boss can work with.

This gets the boss to the starting gate of coaching. (For an example of a boss beginning to shift an unproductive pattern with an employee, reread the conversation between Miriam and Sam in Chapter Seven.) The boss proceeds to coaching only when the role 1 conversation is done and the employee understands and commits to the business goal.

Role 2: Coach and Develop the Employee to Meet Expectations

Now that the employee is committed to meeting the expectation, the question remains as to whether she needs the boss to coach her. This is the third example of what the boss may read as employee resistance: when the employee is either unable or not confident that she can achieve the business goal. Issues of skill level or confidence are two areas that coaching can productively address.

Address Lack of Skill or Confidence

The employee actually is not resisting the expectation but doubts her ability to accomplish it and may in fact not be trained for it. This falls within the coaching work of a boss because the employee understands the expectations, can be emotionally committed to them, and yet lacks initiative only because of the skill or confidence issue, not because of a lack of agreement with the expectation.

The boss can use Ken Blanchard's situational leadership model to tailor his coaching to the specific employee's needs around the issues of competency and confidence. In fact, you can serve your client well by developing his ability to diagnose the employee's developmental needs according to this model. Then the boss can match his coaching style to fit those needs.

Encourage Executives to Customize Their Managing

After a few coaching sessions with a client, I sometimes see that he maintains the same approach toward all employees, despite the different needs of each. He wonders, with a lot of exasperation, why they are not coming through for him. Often an obstacle to a client's effectiveness is the habitual way he manages all employees. A coach can help bosses broaden and customize their approaches to employees and the problems they face. I use the Blanchard, Zigarmi, and Zigarmi (1985) model of situational leadership because it helps bosses see the need to shift their behavior based on specific employee situations. It is an effective tool: bosses experience a breakthrough that helps them choose new directions when they manage others. They can tailor their coaching more appropriately to individual staff members and the specific needs of each.

Rather than applying a one-size-fits-all management style, Blanchard, Zigarmi, and Zigarmi say bosses need to employ the style that brings out the best results. **Managers need to assess each specific employee and the task they face at the time.** They outline different styles arising from two independent variables in the employee:

1. The **skill or competence** to complete a work task
2. The **willingness, confidence, or commitment** to do that same task

These variables are independent because an employee can have any combination of the two. For example, she could be high in competence but low in motivation, or low in competence and high in motivation, or low in both, or high in both. A boss needs to match his leadership style to the employee's combination of the two variables.

The boss's approach to an employee is based on two other independent variables:

- **Directive behaviors:** predominantly one-way communication— for example, tell, explain, give directions, train, and lay out specific expectations
- **Supportive behaviors:** predominantly two-way communication—for example, elicit the employee's opinions and problem-solving skills, ask for information, express empathy and respect (as defined in Chapter Five), and show confidence in the employee

Directive behaviors are more essential when an employee's competence is low, whereas supportive behaviors are important for a low motivation or low confidence level but less crucial when an employee has high confidence or high commitment.

This approach is work-task specific. For example, a boss could have an employee who has this combined profile:

- Low computer competence with low commitment to do computer tasks
- High training skills and high confidence to do the training
- Low supervisory skills with fluctuating commitment to supervise well

The boss needs different management styles depending on which tasks he is addressing. The boss must give high direction and high support regarding the computer tasks, low direction and low support on training skills, and high direction and high support on supervisory skills.

How can a boss keep track of all of this? Actually, it takes very little time to assess where employees stand developmentally on specific tasks. The challenge comes from the boss himself; he usually has his own preferred, dominant style, one that he keeps using on everyone, whether they need it or not.

As the boss's coach, you can help clients think through their approaches to employees and evaluate whether they are effectively matching their style to each. You can spend part of your coaching time teaching your client to evaluate his situational leadership effectiveness.

When the boss matches his style to his employee's needs, he can accelerate the employee's development. He can also decrease the frustration they both may feel if he uses the wrong style. A typical frustrating mismatch occurs when the employee is committed but unskilled and receives negligible direction and training from her boss. Another extreme example results from a boss who constantly looks over the shoulder of a highly committed and skilled employee. Both scenarios can demoralize the employee and frustrate the boss.

Sometimes an employee is totally unfamiliar with and unskilled in key processes that are required to attain the goal. Training becomes necessary in these situations. For an employee to be productive, the boss needs to make sure all the classic stages of training are covered:

- Demonstrate the task.
- Explain how to do it.
- Observe the employee doing it.
- Give feedback on her performance.
- Repeat the steps if necessary.

Employees are shortchanged when they do not receive all of the training steps. A boss is responsible for making sure that he or someone he designates must train the employee in the skills necessary to do her job.

Coaching Phases for the Boss Who Coaches

Once the employee is ready for coaching, the boss can use a variation of the coaching phases covered in Chapters Five through Eight: contracting, planning, live-action coaching, and debriefing. I outline their adaptation here.

Contracting

Contracting from a boss position covers some of the same ground as coaches cover when contracting. **The boss familiarizes herself with the employee's work challenge** and examines it from the employee's point of view. The boss helps the employee **delve into the specifics of the issue.** What in particular is difficult for him? What are the obstacles? What has he tried already? It is important to keep the ownership with the employee, just as it was for the executive coach to ensure that the client maintain ownership of the issue.

The boss also tests the employee's willingness to acknowledge his own contribution to his difficulty. Can he see how he contributes to his dilemmas regarding the business issue? The boss uses immediacy and describes her experience of the employee while she talks with him. This feedback acts as a mirror of the employee's attitudes and actions. Finally, the boss establishes a contract to coach if the employee wants such help from the boss on this particular issue. Once role 1 (commitment to expectations) is completed, role 2 (coaching) is an option that the employee can accept or decline. This option approach to accepting coaching from the boss positions the employee's motivation where it belongs: with the employee. The employee takes advantage of whatever tools he believes he needs, including the coaching he could get from his boss.

There are many opportunities for a boss to **use immediacy in coaching an employee.** The boss gives feedback on her experience of the employee here and now and identifies the very thing the employee struggles with while approaching the business goal. Let's say that an employee tells his boss, "Jane and Darnell constantly argue with each other at the committee meetings and ignore my facilitating." In this example, the boss might use immediacy by saying, "You know, I'm also finding it difficult to follow your agenda during this meeting. You seem unsure as to where you need help. I wonder if Jane and Darnell experience your facilitating in the same way—as somewhat disjointed." This conversation invites the employee to see his own counterproductive pattern of behavior.

Planning

During the planning phase of coaching, the boss helps the employee envision his next step. There may be a pattern barring the employee from resolving the business issue; he may habitually approach or avoid the issue in ways that stagnate him and his professional progress. **The boss helps the employee identify his pattern and determine his specific next step, particularly in changing his side of the pattern.** Here are some examples of patterns:

"Every time I make this a priority, I get distracted by another priority."

"The accounting department isn't cooperating. They don't respond to my requests."

"I never get around to making the calls I need to make to move this thing along because people act so bothered when I call to remind them of the meetings."

The boss needs to be aware, however, that she may uncover more than her employee's ingrained pattern. Some **organizational alignment issues** may emerge as well. In other words, she needs to check to see whether roles are well defined and executed in this particular project. Close-in coaching gives the boss a chance to check whether her staff is aligned or misaligned with each other and with her department goals.

As you help the boss coach her staff, you can foster her thoroughness in attending to the boundaries and responsibilities of the roles of sponsor, agent, implementer, and advocate. Such attention can guide the boss and employee as they determine the best course of action.

In the previous example with Darnell and Jane's arguments, the boss can ascertain the employee's thought process, including which action he thinks should come first. The employee may uncover a core role confusion between Jane and Darnell; their arguments with each other are only symptoms of the lack of role clarity. The employee/meeting facilitator (the agent) cannot resolve the arguments because the boss (the sponsor) should resolve role issues. Or the employee may decide to facilitate the conflict between Jane and Darnell as an interpersonal issue. Alternately, the employee may decide to keep to the agenda in the meeting so the whole group does not get sidetracked. The employee's development is stimulated when he personally confronts issues regarding which direction to proceed in and then solicits the boss's input on the first action to take.

In such situations, the boss wears two hats: the boss hat and the coach hat. Depending on the course of action the employee chooses, the boss has to decide if the employee is ignoring or hiding behind alignment issues. If the employee has misjudged an alignment issue, the boss must step in and course-correct the employee's plan.

> *The boss has to decide if the employee is ignoring or*
> *hiding behind alignment issues.*

If the real issue is role confusion between Darnell and Jane but the employee plans to treat it as an interpersonal conflict (ignoring the alignment role confusion), then the boss needs to step in and clarify the roles between Darnell and Jane, which the employee is in no position to do. When this issue surfaces during a coaching conversation with the employee/meeting facilitator, the boss can clear up the issue fairly quickly, not by coaching the employee to deal with it, but by going directly to Jane and Darnell and distinguishing between their roles on the project. Jane and Darnell can then act more productively in the meetings that the employee facilitates.

Or the actual issue may be that the employee's facilitation style confuses Darnell and Jane, who in turn argue over how to proceed on the agenda. But the employee tells the boss that Darnell and Jane's roles are not clear (hiding behind alignment issues). In this case, the boss needs to challenge the employee to improve his facilitation skills.

The boss must address these issues because the boss has authority to determine what the employee will focus on next. A coach can see the same situations and diagnose them the same way as the boss, but a coach merely recommends rather than mandates a next course of action. If the boss steps in and changes the employee's plan because the employee misreads or hides behind an alignment issue, then the boss must temporarily leave her coaching role to make a "boss decision" about the employee's plan.

Making clear distinctions about when the boss is stepping out of the coaching role and when she is fully in it builds credibility with the employee. He can trust that when the boss makes statements or suggestions or asks questions from the coaching role, they are only coaching interventions (suggestions and recommendations), not disguised boss mandates. The employee can trust this because he knows he will hear directly from the boss when the boss is making a "boss decision" rather than giving coaching help. Once this rhythm is firmly established between the two of them, the employee is free to take the boss's coaching statements as input or recommendations, not as expectations or obligations.

This is the core issue in coaching as a boss. Coaching is a staff development activity, not a sneaky way to get the employee to do what the boss wants. When the boss coaches, she conveys her belief that the employee has the resources to solve the problem. To act on this belief is not to impose help but to offer it when needed. This does not prevent the boss from stating her own positions, but instead of giving answers, she shares her viewpoint to provoke and expand her employee's perspective on the issue. This requires a particular attitude from the boss: the employee is ultimately responsible for producing the results the boss sets for him.

Live-Action Coaching

What? you may be wondering. *Live-action coaching from a boss? Wouldn't that be a little strange?* Actually bosses engage in live-action coaching all the time. It has been called "management by walking around" and "supervising on the floor." **The problem is that the boss is frequently unclear about the structure of that coaching and how much on-the-spot intervening will happen.** If boss and employee do not talk about it beforehand, the employee may be waiting for the boss to intervene when the boss actually wants to see the employee work out the dilemma by himself. Or an employee may want a hands-off approach from his boss so he can learn from his own mistakes. The boss and employee need to reach an agreement about the live-action continuum, ranging anywhere from observer to stop-action intervener.

Another agreement about the boss's intervention is particularly critical if the employee is a manager or supervisor and leads meetings where the live-action coaching occurs. **The boss and the coachee also need to know whether or when the boss will step out of a coaching role and act within her authority as the coachee's boss.**

For instance, the coachee/manager may hold a team meeting where an issue comes up that would normally require the boss's input or decision. If the boss is there as a coach but immediately intervenes without clarifying her role switch from coach to boss, the change can disrupt the group and undermine the coachee's legitimate authority. The group may begin to distrust the boss's on-the-spot "coaching" and assume that everything she says comes from her position of authority.

When the boss preemptively acts as the boss, she denies the coachee the opportunity to decide when it is best to turn to his manager for input on decisions. That moment is lost when the boss jumps in. The boss misses the chance to observe the coachee's maturity in managing the boundary between the boss's authority, the coachee's authority, and the team's authority.

But, you ask, *what if the boss sees red flags in the coachee's meeting? What if she knows the coachee is giving incorrect information or overstepping his authority?* The boss can act but should take care that she does not undermine the coachee in front of his employees. The boss and coachee should determine beforehand the conditions under which the boss will intervene as his boss and how she will do so. You can give some of the following suggestions to the boss about this agreement:

- During the meeting, wait a short time after you are inclined to intervene. Give the coachee/manager a chance to self-correct.
- Address the manager first rather than talking immediately to his team. You can do this respectfully in front of the team. For example, you could say, "Bob, I have some information that is

different from what I gave you earlier, and I believe it would be useful here in the meeting."

- Be clear with the manager and the group that you are temporarily switching hats from the coach role to the boss role: "I'm switching hats from coach to boss at this point because there is some important information I need to add from my director position." Then be clear when you are switching back to coach.

Once the boss learns to manage the boss-coach boundary during live-action coaching sessions, she can turn her attention to the actual coaching itself. The guidelines are those enumerated in Chapter Seven. As coach, the boss works to support the employee's goals, foster changes in the employee's patterns of interaction, and help the employee maintain effective alignment in his organization.

Debriefing

Realistically, when a boss gives coaching feedback to an employee, it is evaluation, not just feedback. Helping the boss understand this can develop her management style further. It is not possible for a boss to split her awareness of an employee into two areas: a "this is just feedback" area and a "this is how I judge your performance" area. She uses any experience of the employee on the job as material for evaluation. It is best when the boss is honest with herself about this, rather than trying unsuccessfully to split her experience of an employee or reassuring the employee that she can engineer such a split. Employees are naturally dubious anyway that bosses could retain a split-screen view of them.

The coach should debrief the employee after he has implemented part of the action plan that he generated during their planning sessions. Debriefing is necessary for both the live-action coaching sessions and the times when the employee is implementing his plan on his own. When it comes to the **boss debriefing the employee regarding his effectiveness,** many of the debriefing activities of executive coaching come into play, with the employee self-assessing first. Discussions of the employee's strengths, challenges, patterns, management of alignment issues, and next steps can catapult the employee to a deeper level of self-understanding and encourage him to take ownership for his performance.

When the boss debriefs her effectiveness as a coach with the employee, she needs to be honest about how much feedback she wishes to receive on her coaching. Encourage her to be as open as possible. It may be difficult for the employee to give his manager an honest evaluation of her effectiveness as a coach. Therefore, **the boss needs to set an inviting tone** in order to get useful feedback. **This is the one case where it is effective for the coach to self-assess first** so the employee experiences the boss's readiness to receive real feedback. True openness means that the boss weighs what the employee says rather than assuming the information is either not useful or a reflection on the employee's performance. ("Of course, I wasn't successful as your coach because you were such a lousy coachee!")

Here are some questions the boss can ask both herself and the employee during debriefing about the boss's coaching effectiveness:

- Did I stick to our contract?
- How clear was I in my roles, stating my parameters as your boss as well as helping you as your coach?
- What are examples of times I was successful and times I was not?
- Can we identify any patterns that I created with you during this coaching that are typical of how we relate to each other?
- Which ones worked, and which didn't?
- Of the ones that didn't work, what can I [or we] do about them?
- What do you [or we] want to strengthen or change as I coach you in the future?

When the boss coaches team members effectively, it has a ripple effect throughout the organization. Many of the boss's other initiatives go more smoothly. She has more highly developed employees who can take on more issues independently and interdependently with peers without the boss's continual micromanaging.

Chapter Eleven Highlights

Role Clarity

1. Help bosses manage the complexity created by the dual role of a boss/coach.

2. Coach bosses to accomplish the separate and sequential activities of roles 1 and 2.

Role 1: Articulate Performance Expectations and Ensure the Employee Commits to Them

1. Help the boss set behaviorally specific expectations.

2. Role 1 is complete when the employee:

   - Understands business goals and outcomes.

   - Is committed to achieving the results.

   - Takes initiative in addressing the issues by using her own ideas.

Coach the Boss to Deal with Resistance That Hinders the Completion of Role 1: Identify the Kind of Resistance, and Brainstorm Ways to Deal with It

1. Legitimate concern about organizational obstacles

   - Listen and respond to their loyal resistance.

2. Unproductive boss-employee pattern

   - Identify an unproductive boss-employee pattern, and change the boss's side of the pattern.

   - Clearly state the goal and outcomes.

- Stay the course through the storm of resistance and push-back.
- Reinforce the change in the employee's side of the new effective pattern.

Role 2: Coach and Develop the Employee to Meet Expectations.

1. Lack of skill or competence:
   - Train if necessary.
   - Apply the situational leadership model.
2. Encourage executives to customize their managing:
   - Help the leader diagnose individual employees' development needs.
   - Ensure the leader matches management style to the development needs of the employees.
3. Contracting. The boss:
   - Becomes familiar with the employee's challenges.
   - Helps the employee get more specific about the issue.
   - Tests the employee's willingness to reflect on the part the employee may be playing.
   - Uses immediacy.
4. Planning. The boss:
   - Helps the coachee identify patterns.
   - Coaches the coachee to identify the next step.
   - Checks for organizational alignment of the coachee's plan.
5. Live-action coaching. The boss:
   - Provides clarity about their agreement of how much and what kind of on-the-spot intervention will occur.
   - Is clear when the boss transitions from the coach's role to the role of boss.

6. Debriefing. The boss:

- Realizes feedback to the employee is evaluation.

- Debriefs the employee's strengths, challenges, patterns, management of organizational alignment, and next steps.

- When evaluating the boss's coaching effectiveness, the boss (1) sets a tone of openness to feedback and (2) self-assesses first, then asks for the employee's feedback on her coaching.

Afterword:
Coaching for the Coach

Now is the time to bring the lessons of *Executive Coaching with Backbone and Heart* full circle. Coaches can most effectively maintain their role by receiving coaching themselves. Can it be any other way? Everyone needs help to stay on track in the powerful interactional fields of organizations. As I have emphasized throughout this book, coaches, like everyone else, never evolve to a state in which they are totally immune to these forces.

I stay on track in two ways. First, I often partner with another coach for live-action team coaching work. One of us is in the lead position, and the other is in a secondary position. Two pairs of eyes see more than one. By virtue of her position, the lead coach feels more strongly the power of being pulled into the client's anxiety. A telltale symptom is the loss of balanced backbone and heart work with the client. The second consultant enjoys a less anxious position and thus can see the system patterns more easily, notice gaps in the process, and assist the lead coach to do a thorough job and to bring her backbone and heart back into balance.

Notice that I say "by virtue of her position." The paired coach method allows one person to function differently given different roles within the system. I have played both lead and second coach roles, sometimes in the same organization. I can feel my anxiety shift, as well as my ability to see peripherally, as I make the transition from one position to the other. I also work with colleagues who seem quite calm in the second position and then lose some of their creativity and equilibrium as they become the lead coach.

I have learned not to personalize these shifts as signs of declining competence. It is a function of my position in the system rather than a sign of my character. Observing the differences in anxiety and clarity of one's vision according to position has been instructional, reminding me of what my clients go through when they experience the stress inherent in the leadership position.

A second way I keep my bearings is by maintaining access to my own coach when I work alone in an organization. This coach is often a colleague who knows me well and consults with me behind the scenes, either to plan for a client session ahead of time or to debrief after I've had a client session.

I used to think my need for a coach would diminish once I had worked with numerous clients and had many years under my belt. After twenty years and scores of clients later, my effectiveness has dramatically increased. My need to use a coach, however, has not diminished. I no longer see using a coach as a sign of incompetence but as a smart investment (thank goodness, since that is what I tell my clients!).

It remains true after all these years that the more I open myself to being coached, the more I know in my bones what my clients experience. Intellectually, I no longer see my need for a coach as a weakness, but there are still times when I get embarrassed about using a coach. It happens when I am particularly anxious about a specific client. I have learned to recognize that this embarrassment is in itself a sign of how inducted I have become in the client's system. Turning to a colleague for coaching is the first step toward climbing out of the vortex and recovering my bearings, clarity of thinking, and sense of humor. It helps me regain the Toddler's Mind I referred to earlier.

I mention both my need for coaching and my approaches to getting coached as encouragement to you. To the extent that you share any of my early biases against getting coaching help to become a better coach, I hope my story invites you to be more accepting of using a coach yourself.

Appendix A

THE CORE ACTIVITIES AND OUTCOMES OF THE COACHING PHASES

This Appendix provides a brief overview of the activities for each of the coaching phases and links those activities with the outcomes you are working toward in each. When you have achieved all four of the outcomes for a particular phase, you are ready to move with your client to the next phase.

You can develop your coaching skills more quickly when you take the time to evaluate your coaching sessions and incorporate what you learn as you plan the sessions to follow. Use the following pages both as a checklist to prepare for meeting a client and as a way to review your own performance after a coaching session.

Phase 1: Contracting

Activities
1. Elicit and **show understanding** of the client's core concerns.

2. **Give feedback, using immediacy,** your here-and-now experience of the client, raising the client's awareness of her role in the situation.

3. **Negotiate mutual expectations** of the responsibilities in the coaching contract.

Note: My colleague Roger Taylor codeveloped the pairing of outcomes to the four-phase coaching activities for the trainings we do in the Executive Coach Training Seminar Series. The series trains experienced coaches in the four-phase coaching model explored in Chapters Five through Eight.

4. Focus the client on **the Three Key Factors** in this situation and help the client identify specific, **measurable goals.**

Outcomes

1. The coach's accurate paraphrase of the client's core concerns.

2. The coach gave the client immediate feedback, and the client responded to the feedback.

3. Written mutual expectations of the contract.

4. A completed Three Key Factors worksheet, with a single specific business issue and specific, measurable goals in each category, to which the client is committed.

Phase 2: Planning

Activities

1. Help the client **identify a next step,** with specific actions to be taken.

2. Ensure the client's strategy **aligns with key change management models.**

3. Direct the client's attention to **a key pattern** that needs to shift.

4. Prepare the client to deal with both the **positive and corrosive effects** of resistance to the change.

Outcomes

1. A clearly articulated, challenging action step the client will take next.

2. A diagnosis of the alignment or misalignment of the business issue and the people involved.

3. An explicit description of a pattern, with "from" and "to" behaviors described.

4. A clear plan for how the client will respond to resistance during the next step.

Phase 3: Live-Action Coaching

Activities Behind the Scenes

1. **Clearly define your role** in the specific type of live-action option chosen.

2. **Ensure sponsorship** and clarity of structure for the live-action session.

Activities During Live Action

1. Follow and **intervene around the client's goals** (business and work relationship challenge goals) for this live-action session.

2. Intervene effectively on the level of **pattern change.**

Outcomes

1. An explicit contract for how the coach will (and will not) intervene during the action.

2. An accurate description by the client that clearly sponsors the coach and clarifies the structure and process of the next step.

3. Coaching interventions that align with the contracted goals (both business and work relationship challenge goals).

4. The client transforms his interactional behavior and co-creates a new pattern with others.

Phase 4: Debriefing

Activities

1. **Encourage the client to self-assess** the results of her actions: strengths, challenges, pattern changes, and change management issues.

2. **Give supportive and challenging** feedback to the client.

3. Help the client **identify specific next steps.**

4. **Invite the client to give feedback** on the effectiveness of your coaching.

Outcomes

1. The coach's accurate paraphrase of the client's self-assessment.

2. The client's accurate paraphrase of the coach's feedback to the client.

3. Specific, articulated next steps.

4. The coach's accurate paraphrase of the client's feedback to the coach and the coach's self-assessment given to the client.

Appendix B

EXECUTIVE COACHING SKILLS SELF-ASSESSMENT SURVEY

This Appendix presents a survey you can take regarding your current level of knowledge and skill relative to the four main activities outlined for each of the executive coaching phases detailed in Chapters Five through Eight. By taking the survey you can see a quick snapshot of three major professional skill areas needed to use the executive coaching approach in this book:

1. **Foundational coaching ability.** These skills are necessary for all coaches, whether they are personal, career, or business coaches.

2. **Use of your signature presence with clients' work relationship challenges.** These skills come from your ability to use yourself as the main intervention tool. You use your presence with your clients to help them tolerate their discomfort enough to head in new directions in which they have not had success in the past.

3. **Knowledge and use of organization models to increase the impact of your interventions with clients.** These skills allow you to choose the most relevant maps to use with your clients and target your coaching interventions specifically to the situations they face. This gives you much greater flexibility than using only one perspective with executives.

Once you take and score your self-assessment survey, you can then decide how satisfied you are with your results.

Executive Coaching Skills
Self-Assessment Survey

Rate yourself on a scale of 1 to 6 (see rating scale) on each skill as you see your ability at this time.

Rating Scale

1. *I **don't understand** this idea.*
2. *I understand the idea but **do not notice opportunities** to use it.*
3. *I notice opportunities but **do not know how to apply relevant tools.***
4. *I apply this with **limited effectiveness.***
5. *I **occasionally** apply this with **moderate to high effectiveness.***
6. *I **consistently** apply this with **moderate to high effectiveness.***

Executive Coaching Phase 1: Contracting

1. Elicit and show understanding
   of the client's core concerns.   _____

2. Give feedback, using immediacy—
   your here-and-now experience of the
   client, raising the client's awareness of
   her role in the situation.   _____

3. Negotiate mutual expectations of the
   responsibilities in the coaching contract.   _____

4. Focus the client on the Three Key
   Factors in this situation, and help her
   identify specific, measurable goals.   _____

Executive Coaching Phase 2: Planning

5. Help the client identify a next step,
   with specific actions to be taken.   _____

6. Ensure the client's strategy aligns with key change management models.   _____

7. Direct the client's attention to a key pattern that needs to shift.   _____

8. Prepare the client to deal with both the positive and corrosive effects of resistance to the change.   _____

Executive Coaching Phase 3: Live Action

9. Clearly define your role in the specific type of live-action option chosen.   _____

10. Ensure sponsorship and clarity of structure for the live-action session.   _____

11. Follow and intervene around the client's goals (business and work relationship challenge goals) for this live-action session.   _____

12. Intervene effectively on the level of the pattern change.   _____

Executive Coaching Phase 4: Debriefing

13. Encourage the client to self-assess the results of her actions: strengths, challenges, pattern changes, and change management issues.   _____

14. Give supportive and challenging feedback to the client.   _____

15. Help the client identify specific next steps.   _____

16. Invite the client to give feedback on the effectiveness of your coaching.   _____

Scoring Your Results

Transcribe your answers for each of the sixteen skills in the following list. You will notice that a couple of the skills are listed in two of the columns because they apply to both areas. When you have filled all three columns with your results, add up each column. The sum of each column will be between 0 and 36.

Foundational Coaching Ability	Using Your Signature Presence with Clients' Work Relationship Challenges	Knowledge and Use of Organization Models to Increase the Impact of Your Interventions with Clients
1 _____	2 _____	4 _____
3 _____	7 _____	6 _____
5 _____	8 _____	7 _____
13 _____	11 _____	8 _____
15 _____	12 _____	9 _____
16 _____	14 _____	10 _____
Total: _____	Total: _____	Total: _____

The results can be interpreted as follows:

0–18 Low knowledge of these skills. You need more conceptual training to increase your understanding of the skills and to learn to recognize when to use them.

19–29 You have conceptual understanding of these skills but have low skill in using them, have just become aware of them and have yet to put them into practice, or have limited opportunities to use them. You could benefit from further training, or you need additional repetitions of these skills in order to increase your effectiveness.

30–36   You have knowledge and moderate to high skill level in this area. The more you use these skills, the more they can become a strength area of your coaching practice.

There may be one or more areas where you want to further develop your skills. This can be done through a variety of methods depending on your needs: going through a foundational coaching training course, working with a coach to increase your skills, creating a peer consult group to debrief and prepare for your challenging situations with clients, or further training explicitly in these executive coaching phases. (MBO Consulting offers further training through the Executive Coach Training Seminar Series. You can learn about the series by going to www.mboExecutiveCoaching.com.)

Appendix C

QUESTIONS FOR CLIENTS

This Appendix contains examples of questions that you can ask your clients at various stages throughout the coaching process. You will recognize them as the questions that are embedded throughout the chapters and stories of this book. They are not meant as a prescription or recipe for conversations with executives. They are intended as a stimulus to your thinking as you customize your conversations with clients.

All of these questions are intended to inspire ownership and resilience in your client. Use whichever ones you find helpful to get you started in the conversation. Ultimately, you will create your own questions, which will engage both your resourcefulness and the resilience of the leaders with whom you work. You may wish to create your own list of questions that you find useful in coaching sessions.

Contracting

What business challenges do you face?

Have you met this challenge successfully before?*

What is your best thinking about this issue?*

What are the barriers to surmounting the same kind of challenge this time?*

Note: Questions marked with an asterisk are excerpted, adapted, and used with the permission of Rob Schachter, from "Questions When Contracting with Leaders," unpublished manuscript, 1997.

What is keeping you from getting the results you want?

How do you account for not being able to accomplish this?*

How have you responded to this issue?

Do you have any sense of your part in not meeting the challenge this time?*

How urgent do you feel this issue to be?*

How much time do you have to achieve this?

What do you find personally challenging about leading this effort given the results you have so far?*

How do you think I could be useful to you?

Do you have the authority to sponsor this plan, or do you need a sponsor?

Goals

What do you want to accomplish in this effort?*

What outcomes do you want?*

What would be achievable results and in what specific time frame?*

What would successfully fulfilling those goals look like? How would you measure it?

What team behaviors need to change to accomplish the results?

In your position as leader, what challenges do you personally feel regarding this effort?*

What behaviors will you need to strengthen or change?

How does this challenge fit into goals you have for yourself?*

To what extent do the people who report to you hold the same perspective or urgency that you do?*

Does your team know as much about what you're thinking as I now know?*

Planning

Have you clearly expressed your commitment to this challenge so that your team knows your level of commitment?

What do you know, and what don't you know? Can you be clear about both? What information and support do you need, and from whom?

How can you increase participation within the work group?

How clear have you been about your performance expectations?

Are these expectations compromised in some way by the surrounding context?

Are matrixed groups clear about their roles on this issue? Do they know to whom they are accountable and for which items?

Are you the decision maker? Which decisions will you make, and which will you delegate?

What strengths do you have as a leader that you want to preserve and build on?

Patterns

What pattern are you playing out with the other person? Is the pattern effective? If not, how does it detract from your success?

What does the other person do or not do that triggers your response? Does this interaction have a familiar ring to it? Can you count on people (yourself included) to react in familiar ways? Is this so recurring that you can anticipate it? How would it be reframed as a news headline or a two-verb reinforcing circle?

How do you enable others to maintain counterproductive patterns? What is your contribution to this pattern? What do you do that starts them down that path in the first place?

What pulls you off course?

What can you do to stay on course? And then what can you do when that doesn't work?

Boundaries

Do people know what is expected of them?

What are the boundaries of this system?

How frequently are they compromised so that work is made more difficult?

Does their rigidity make it hard for people to get essential information and resources from other parts of the organization?

Debriefing

How do you think you did?

To what extent did you achieve your goal? What did you do well?

Did you follow the mandate of your role as sponsor, implementer, advocate, or agent?

Did you match your managing style to the developmental needs of the employee?

Did you establish a pattern that enhanced the interaction?

What internal cues can you identify when you get into this pattern (for one that works or one that does not work)?

What loose ends around decision making, participation, and other issues need to be resolved?

What challenges do you continue to face?

What next step do you want to take?

What do you want to strengthen or change as I coach you in the future?

Appendix D

COMBINING COACHING AND CONSULTING FOR POWERFUL RESULTS

Executive Coaching with Backbone and Heart has detailed the methods and skills essential to coaching leaders. I've focused largely on the one-to-one relationship between the coach and the executive. While Chapter Ten is addressed to consultants who want to develop a larger coaching practice, this Appendix provides ideas for coaches doing one-to-one work who want to tackle larger organizational change efforts. Your clients may request your assistance in larger change agent arenas or invite you to join them in the live-action work within their organizations.

Most of my coaching is part of a larger partnership with the executive concerning an organizational initiative that she launches. Since consulting and coaching are mutually reinforcing, the client efforts benefit from such a powerful combination. The consulting/coaching process allows the executive to have an impact on a larger part of the organization in a shorter time. In addition, the coaching deepens the executive's commitment to sustain her organizational change goals and outcomes. Any effective consultation process includes ongoing coaching as an integral part of the work and can make significant contributions to organizations.

These gains result when the leader strongly sponsors both the executive coaching and other organizational change efforts. Then the coach-consultant can intervene on multiple levels in the company by using many change agent roles: interviewing, facilitating, training, coaching of other leaders in the system, and other roles as well. Ongoing coaching of the executive empowers these extensive organizational efforts with greater effectiveness.

Before turning to how coaching and consulting can be combined, I briefly discuss the results of such an undertaking. They highlight the benefits of offering a fuller set of services to executives.

The Client's Results

Following are actual results clients have achieved during executive coaching processes that link executive coaching with larger consulting interventions in the executive's company:

- The company's market share moved from bottom to top rank.
- The manufacturing plant ascended from the lowest to highest production quantity.
- Where previously no department connected its work to the organization's bottom-line goals, every department reorganized to deliver on the three major goals of the company. This change resulted in sustaining membership in the "top three" rating on a national customer satisfaction index.
- An HR department that delivered basic personnel benefits and policies transformed itself into a full-service HR department linking organizational development work along with personnel administration and delivery.
- In a company in which executives were protected from hearing bad news from peers and direct reports, subordinates began giving consistently straight feedback throughout the company. This led the company to be rated by outside auditors as the least politicized company they had experienced.
- Strained and combative management-union relationships were replaced by significant collaboration on business decisions.

Combining Coaching and Consulting

There are numerous approaches to creating organizational change. Surveying the theory and process of organizational consulting is beyond the scope of this book.[1] Following, however, is a sample of how putting consulting and coaching together can produce powerful results. Five tenets underlie this work:

1. Link business results to work relationship behaviors.
2. Build the leadership capabilities of the executive, particularly in the areas of articulating positions clearly (backbone) and staying in a strong relationship with the team (heart). This includes the ability to manage productive conflict (backbone and heart).
3. Provide live-action coaching and consulting interventions while the executive and the team are conducting real work.
4. Develop individuals within the work group to bring their own leadership forward as they take initiative involving productive collaboration and challenge.
5. Encourage and stimulate a stronger relationship between the executive and her team of direct reports.

Encouraging the interplay of these items between an executive and a work team produces powerful results such as those listed above.

Here are some of the consulting activities that, with strong sponsorship from the client, can contribute to this productive dynamic. Notice the classic blend of consultation with coaching. Effective outcomes result when you work this traditional blend along with a systems perspective to uncover, identify, enhance, or change the strong patterns operating in the executive and the team arising from their co-created interactional field. Many moments of individual discovery and behavioral change create the possibility for greater team effectiveness. The classic consulting process has listed the companion coaching activities in each category.

Consulting and Coaching Activities

- Consulting: Contract with the executive for work with him and his immediate team.

  Coach the executive during the contracting process outlined in Chapter Five.

- Consulting: Conduct individual interviews of team members.

  Coach individuals to identify unique, specific goals to increase their own effectiveness during team meetings.

- Consulting: Hold business meetings, facilitated by the leader, to address actual organizational issues. Provide just-in-time training by using models that develop crisper visions, goals, decisions, commitments, and action plans regarding the business issues.

  Coach the leader and the team in live-action sessions while they conduct their business.

  Coach the leader in debriefing and planning sessions between meetings.

- Consulting: Train the leader and the team in interactional skills to develop their resources in uncovering information, talking directly to each other, managing conflict, and making decisions.

  Coach individuals during training practice sessions.

  Coach during training debriefings.

- Consulting: Identify staff and operations areas of the organization that need further development.

  Coach the executive to build strong sustaining sponsor leaders across the organization.

  Coach the executive during meetings she leads with these sustaining sponsors.

  Coach the executive to ensure successful project management implementation across the organization.

Coach designated leaders in the organization who have a
high impact on the business.

- Consulting: Train designated executives to become more
effective coaches to their direct reports.

    Coach leaders as needed on their coaching skills.

- Consulting: Train an internal group to become coaches and
continuing change agents in the organization.

    Coach these individuals as needed.

A range of skills is required for the activities catalogued above.
The list of competencies in the next section gives you a sense of
what is necessary to expand your practice to include a blend of
consulting with coaching.

Consultant Competencies

Although one-to-one coaches need to have many of the competencies listed here, consultants need to master all of them. They
work on larger processes, ones that often affect a whole department, division, or the entire company. They intervene in multiple
arenas simultaneously. Consultants play the other roles listed here
that exceed coaching—for example, project manager, trainer, and
meeting facilitator.

There is a great deal of overlap between these skills and the
management competencies cited in Chapter Eight. When it comes
to enhancing people's performance at work, executives and consultants share much of the same people skill requirements, though
they use them in distinctly different roles. You can use this list to
assess the range and depth of your current change agent skills.

Systems functioning	Expands awareness of the present-ing issues to include (1) the systems patterns at play, (2) the function of the organization's infrastructure, (3) the emotional tugs underlying

organizational issues, and (4) the larger communities that affect the organization.

Includes oneself as an important player in co-creating the patterns at work in the system.

Works to increase own and others' resilience in functioning within the system and between intertwined systems.

Strengthening sponsorship	Educates and coaches clients in sustaining critical dimensions of their sponsorship.
	Ensures that clients create role clarity and distinctions between themselves as sponsors and their change agents.
	Declines duties that undermine the relationships and responsibilities that sponsors and implementers have to one another.
Project managing	Educates and coaches clients to (1) give specific direction and identify key roles, responsibilities, and time frames for projects, (2) allocate the people resources necessary for each project, (3) identify the decision makers, (4) clarify the single point agent for the project, and (5) sponsor the kickoff.
	Acts as single point agent in designated projects to monitor processes and ensures that leaders sustain cross-functional sponsorship.

Facilitating meetings	Develops an agenda, prioritizing items for best use of time.
	Facilitates discussion to gain maximum participation and input.
	Helps group members identify key needs, ideas, and plans for actions.
	Uses a variety of group process methods to achieve effective engagement, leading to synergistic results and productive outcomes.
Decision making	Ensures that the sponsor is clear about who has authority for making decisions.
	Helps the client use several decision styles effectively, for example, consultation, delegation, majority vote.
Promoting conversations	Clarifies the parameters of discussions to maximize their effectiveness.
	Helps all constituents to be heard and speak to each other directly.
	Seeks to unearth information and break habitual thinking.
	Addresses underlying issues.
	Talks about the tough issues.
	Takes a learning stance in conversations, that is, can expand one's position based on others' input.
Coaching	Promotes leadership and initiative in coachees across all roles in the organization.

	Gives specific feedback to others about their strengths and challenges, thus building competence and commitment in others.
	Helps people clarify their positions while staying connected in their work relationships.
Training	Designs and delivers training linked to strategic organizational goals.
	Engages trainees' participation while achieving the intended objectives.
	Is capable of facilitating knowledge, attitude, and skill training. Provides clear theory sessions.
	Gives easy-to-follow instructions for skill practice.
Advocating	Effectively advocates for ideas and for one's role in the organization in order to achieve the goals.
	Uses advocacy to enhance the broader strategic vision of the whole organization.
	Communicates understanding and commitment to the larger goals when advocating.
Strategic thinking	Understands the whole picture. Sees complex functions from the broadest perspective.
	Can weigh external and internal variables that affect the organization's productivity and results.

	Comprehends business issues and how an organization works. Can develop ideas to maximize the organization's effectiveness.
Understanding customer relations	Perceives the customer, vendor, internal customer (employee), and larger community (civic contexts) relationships as mutually reinforcing.
	Works to streamline processes to aid these relationships.
Visioning	Develops a clear vision for oneself as part of the larger organization.
	Helps executives identify specific and measurable goals to achieve the vision, and communicates the vision and goals effectively.
	Helps clients to engage constituents in conversations to further the vision, gain greater clarity, and increase communal commitment.

Notes

Chapter Two

1. My colleague Rob Schachter says, "Take the bull by the horns and then hand it back to them." This applies to those delicate situations that call for both bold initiative and following a client's lead simultaneously.

2. *Self-differentiation* was defined by Murray Bowen and later used by Edwin Friedman. I give it only the barest definition here. For an accessible introduction to the journey of self-differentiation, see Friedman (1985) and Kerr and Bowen (1988).

3. One path that can lead to greater mastery is called "family-of-origin" work. Since it is a developmental therapeutic process, it is beyond the scope of this book. For those interested in this topic, see Gilbert (1992) and Richardson (1984). For a related resource with the distinctive exploration of personal authority, see Williamson (1991).

4. The interplay of order and chaos and the experience of ambiguity and confusion mentioned here give a cursory explanation of an approach to organizations that is informed by the new science in biology and physics. For an accessible introduction, see Wheatley (1992).

5. See note 3. For brain research on reactivity, see Goleman (1995).

6. If you are interested in being trained to recognize and use moments of immediacy, the Leadership Institute of Seattle provides that training in its seminar entitled, "InterAct: Quality Workplace Relations." For more information, go to www. lios.org.

Chapter Three

1. I am fortunate to have been colleagues with the faculty members at the Leadership Institute of Seattle/Bastyr University who are practitioners in the fields of consulting and coaching, as well as systems counseling. In their work, they also use many of the key systems theory assumptions I bring to coaching and successful change efforts. Two other significant conversation partners regarding this theory have been consultant colleagues Rob Schachter and Roger Taylor.

2. I use the terms *interactional force field* and *social interactional field* because they are conducive to a work environment. The actual term used in the discipline of family systems is *emotional field*. For a more in-depth exposition on the term, see Kerr and Bowen (1988).

3. See note 3 in Chapter Two.

4. My introduction to pattern thinking was through Ronald Short (1985a, 1985b), a former director of the Leadership Institute of Seattle. Short studied with Salvador Minuchin (1974) and found a way to apply Minuchin's structural systems thinking to organizations.

Chapter Four

1. These questions and others that can help coaches better understand patterns are listed in Appendix C.

2. A current boundary issue between an organization and other systems that is gaining in importance is the amount of time

increasingly expected from middle- and upper-level leaders to do their jobs. There is a corporate cultural expectation that community and family boundaries will be routinely violated for the sake of the organization's increased demand on leaders' time. Some corporate systems are creating a new class of indentured servant—highly paid, time-starved executives, whose time is not their own, who work six or seven days a week, while personal pursuits with family, community, and individual rejuvenation get what little is left over of the executive's energy and time. This is a formidable, large-scale societal pattern. Executive coaches can help clients recognize and face this boundary issue, see how they play into it, and make decisions to create healthy boundaries among all the systems of which they are members, while they work for increased skill and effectiveness in their positions. Facing and changing these boundary issues is daunting because of external and internal systemic resistance.

3. Conner (1998) follows up his change management approach by describing the nimble organization and what it takes to get there.

Chapter Five

1. I use a guiding motto for each of the phases, which are the chapter subtitles in the chapters addressing the phases.

2. For an excellent introduction to action research, see Block (1981). Dotlich and Cairo (1999) present another coaching approach that draws from the stages of action research in broad strokes. Readers may note that explicit mention of data collection, one of the steps in action research, seems to be missing from the coaching phases. Actually it is embedded in all four. A coach's direct experience with leaders provides this information as they go through these phases. That is why it is instructive to observe leaders and their interactions

with team members within their work settings (see Chapter Seven). In a sense, I collect information on how leaders collect data and receive feedback about themselves and their business issues.

3. These are some of the listening skills that Carkhuff (1969), drawing from Carl Rogers, defines as crucial to helping clients solve their own problems. Carkhuff's technical definitions of these skills differ from typical cultural use, particularly for confrontation and respect.

4. Three resources for assisting clients in goal setting are Hargrove (1995), Craig (2006), and Schaffer (2002). Hargrove discusses the use of breakthrough thinking to achieve "stretch goals." Craig discusses "backplanning" as a way to ensure that goal setting is strategic and outcome based in a way that instills an organizationwide urgency to achieve results. Schaffer talks about avoiding the "five fatal flaws" in setting up a coaching contract as a way to ensure that both the client and the consultant are focused on bottom-line results, with the client taking responsibility for the outcome.

5. The Executive Coach Training Seminar Series explores in depth the methodology of working with the Three Key Factors when coaching executives. For more information, go to www. mboExecutiveCoaching.com.

6. The story of Anne and the development of her Three Key Factors is excerpted and revised from O'Neill (2005).

Chapter Six

1. David Schnarch is a marriage and sex therapist. His book (both highly theoretical and graphic) is written for couples' personal use. But his descriptions of the dynamics of anxiety, reactivity, resilience, and differentiation are some of the best available in the field of systems theory.

Chapter Nine

1. For a concise study that includes different approaches to measuring the impact of executive coaching see McGovern and others (2001). Those with responsibility for the HR function who want to contribute more to identifying process and human capital ROI, see Fitz-enz (2000).

2. Why do I prefer benefit-cost ratio? A ratio is easier to grasp and visualize ("Oh, I got ten times more out of this project than I paid into it. That's great!"). ROI that is expressed as a percentage requires an extra mental calculation to determine, relatively, how much was paid out compared to what was received. For a more in-depth explanation regarding how to choose the best formula to use, see note 5 in this chapter.

3. Anderson (2003) recommends that the coach ask the client to assign a percentage of confidence for her estimate when linking the bottom-line results to any human performance intervention. You can multiply the actual impact by this percentage.

4. Anderson and Anderson (2005) list ways to isolate and identify effects, such as control groups. You could also compare Anne's performance this year to her performance in a previous year (as you recall, she brought in 10 percent more revenue than the year before). You can see that the 6 percent difference from the next best peer's team in the same year is the more conservative number.

5. I did not include fully loaded costs (for example, percentage of team salaries, benefits). I have found that some clients are actually less swayed by fully loaded costs than by the cost of the coaching contract itself. Therefore, I offer the following perspective to add flexibility to your conversations with clients about their financial return on executive coaching.

Customize tools to the client. These multiple options (ROI percentage versus benefit-cost ratio, fully loaded costs versus only coaching costs) provide an array of analytical tools that meet clients' needs and maximize your credibility with them.

Benefit-cost ratio. I typically use the following benefit-cost ratio formula:

$$\text{Benefit-cost ratio} = \frac{\text{Business results} \times \% \text{ of impact of coaching}}{\text{Cost of coaching}}$$

The formula renders a ratio that is clear and comprehensible for the client. To use this formula, the client needs to focus on business results during the time of the coaching contract. They could include any of the following: revenue, profit, costs, market share, customer retention, and employee turnover. This formula hones in on what the client most cares about in terms of calculating a financial benefit. It does not calculate net contribution. Depending on what the client wants to calculate, this formula would be sufficient, or have to be replaced with calculating net contribution.

ROI percentage. Jack and Patricia Phillips (Phillips, 2002; Phillips, 2003; Phillips and Phillips, 2004) use the following ROI formula to calculate return:

$$\text{ROI percentage} = \frac{\text{Program benefits} - \text{program costs}}{\text{Program cost}} \times 100$$

This is not calculating net contribution of the client's entire operation either, which would need to be done for a full ROI. It does, however, figure net benefits of the coaching program itself. When using this formula, I would still multiply the net benefits by the percentage of the coaching impact so that coaching receives only the portion of credit that it deserves as one of the many variables. Then the formula would look like this:

$$\text{ROI\%} = \frac{(\text{Business results} - \text{coaching costs}) \times \% \text{ of impact of coaching}}{\text{Coaching cost}} \times 100$$

Fully loaded costs. Jack and Patricia Phillips (Phillips, 2002; Phillips, 2003; Phillips and Phillips, 2004) advocate using fully loaded coaching costs to calculate the ROI or benefit-cost ratio. This includes not only the coaching fees and the coach's travel expenses but also facilities costs, employee travel expenses (if applicable), and the salary and benefits costs attributed to the time the leader and team took out of their workdays to engage in the coaching effort.

I see this as a judgment call for the client with whom I have the contract in any given coaching assignment. Some clients want the fully loaded costs, and some do not. For example, one of my clients found the fully loaded costs less compelling. When I asked if she wanted to use them, she said, "I only want to see the coaching travel expenses and fees. The other costs I would incur anyway. I regularly take my team—quarterly—to off-site meetings, and I'm paying the same salaries and benefits no matter what they are doing." The case might be different for clients who measure and work to specifically increase staff productivity. In that case, tracking fully loaded costs is much more relevant.

Appendix D

1. For further resources, see Lippitt and Lippitt (1986), Schein (1987, 1988), Bunker and Alban (1997), and Weisbord (1987).

References

Anderson, D., and Anderson, M. *Coaching That Counts*. Burlington, Mass.: Elsevier, 2005.

Anderson, M. *Bottom-Line Organization Development: Implementing and Evaluating Strategic Change for Lasting Value*. Burlington, Mass.: Elsevier, 2003.

Bell, C. R. *Managers as Mentors*. San Francisco: Berrett-Koehler, 1996.

Blanchard, K., Zigarmi, P., and Zigarmi, D. *Leadership and the One Minute Manager*. New York: Morrow, 1985.

Block, P. *Flawless Consulting*. San Diego: University Associates, 1981.

Bunker, B., and Alban, B. *Large Group Interventions*. San Francisco: Jossey-Bass, 1997.

Carkhuff, R. *Helping and Human Relations*. New York: Holt, 1969.

Conner, D. *Managing at the Speed of Change*. New York: Villard, 1993.

Conner, D. *Leading at the Edge of Chaos*. Hoboken, N.J.: Wiley, 1998.

Craig, N. "Using Results-Driven Backplanning to Improve Strategic Implementation." *Employee Relations Today*, 2006, *32*(4), 15–24.

Dotlich, D., and Cairo, P. *Action Coaching*. San Francisco: Jossey-Bass, 1999.

Fitz-enz, J. *The ROI of Human Capital*. New York: Amacom, 2000.

Fournies, F. *Coaching for Improved Work Performance*. New York: McGraw-Hill, 1998.

Friedman, E. *Generation to Generation*. New York: Guilford Press, 1985.

Gilbert, R. *Extraordinary Relationships*. Minneapolis, Minn.: Chronimed, 1992.

Goleman, D. *Emotional Intelligence*. New York: Bantam Books, 1995.

Hargrove, R. *Masterful Coaching*. San Francisco: Jossey-Bass/Pfeiffer, 1995.

Kerr, M., and Bowen, M. *Family Evaluation*. New York: Norton, 1988.

Kinlaw, D. *Coaching for Commitment*. San Diego: Pfeiffer, 1993.

Kouzes, J., and Posner, B. *The Leadership Challenge*. San Francisco: Jossey-Bass, 2002.

Kouzes, J., and Posner, B. *The Leadership Challenge Workbook*. San Francisco: Jossey-Bass, 2003.

Lencioni, P. *The Five Dysfunctions of a Team: A Leadership Fable*. San Francisco: Jossey-Bass, 2002.

Lencioni, P. *Overcoming the Five Dysfunctions of a Team: A Field Guide*. San Francisco: Jossey-Bass, 2005.

Lippitt, G., and Lippitt, R. *The Consulting Process in Action*. San Francisco: Jossey-Bass/Pfeiffer, 1986.

McGovern, J., and others. "Maximizing the Impact of Executive Coaching: Behavioral Change Organizational Outcomes, and Return on Investment." *Manchester Review*, 2001, 6(1), 1–9.

Minuchin, S. *Families and Family Therapy*. Cambridge, Mass.: Harvard University Press, 1974.

O'Neill, M. B. "An ROI Method for Executive Coaching: Have the Client Convince the Coach of the Return on Investment." *International Journal of Coaching in Organizations*, 2005, 3(1), 39–52.

Phillips, J. *Return on Investment*. Burlington, Mass.: Elsevier, 2003.

Phillips, J., and Phillips, P. "Measuring ROI in Executive Coaching." *Executive Coach Magazine*, Spring 2004, pp. 18–21.

Phillips, P. *The Bottomline on ROI*. Atlanta, Ga.: CEP Press, 2002.

Pomerantz, S. *Seal the Deal: The Essential Mindsets for Growing Your Professional Services Business*. Amherst, Mass.: HRD Press, 2007.

Richardson, R. *Family Ties That Bind*. Vancouver, B.C., Canada: Self-Counsel Press, 1984.

Schachter, R. "Questions When Contracting with Leaders." Seattle: LIOS Consulting Corporation, 1997. Unpublished document.

Schaffer, R. *High-Impact Consulting*. San Francisco: Jossey-Bass, 2002.

Schein, E. *Process Consultation: Lessons for Managers and Consultants*. (Vol. 2.) Reading, Mass.: Addison-Wesley, 1987.

Schein, E. *Process Consultation*. (Vol. 1, 2nd ed.) Reading, Mass.: Addison-Wesley, 1988.

Schnarch, D. *Passionate Marriage*. New York: Holt, 1997.

Senge, P. *The Fifth Discipline*. New York: Doubleday Currency, 1990.

Short, R. "Structural Family Therapy and Consultative Practice: A Paradigm Shift for OD." *Consultation, an International Journal*, 1985a, 4(2), 1–17.

Short, R. "Structural Family Therapy and Consultative Practice: A Paradigm Shift for OD." *Consultation, an International Journal*, 1985b, 4(3), 1–12.

Weisbord, M. *Productive Workplaces*. San Francisco: Jossey-Bass, 1987.

Wheatley, M. *Leadership and the New Science*. San Francisco: Berrett-Koehler, 1992.

Whitmore, J. *Coaching for Performance*. (2nd ed.) London: Nicholas Brealey, 1996.

Whitworth, L., Kimsey-House, H., and Sandahl, P. *Co-Active Coaching*. Palo Alto, Calif.: Davies-Black, 1998.

Williamson, D. *The Intimacy Paradox*. New York: Guilford Press, 1991.

Index

C

T